MONEY, POLITICS, AND DEMOCRACY

MONEY, POLITICS, AND DEMOCRACY
Canada's Party Finance Reforms

Edited by Lisa Young and Harold J. Jansen

© UBC Press 2011

All rights reserved. No part of this publication may be reproduced, stored in a retrieval system, or transmitted, in any form or by any means, without prior written permission of the publisher, or, in Canada, in the case of photocopying or other reprographic copying, a licence from Access Copyright, www.accesscopyright.ca.

21 20 19 18 17 16 15 14 13 12 11   5 4 3 2 1

Printed in Canada on FSC-certified ancient-forest-free paper
(100% post-consumer recycled) that is processed chlorine- and acid-free.

Printed in Canada on acid-free paper

Library and Archives Canada Cataloguing in Publication

Money, politics, and democracy : Canada's party finance reforms /
edited by Lisa Young and Harold J. Jansen.

Includes bibliographical references and index.
ISBN 978-0-7748-1891-9 (cloth); 978-0-7748-1892-6 (pbk.)

1. Campaign funds – Canada. 2. Campaign funds – Law and legislation – Canada. 3. Canada – Politics and government – 2006-. I. Young, Lisa, 1967- II. Jansen, Harold J., 1966-

| JL193.M6584 2011 | 324.7'80971 | C2010-907382-7 |

e-book ISBNs: 978-0-7748-1893-3 (pdf); 978-0-7748-1894-0 (epub)

Canadä

UBC Press gratefully acknowledges the financial support for our publishing program of the Government of Canada (through the Canada Book Fund), the Canada Council for the Arts, and the British Columbia Arts Council.

This book has been published with the help of a grant from the Canadian Federation for the Humanities and Social Sciences, through the Aid to Scholarly Publications Program, using funds provided by the Social Sciences and Humanities Research Council of Canada.

UBC Press
The University of British Columbia
2029 West Mall
Vancouver, BC V6T 1Z2
www.ubcpress.ca

Contents

Acknowledgments / vii

1 Reforming Party and Election Finance in Canada / 1
Lisa Young and Harold J. Jansen

2 State Funding of Political Parties: Truths, Myths, and Legends / 19
Justin Fisher

3 Public Funding of Political Parties: The Case for Further Reform / 37
F. Leslie Seidle

4 Finance Reform and the Cartel Party Model in Canada / 60
Richard S. Katz

5 Cartels, Syndicates, and Coalitions: Canada's Political Parties after the 2004 Reforms / 82
Harold J. Jansen and Lisa Young

6 The Impact of Election Finance Reforms on Local Party Organization / 104
David Coletto and Munroe Eagles

7 The Quarterly Allowance and Turnout: Old and New Evidence / 130
Peter John Loewen and André Blais

8 Financing Party Leadership Campaigns / 145
William Cross and John Crysler

9 Lessons from the American Campaign Finance Reform Experience / 173
Robert G. Boatright

10 Conclusion / 198
Harold J. Jansen and Lisa Young

Contributors / 206

Index / 208

Acknowledgments

The genesis of this project was a research workshop held in May 2006 at the University of Calgary. That workshop was generously funded by the Social Sciences and Humanities Research Council of Canada through an Aid to Research Workshops and Conferences Grant. We are grateful to the authors of the chapters in this book for their patience in waiting for us to sort out what kind of book should come out of the workshop as we slowly moved from workshop papers to edited volume. Their speed and professionalism in updating their work to account for the intervening years made this book possible. We also appreciate the patience and encouragement offered by our editor, Emily Andrew, and her colleagues at UBC Press.

This book has been published with the help of a grant from the Canadian Federation for the Humanities and Social Sciences, through the Aid to Scholarly Publications Program, using funds provided by the Social Sciences and Humanities Research Council of Canada.

Finally, we would like to thank our families for their support while we worked on getting this project out the door. Thank you to Shobha George, Benjamin, Joel, and Aliya Jansen, and Mike, David, and Josh Griffin for their encouragement and patience.

MONEY, POLITICS, AND DEMOCRACY

1

Reforming Party and Election Finance in Canada

LISA YOUNG AND HAROLD J. JANSEN

In December of 2008, an extraordinary political drama transfixed Canadians. The Liberal and New Democratic parties reached an agreement to form a coalition that would govern with the support of the Bloc Québécois after defeating the Conservative minority government that had been formed a few weeks earlier. Ultimately, the attempted coalition crumbled after Prime Minister Stephen Harper convinced Governor General Michaëlle Jean to prorogue Parliament, thus postponing the vote of non-confidence. Although the attempted coalition was generally considered constitutionally legitimate, many Canadians nevertheless objected to it on the grounds of popular sovereignty (Russell and Sossin 2009). Whatever the public might have concluded about the dramatic events in Ottawa, it was clear that the Liberal-NDP move was a sharp break from the way politics had been conducted in Canada. Although coalition governments are common elsewhere, Canadians had very little experience with them outside of times of national emergencies, such as the World Wars.

The trigger for this unprecedented episode in Canadian politics was an attempt by the Conservatives to eliminate the annual financial subsidy to political parties, ostensibly as part of the government's response to the economic crisis that unfolded in the fall of 2008. Although the opposition parties presented their coalition as driven by a more general lack of confidence in the direction of the government, there is little doubt that the changes to party finance were the impetus for the move. The elimination of the subsidy would have been disastrous for the opposition parties in Parliament (and for the Green Party, which lent its support to the coalition as well). In practical terms, the opposition parties had little choice but to oppose the Conservatives' proposal.

This book examines the series of reforms to the laws governing political finance in Canada that led to this dramatic showdown. The chapters included in it seek to understand the reasons for the significant revisions to the legislation, and the ways in which these changes have affected the internal organization of political parties and the dynamics of inter-party competition. In one respect, the book is very much focused on understanding the new dynamics of party organization and competition in the Canadian case. But in a second respect, the book seeks to speak to a broader international audience interested in the patterns of reform to political finance and the implications of these rules for political parties as organizations and as electoral competitors.

Institutional Context and Party System

Canadian political institutions are fixed firmly within the Westminster political tradition, featuring a single member plurality electoral system and parliamentary government characterized by tight party discipline and a concentration of power in the office of the prime minister. These institutional characteristics are important context for understanding the Canadian experience with public funding and election finance reform in comparative perspective. Canada is unusual in its coupling of Westminster institutions with extensive public funding of its political parties at the national level. As a result, it offers an intriguing test of theoretical propositions derived from the experience of more consensual political systems that have experimented with the regulation of political finance.

The British tradition holds a view of political parties as appropriately private organizations. Gauja (2008) notes that in established democracies with Westminster constitutional traditions (Canada, Australia, New Zealand, and the United Kingdom), there is no mention of parties in constitutional documents. This absence reflects a dominant constitutional theory that sees political parties, with their socially divisive character, as essentially incompatible with liberal democratic traditions. The reticence to acknowledge parties as key players in these democracies has translated, in practical terms, into a relative reluctance to regulate the internal workings of parties or to offer them substantial financial support from the public purse. Over time, this reluctance has conflicted with pressure to acknowledge the extensive role parties play in selecting candidates and structuring electoral competition, and the necessity of regulating these critical actors as part of broader efforts to prevent corruption and encourage transparency, accountability, and equitable electoral competition. As a result, the Westminster democracies have, to varying degrees, come to recognize political parties in law, register them, and regulate their financial dealings. Among the Westminster democracies, however, Canada stands out. Canada established legislation governing the registration of political parties in 1974, whereas the other Westminster systems did not follow until 1983 (Australia), 1993 (New Zealand), and 1998 (United Kingdom). Similarly, public funding of parties' electoral campaigns began in Canada in 1974 but only later (if at all) in the other Anglo-American systems. Because it couples Westminster institutions with a more continental propensity to regulate and fund political parties, Canada serves as a critical case for testing some of the propositions within the academic literature regarding the impact of regulation and public funding.

In 2004, a series of reforms to the Canada Elections Act further extended both the funding and regulation of political parties. These reforms coincided with an unusual period in Canadian electoral politics, interrupting a relatively stable two-and-a-half-party system characterized by the rotation of the Liberal and Progressive Conservative (PC) parties in office. The 1993 general election ushered in a decade of highly regionalized politics at the national level. In the 1993 electoral "earthquake," the PC Party was reduced from a majority government to only two seats in the House of Commons. Its base of support had effectively splintered to support three parties: the remnants of the PC Party, the sovereignist Bloc Québécois, and the western-based Reform Party (which later morphed into the Canadian Alliance). The electoral collapse of the PCs and the resulting regionalization of the party system benefited the Liberal Party, which was able to form a majority government with its support in Ontario and major urban centres elsewhere in the country (Johnston 2000). Having governed for a decade, by 2003 the Liberal Party had been damaged politically by a series of scandals and an internal struggle for the party's leadership. Nonetheless, by virtue of a seemingly popular new leader in Paul Martin and the ongoing fracture of the opposition parties, the Liberals appeared poised to continue their electoral domination. The unexpected merger late in 2003 of the Canadian Alliance and the Progressive Conservative Party into the Conservative Party, coupled with the electoral fallout of the sponsorship scandal in Quebec, disrupted these plans, leaving Paul Martin's Liberals with only a minority of seats in the House of Commons after the 2004 federal election. Since 2004, Canada has been governed by a series of minority governments: first the Liberals from 2004-06, and then two consecutive Conservative minorities – from 2006-08 and then 2008 until the present. With the two right-of-centre parties merged into the Conservative Party, the Bloc Québécois still dominant in Quebec, and the Liberal Party struggling with ongoing internal leadership politics, electoral majorities have proved elusive.

As a consequence of these unsettled political conditions, our ability to understand the adaptation of actors to the new set of incentives in the system is curtailed. Canadian political parties have fought three general elections over a period that would normally have seen only two; the precarious minority status of the three governments since 2004 has required parties to maintain a constant state of electoral readiness, focusing their attention on electoral considerations to the exclusion of other issues. The Liberal Party has also had three leaders over the six-year period during which the new legislation has been in place. These unsettled electoral conditions may have led Canada's parties to adapt to the new finance rules differently than they would have under "normal" circumstances.

The Reforms

The reforms came into effect in 2004 but were first brought forward before the House of Commons as Bill C-24 in 2003, Liberal prime minister Jean Chrétien's last year in office. Leading a government beset with scandals, the prime minister introduced the bill as an element of a broader ethics package designed to defuse criticism of the governing party. The effects of this legislation have been amplified by further reforms to election finance introduced by Stephen Harper's Conservative government in 2006, under the rubric of the federal Accountability Act. In December of 2008, an effort to reverse part of the 2004 reforms almost led to the defeat of the Harper government.

Prior to the 2004 reforms, the regulatory regime governing Canadian parties and elections relied on disclosure of the size and source of contributions to discourage political corruption, and employed spending limits at the local and national level to encourage equitable competition and limit the demand for political contributions. Parties and candidates received significant state support via election expense rebates and tax credits for donations, but private funds constituted the dominant source of income for both parties and candidates.

The reforms introduced in 2004 and 2006 maintained these existing rules but added to them significant restrictions on the size and source of contributions and introduced extensive public funding and state regulation of party nomination and leadership contests. A summary is provided in Table 1.1. Under the new legislation, only individuals could contribute to national political parties, and the amount of this contribution would be limited to $5,000. The Harper government's 2006 Accountability Act further reduced this to $1,000 (indexed for inflation). The 2004 reforms allowed entities other than individuals – mainly corporations and unions – to contribute a maximum of $1,000 per year to candidates or local associations; the 2006 Accountability Act eliminated this provision, making individuals the only legal contributors to any partisan entities at the federal level.

To replace parties' lost income, the 2004 reforms substantially increased the public funding available for political parties. First, there was an increase to rebates for candidates' and parties' election expenditures. Second, the reforms instituted a system of quarterly public funding for national political parties based on the number of votes the party won in the most recent election. The latter was a significant change from past provision of public funding to political parties. Taken together, the clear intention of the legislation was to make public funds the primary source of income for major political parties. The 2006 legislation did not affect the provision of public funding. The Conservative government attempted to eliminate the per-vote subsidy in 2008 but had to retreat in the face of the determined opposition of all of the other parties.

Finally, the 2004 reforms extended the scope of the regulatory regime beyond the affairs of national parties and the official election period to govern parties' nomination and leadership contests. Candidates both for a party nomination and a party's leadership became governed by the same limits on the size and source of contributions that applied to other registered entities, and candidates for a party nomination also became subject to spending limits in the nomination contest.

Why Reform?

The 2004 reforms came as a surprise to observers, as there was little pressure on government to amend the existing rules. Appointed in 1988, the Royal Commission on Electoral Reform and Party Financing (RCERPF) had recommended changes to the regulation of third-party advertisers during election campaigns and alterations to the formula for reimbursement of election expenses but did not recommend adopting the Quebec system of

TABLE 1.1

Summary of regulation of party and election finance in Canada

Transparency
- Reporting names of all contributors over $200, including contributions to nomination and leadership contestants
- Reporting party, candidate, nomination candidate, and leadership candidate election expenses
- Reporting contributions to registered third parties
- Reporting expenditures by registered third parties
- Reporting assets held by electoral district associations

Spending limits
- Candidates' election expenses (based on number of electors in district)
- Registered political parties' election expenses (based on number of candidates running for party)
- Registered third-party election expenses ($3,666 in an electoral district; $183,300 nationally)
- Candidate nomination expenses (20% of election spending limit for electoral district)

Public funding
- Political Contribution Tax Credit (75% credit on contributions up to $400, sliding scale on larger contributions)
- Election expense reimbursements:
- 60% for candidates winning at least 10% of popular vote
- 50% for registered parties (winning 2% of national popular vote or 5% of vote in districts where the party ran candidates)
- Per-vote quarterly allowance to registered political parties winning 2% of national popular vote or 5% of vote in districts where the party ran candidates

Contribution limits
- Only Canadian citizens/permanent residents can make political contributions, in the following amounts:
- Maximum $1,100/annum to each registered party
- Maximum $1,100/annum in total to various entities of each party (registered association, nomination contestants, candidates)
- Maximum $1,100/annum to each independent candidate in a particular election
- Maximum $1,100 in total to leadership contestants in a particular leadership contest

Note: All dollar amounts are indexed to inflation; they are adjusted annually.

financement populaire, which banned political contributions from any entity except an eligible voter. Instead, the commission concluded that "Canadian organizations with a stake in the political future of the country should not be prevented from supporting parties and candidates who share their policies and values, provided the public has full opportunity to be informed about these financial activities" (Canada, RCERPF 1991, 450). This view, although accepted by policy makers responding to the commission's report, was not widespread in Quebec, where the provincial legislation banning corporate and union contributions to parties and candidates has long received significant support. For most of its history, the Bloc Québécois, in fact, opted to adhere to the ban on corporate and union contributions in its own fundraising efforts. Beyond this, however, there was little pressure to amend Canada's regulatory framework for election finance. Given a relative absence of public concern and elite policy debate over the regulation of political finance, we are left with the question of why the reforms were adopted when they were.

Electoral law is unique in that the primary subjects of regulation – political parties and candidates – are themselves developing the rules for the next round of the game in which they will be players. Consequently, an extensive literature examining the patterns of change in election finance law has emerged. Self-interest inevitably comes into play in these explanations, although competing theoretical and empirical accounts suggest that self-interest of various actors plays out in different ways. In Chapters 2 and 4 of this volume, Justin Fisher and Richard Katz examine these competing theoretical accounts. Katz elaborates on the cartelization thesis, which holds that self-interested parties unable to raise sufficient funds from private sources collude to use the resources of the state to support their functions (see Katz and Mair 1995). Fisher critiques this argument, holding that empirical evidence from several European countries refutes the contention that parties act largely as rational strategic agents; rather they are constrained by dominant norms and values framed by critical historical choices.

Although the institutionalist approach Fisher outlines does not help to account for the government's decision to reform electoral finance, it does offer insight into the choice of regulatory tools employed in the reforms. The decision to all but ban contributions from entities other than individuals and place limits on the size of these contributions largely replicated the regulatory regime of *financement populaire* introduced in Quebec in 1977. Quebec politicians were familiar with this regime, and many favoured its use at the federal level. Likewise, the form of the public funding introduced in the legislation bore remarkable similarity to the formula for party reimbursements put forward by the RCERPF in 1991 (Canada, RCERPF 1991, 372). The fingerprints of the RCERPF report can also be found in the measures extending regulation to the nomination and leadership selection practices of the registered parties.

To provide a more convincing answer to the question of why the reforms were introduced in 2003, we must examine the patterns of partisan self-interest brought to bear on the reform process. In Katz and Mair's cartel model, extensive state finance is the product of major parties' collusion. In essence, parties agree to employ state resources to fulfil their financial needs, turning away from private sources of finance in favour of the state (Katz and Mair 1995). Examining the Canadian experience through this lens, one might argue that the major parties agreed to accept the loss of revenue from corporate and union contributors and large individual contributions in exchange for a relatively predictable and secure stream of income from the state.

Evidence of collusion in the Canadian experience is, however, incomplete. Although two of the smaller parliamentary parties (the NDP and the Bloc Québécois) supported the Liberals' legislation from the outset, two other parties (the Progressive Conservatives and the Canadian Alliance) opposed it. The Canadian Alliance, then the official opposition, was vocal in its criticism of the legislation, most particularly on the extensive provision of state funding. Canadian Alliance leader Stephen Harper argued that "the worst idea in the legislation is new direct stipends to parties themselves based on previous electoral performance. In this case not only would parties be isolated from the feelings they may have from their own former supporters, but frankly even people who never supported them would be asked to support the party, whether it be the Bloc Québécois or the NDP or ourselves" (Hansard, 11 February 2003).

Although vociferous in its opposition, the Canadian Alliance was in a position to reap the benefits of the legislation without paying any political cost that might be associated with supporting it. The governing Liberals had signalled that they would use their majority in the House of Commons to ensure that the legislation passed, so the Canadian Alliance could achieve both revenue maximization and electoral economy simultaneously, gaining any electoral benefits to be won by criticizing the turn to the state for funding without refusing the new source of revenue.

Because the notion of collusion is not entirely satisfactory for explaining the 2004 reforms, we turn our attention to the financial and electoral self-interest of the governing party. As presented by the Liberal government, the new electoral finance rules were a high-minded effort to enhance public confidence in the integrity of the electoral system by taking corporate and union contributors out of the process. Addressing the House of Commons, then-prime minister Jean Chrétien proclaimed that this legislation would "address the perception that money talks, that big companies and big unions have too much influence on politics, a bill that will reduce cynicism about politics and politicians, a bill that is tough but fair" (Hansard, 11 February 2003). Although the prime minister and other Liberals were careful to deny the reality of corporate influence over public policy making, they placed considerable emphasis on the importance of correcting a perception that political contributions bought influence for donors. In this account, public funding was incidental: a means of compensating parties for lost income. In fact, as the legislation moved through committee, the formula for funding was adjusted from $1.50/vote to $1.75/vote to ensure that the Liberal Party would be adequately compensated (Clark 2003, A4).

Stephen Harper, then Leader of the Opposition, suggested in the House of Commons that the legislation was motivated at least partially by a "need to deal with the bank debts of the Liberal Party itself" (Hansard, 11 February 2003). At the end of 2002, the Liberal Party reported total liabilities of over $2.7 million, offset by just under $1.4 million in assets, leaving the party with net liabilities of some $1.3 million (Federal Liberal Agency of Canada 2003). This was reduced substantially in 2003, when the party's leadership convention and related fundraising (including the last round of fundraising from corporate donors) left the party with $4.6 million in assets, against $5.1 million in liabilities, for a net liability of just over $0.5 million. In short, this level of indebtedness was in all probability manageable for the party, particularly given that it was poised to elect a new leader with extensive corporate ties and capacity to fundraise. This renders improbable the notion that narrow pecuniary self-interest drove the reforms.

More probable is Harper's allegation that the legislation was motivated "by internal Liberal politics and needs: the need of the Prime Minister to whitewash various scandals from his record before he retires" (Hansard, 11 February 2003). The amendments to the Canada Elections Act were included as part of a broader ethics package introduced by the government after several scandals emerged. The incidents in question did not pertain to election finance; rather, they related to untendered contracts and other similar issues (see Greene 2006). More significant politically than these incidents was the sponsorship scandal, which was slowly being revealed by journalists. The full details of the sponsorship scandal did not become public knowledge until the Gomery Commission's hearings in 2004. Presumably, however, the prime minister and his advisers were aware of at least the general outlines of what had gone on in Quebec and were introducing amendments to the Canada Elections Act in a pre-emptive effort to respond to allegations that would later emerge.

When the Gomery Commission thoroughly investigated the sponsorship program and individuals associated with it, it discovered that individuals associated with the Quebec wing of the Liberal Party of Canada were successfully soliciting significant contributions from companies and individuals in receipt of lucrative sponsorship contracts from the federal government. Referring to these transactions as "kickbacks," Justice Gomery concluded that "the LPCQ [Liberal Party of Canada (Quebec)] as an institution cannot escape responsibility for the misconduct of its officers and representatives. Two successive Executive Directors were directly involved in illegal campaign financing and many of its workers accepted cash payments for their services when they should have known that such payments were in violation of the *Canada Elections Act*" (Commission of Inquiry 2005, 435). The reforms that the Liberals proposed to the Canada Elections Act did not directly address all of the improper activities outlined in the Gomery report. Certainly, banning corporate contributions would prevent party officials from requesting contributions directly from companies receiving lucrative government contracts. The reforms said nothing about the other illegal activities, such as cash-stuffed envelopes being delivered to party representatives and illegal payments being made to campaign workers, reported by witnesses appearing before the Gomery Commission. The legislation did, however, serve to signal the government's commitment to increasing public confidence in the regulatory system.

The Impact of State Funding

At the heart of the 2004 reforms was the replacement of parties' revenues from corporate, union, and large individual donors with extensive state funding. A core question that links many of the chapters in this volume is the question of how public funding has – and might – affect party organization and electoral competition in the context of a Westminster system. As public funding for parties has become a routine feature of many established and emerging democracies, these questions have become central to the study of party organization, as scholars contend with Katz and Mair's contention (1995) that contemporary parties are characterized in part by their reliance on public funds.

Although the practice has become common in both emerging and established democracies, the provision of public funding for political parties and candidates remains contentious both in principle and in its effects on party competition. In Chapter 2, Justin Fisher examines the debate over public funding of parties and candidates, noting that proponents of state funding suggest that this practice recognizes the fundamental role of political parties in representative democracy, promotes equality of competition among parties, and limits the influence of private money on politics. These salutary characteristics of public funding are not uncontested, however. The most comprehensive critique of the negative consequences of state funding for party organization and electoral democracy is embedded in Katz and Mair's cartel model, which holds that state-dependent parties have diminished need or desire to link society and the state, their linkages to society weakening as they increasingly become institutions of the state.

In Chapter 4, Richard Katz examines the experience of state funding of political parties in Canada through the lens of the cartel hypothesis and concludes that the evidence thus far is not incompatible with the expectations of the cartel model. The reforms introduced serve to protect parties against the vagaries of private fundraising, reduce the difference in resources between the governing party and the parties within the cartel, and insulate party leaders from constraints, either from large donors or from the party on the ground. Katz notes, however, that the regime does not fully skew the advantage in the direction of the major parties. Although the very smallest parties are excluded from the benefits of the funding regime, two of the smaller parties – the Bloc and the Greens – are some of the biggest beneficiaries of the regime, as Jansen and Young show in Chapter 5.

In that chapter, Jansen and Young argue that there is evidence not of a cartel but of a syndicate, with the Liberals, NDP, Bloc Québécois, and Greens forming a group of state-dependent parties whose behaviour is driven in part by this dependence. The Conservatives are the anomaly among Canada's political parties. Rather than relying on a stable, but limited, state income, the Conservative Party has pursued an aggressive fundraising strategy that has yielded significant additional revenues for the party. As a result, the party is able to outspend its rivals between elections and is better positioned to fight an election at any time. The dynamics of the syndicate, Jansen and Young argue, were laid bare in November of 2008 when the Harper government tried to eliminate public subsidies for parties. The three opposition parties, with support from the Greens, threatened to defeat the Conservatives and back a Liberal-led coalition government.

The potential impact of state funding goes beyond the competitive dynamic among parties. Because public funds are delivered to the national party, there is potential that the balance between national and local associations might be disrupted. In Chapter 6, David Coletto and Munroe Eagles examine this proposition and conclude that there is little evidence to suggest that local associations have been rendered anachronistic in the new regime. Most local associations have been able to maintain some assets; some parties have continued the practice of taxing their local associations in order to raise money for central party initiatives. In short, reforms to the Canada Elections Act have not significantly weakened local associations relative to their national organization.

The introduction of state funding has also been hypothesized to affect voter turnout. Under the provisions of the 2004 reforms, each party's quarterly allowance is based on the number of votes it won in the most recent election. At least theoretically, this creates an incentive for parties to try to maximize their electoral support, even in constituencies the party cannot win. All other things being equal, a party trying to maximize its income should try to increase turnout among its supporters. In Chapter 7, Loewen and Blais test this proposition. Analyzing both aggregate and individual-level data pertaining to the 2004 and 2006 elections, they find no evidence to support the hypothesis that the public funding of parties has increased voter turnout from what it would otherwise have been. The only qualification to their finding is modest support for the proposition that the Green Party has used the per-vote subsidy as a way to encourage turnout among voters who otherwise would not have cast a ballot.

Regulation of Parties' Internal Affairs

The Westminster conception of political parties as primarily private entities stands in sharp contrast to the constitutional recognition of political parties as essential elements of electoral democracy in many west European states and new democracies (van Biezen 2008). Increasingly, the idea that political parties are best understood as public utilities has resulted both in state financial support for parties and in state regulation of their internal affairs. Van Biezen (2008) notes that an important motivation for state regulation of political parties is declining public confidence in parties, most notably as institutions susceptible to corruption. This underlies the view that "higher levels of external control and monitoring of party activity and behaviour are warranted in order to ensure that they perform their democratic functions more effectively" (ibid., 338).

In Canada, some of this logic is seen in the 1991 report of the RCERPF, which advocated several measures that would have encroached on the notion of political parties as private entities. It recommended that parties be required to adopt a party constitution mandating internal democracy as a prerequisite for registration, that parties establish policy foundations, that parties' funding be partially contingent on their success in electing women, and state regulation of spending in nomination contests. The parties resisted all these recommendations, and it was not until the 2004 reforms that the internal affairs of political parties came under any state regulation. The 2004 reforms were much more modest than those recommended by the RCERPF: they included only the regulation of contributions to candidates running for a party leadership and regulation of contributions to and spending by candidates running for a party nomination.[1]

This is the logic that underlies Leslie Seidle's calls for state regulation of various elements of Canadian parties' internal affairs. In Chapter 3, Seidle lays out the case for demanding more of Canada's increasingly state-supported parties. Noting the Royal Commission on Electoral Reform and Party Financing's conceptualization of political parties as "primary political organizations," with emphasis placed on their role in providing citizens with access into the political system, Seidle proposes a series of further reforms. He suggests that the threshold for a party to receive public funding should be lowered, that parties should be given financial incentives to increase the number of women in the House of Commons, and that parties be required to establish policy foundations that would enhance the policy development role of parties.

Although rooted in a very different political tradition from the state-subsidized European parties discussed above, American political parties are also subject to extensive state regulation of elements of their internal affairs, notably the selection of candidates via primary elections. American direct primaries were legislated by state governments early in the twentieth century at the behest of progressive reformers outside the parties, along with the parties' elite. Both groups shared an ideological commitment to broad public participation in party affairs, and primary elections were a means of achieving this end (Ware 2002).

The state regulation of internal party contests in Canadian elections that came as part of the 2004 reforms did not reach nearly as far into the internal affairs of Canadian parties as is the case in the American direct primaries. Under the new rules, political parties remain free to structure their internal party leadership and nomination contests largely as they see fit. Although the Canada Elections Act now recognizes and regulates party leadership and nomination contests when parties declare them to occur, it does not require parties to conduct such contests. Parties remain free to appoint leaders and candidates as they see fit. Should they conduct an election for either position, however, financial aspects of the contest fall under the regulatory framework of the act.

In Chapter 8, William Cross and John Crysler place the new rules governing party leadership contests in historical context, arguing that parties' efforts to self-regulate have been largely unsuccessful. Wealthy candidates and candidates able to attract support from wealthy donors have enjoyed significant advantages in past party-leadership contests, at the expense of qualified candidates without the same networks or personal resources. Noting that political parties play a central and privileged place in Canadian democracy, and that the leaders they choose are highly significant players in Canadian politics, Cross and Crysler judge the legislation governing party-leadership contests as appropriate but insufficient. Reviewing the experience of the Liberal Party in selecting its new leader in 2006, they suggest that the era of big money dominating party leadership contests has come to an end.

Impacts on Electoral Democracy

It would be remarkable if the extensive changes to the regulation of party and election finance contained in the 2004 and 2006 reforms did not affect the patterns and quality of electoral democracy. Some of these effects will not be immediate, as diffusion of information regarding the changes may be slow in some instances, and actors do not immediately respond to the incentives and disincentives embedded in the new regulatory regime. Nonetheless, the initial experiences from the first six years working under the rules are useful indicators of the possible patterns of competition and other effects. The three general elections held during this period make it possible to examine some of the potential electoral effects in greater detail.

Availability of funds is an important, but not definitive, factor affecting a party's electoral success. A financial advantage may translate into an electoral advantage for either a party or a candidate and will usually have a positive impact on the party's or candidate's ability to communicate a message to voters (see Rekkas 2007). In the Canadian context, spending limits for both candidates and parties during election campaigns limit the extent to which inequities in finances affect the campaign itself (assuming, of course, that the party or candidate in question is able to spend up to or near the limit). Canadian election campaigns are relatively brief, however, and the ability to spend money in advance of the campaign is also important. The Conservative Party's series of television ads attacking Liberal Party leader Stéphane Dion shortly after his election as party leader illustrate the potential impact of these disparities. In this respect, it is important to examine the disparities in income among the parties.

As Jansen and Young show in Chapter 5, the overall impact of the reforms has not been a level playing field for parties. The Conservatives have raised more than the four other parties combined. Paradoxically, all of the parties except the Liberals are better off in absolute terms than they were in the past. The fundraising prowess of the Conservative Party, however, has raised the bar in comparative terms, so the opposition parties find themselves at a significant financial disadvantage when compared with the governing Conservatives.

The Conservative Party's financial advantage is replicated at the local level. David Coletto and Munro Eagles show in Chapter 6 that Conservative associations boast much larger war chests than their counterparts from other parties. This is not simply a product of being in government: Table 6.3 of their chapter demonstrates that in 2004 there was only a modest difference of just over $6,000 on average in the assets held by Liberal and Conservative Electoral District Associations (EDAs) that elected a candidate in the 2004 election. By 2006, the average Conservative EDA that had elected a candidate in 2004 had over $46,000 more in assets than the average Liberal EDA that had elected a candidate in 2004. The relative affluence of Conservative EDAs is at least in part a spillover from the national party's fundraising capacity: Coletto and Eagles demonstrate that by 2006 the net internal flow of funds within the Conservative Party was from the national level to the EDAs. For all the other parties, the net flow was in the opposite direction.

From 2004 through 2010, Canadian electoral politics have been unusually competitive, with no party able to form a majority government. This is in large part a function of the electoral success of the Bloc Québécois and the collapse of Liberal Party support in the province of Quebec. Although changes to the electoral finance regime did not cause these phenomena, the Bloc's improved financial standing has facilitated its electoral success. Likewise, the Liberal Party's financial woes have made it all the more difficult for the party to rebuild its popularity. In this sense, political finance has provided the backdrop for an unusual period in Canadian politics.

With the changes to the regulatory regime, the incentives facing a variety of political actors changed. These included unions, corporations, and interest groups. Now banned from contributing to parties or candidates, would these actors choose to engage directly in the electoral process as third parties? Would they seek to find ways to circumvent the new rules? Or would they disengage from the electoral process? The American experience with bans on contributions suggests that these non-partisan actors would opt for the two former routes. As Robert Boatright observes in Chapter 9, however, this has not proven to be the case. Canadian groups have never been as focused on electoral politics as their American counterparts, and the Canadian institutional framework does not lend itself to their direct engagement. Noting that it is entirely appropriate that actors other than parties and candidates be able to have a voice in the conduct of elections, Boatright concludes that the new regime allows them to do this but does not in any way threaten the primary role of political parties in Canadian elections.

Conclusion

When Jean Chrétien introduced Bill C-24 to Parliament in 2003, he could not have foreseen the extraordinary political circumstances that would emerge once he left the political stage. Responding to an immediate political problem, he instituted a set of reforms that have shaped political competition in Canada since 2004. In this new era of political competition, parties are much more creatures of the state, dependent on it for financial support and subject to its regulatory authority. As the chapters in this volume demonstrate, both the extent of the state regulation of parties and its merits are subject to debate.

What is evident, however, is that the terrain on which Canadian parties compete has been altered significantly. The formula for dispensing funds to parties, and the strategies that parties have adopted under this new regime, have created financial advantages for some parties and disadvantages for others. In calculating their electoral strategies, parties must now take into account not only the imperative to maximize the number of seats they win but also the number of votes they receive, as that will affect their financial future. The players in the game have also changed, as businesses and unions have been replaced by individual donors as the revenue source to be courted. Within parties, the financial centre of gravity is shifting, recasting the balance of power between national and local organizations. The chapters that follow examine the new dynamics shaping party organization and electoral competition in Canada to provide a guide to understanding the new political world Canadians inhabit.

NOTE

1 The resistance of Canadian parties to the recommendations of the Royal Commission on Electoral Reform and Party Financing was highlighted in May of 2004, when the Supreme Court's *Figueroa* decision required that new legislation be written establishing rules for the registration of political parties. The new legislation required that a party applying for registered party status run at least one candidate, and that its leader attest that one of the party's fundamental purposes is to participate in public affairs by endorsing one or more of its members as candidates and supporting their election. The government did not take the opportunity to require that a party have a constitution that required it to be internally democratic.

WORKS CITED

Canada. RCERPF (Royal Commission on Electoral Reform and Party Financing). 1991. *Reforming Electoral Democracy*. Ottawa: Ministry of Supply and Services.

Clark, Campbell. 2003. PMO Strikes Compromise with Key MPs on Financing. *Globe and Mail*, 5 June, A4.

Commission of Inquiry into the Sponsorship Program and Advertising Activities. 2005. *Who Is Responsible?* Ottawa: Government of Canada.

Federal Liberal Agency of Canada. 2003. Financial Statements, 31 December 2003. http://www.elections.ca/fin/rep/2003/liberal_2003.pdf.

Gauja, A. 2008. State Regulation and the Internal Organisation of Political Parties: The Impact of Party Law in Australia, Canada, New Zealand and the United Kingdom. *Commonwealth and Comparative Politics* 46(2): 244-61.

Greene, Ian. 2006. The Chrétien Ethics Legacy. In *The Chrétien Legacy: Politics and Public Policy in Canada*, ed. Lois Harder and Steve Patten, 276-99. Montreal and Kingston: McGill-Queen's University Press.

Johnston, Richard. 2000. Canadian Elections at the Millennium. *Choices* 6(6): 4-36.

Katz, R., and P. Mair. 1995. Changing Models of Party Organization and Party Democracy: The Emergence of the Cartel Party. *Party Politics* 1(1): 5-28.

Rekkas, Marie. 2007. The Impact of Campaign Spending on Votes in Multiparty Elections. *Review of Economics and Statistics* 89(3): 573-85.

Russell, Peter, and Lorne Sossin, eds. 2009. *Parliamentary Democracy in Crisis*. Toronto: University of Toronto Press.

van Biezen, I. 2008. State Intervention in Party Politics: The Public Funding and Regulation of Parties. *European Review* 16(3): 337-53.

Ware, A. 2002. *The American Direct Primary: Party Institutionalization and Transformation in the North.* Cambridge: Cambridge University Press.

State Funding of Political Parties
Truths, Myths, and Legends

JUSTIN FISHER

The Canadian party finance reforms of 2003 and 2006 raise some very interesting questions, especially in relation to the adoption of state subventions as a core method of funding major parties. In particular it taps into two key debates: why certain party funding systems are adopted and what are the wider consequences of any such reforms. Comparative political experience as well as political science should be able to offer some guidance here. Yet, unfortunately, political finance in general, and the state funding of political parties in particular, is an often under-researched and under-theorized area, and many myths persist about the desirability and effects of party funding systems. Indeed, some myths have the ability to become legends – repeated and reinforced by successive political scientists. Other myths are perpetuated by politicians and political commentators, and periodically resurface when the issue of party funding comes under the spotlight.

Perhaps the first myth to expose, and therefore discount, is that of the mass party. As Katz and Mair (1995, 5-6) note, the mass party has tended to be set up as the one against which all other models of party organization, and more specifically party funding, should be judged. Yet, such a comparison is arguably pointless. First, in most democracies, even if genuine mass parties ever existed, they are now effectively a historical curio. This mythical party, where funds are raised principally from small donations and small fundraising events, belongs to another age. But this has not prevented politicians and commentators from calling for a return to these mythical times. Nevertheless, mass parties may themselves be undesirable. Moisey Ostrogorski's criticisms, for example, indicate that the view that mass parties are a gold standard against which all other models should be judged is, at the very least, evidence that opinion is divided (McKenzie 1955, 8-9). And as Hopkin (2004) shows, there are good normative cases to be made for party funding models other than those of the mythical mass party. In sum then, political scientists, politicians, and commentators may all yearn for the golden age that never was, but this is not a fruitful way of thinking about party finance in more modern times. If mass parties therefore neither exist nor are universally praised, parties must be funded in other ways. Canada has opted to use state monies as the primary source of income for major parties, and this is a model of party funding that attracts perhaps the most truths, myths, and legends.

State Funding – The Theoretical Cases For and Against

Some form of state funding is prevalent in many, if not most, established democracies, as well as in many new democracies (van Biezen and Kopecký 2007, 242-23). One important consideration in any such discussion is that state funding can include small-scale as well as comprehensive support for parties. In the United Kingdom, for example, state support for party activity could arguably be said to date back to 1911, when the parties were freed from the burden of paying their MPs' salaries. Since then, small additions to state support (both direct and indirect) have been made, such that British parties are, to a very limited degree, dependent upon state money, despite state subventions in the United Kingdom being at a far lower level than those enjoyed in many other European countries (Fisher 2002, 393; 2009, 304). Thus, the principle of at least some state involvement in party politics is almost universally accepted even if, in truth, it may not be widely appreciated.

The Cases For

Most discussions surrounding the introduction of more comprehensive state funding, or extending the provision of state support, have focused on the following arguments in its favour, based in the reality that the genuine mass party as a means of funding parties is a non-achievable goal. First, there has been a recognition that party income has failed to keep pace with the demands on party expenditure, which are constantly rising. The increased use of mass media, more cost-intensive campaign techniques, internal professionalization within party organizations, and the increasing number of elections contested by parties have all contributed to the rising "costs of democracy," especially as campaigning has become almost permanent. The general decline in party membership has exacerbated these trends. Although its effects are probably overstated, parties have suffered a decline in income from membership dues. In addition, the decline in members has led to a decline in the number of volunteer workers available to engage in party activities – particularly, but not exclusively, at the time of elections. This, in part, has led parties to use campaign techniques that cost money, rather than the free services of members. In truth, this is partly because more modern techniques may be seen as being more efficient, but faced with membership decline, parties have little choice but to increasingly engage in non-volunteer based activities (Fisher and Denver 2008). This trend is clearly illustrated in Britain. Using measures of traditional (labour intensive) and modern (technology intensive) campaigning, Fisher and Denver (2008) show how district-level party campaigns have changed – by and large traditional campaigning has declined, whereas modernization has increased. And comparing overall change, the trend is relatively clear – each election has seen the balance of campaigning tilting more toward modernization, with 2001 being the tipping point.

The response to these problems by advocates of state funding is that parties should be seen as a fundamental part of a modern democracy and, as such, the state has a legitimate interest in providing an alternative or additional source of income in the wake of the imbalance of party income and expenditure needs. Thus, parties should not be punished for failing to keep financial pace with the demands of modern democracy. Rather, the state, acknowledging that membership decline may be a function of social as well as political trends, seeks to help maintain the parties' key role as the link between the citizen and the state by offering financial assistance. As van Biezen (2004) argues, parties have often come to be regarded less as voluntary organizations and more as public utilities. This in effect recognizes that a reliance of voluntary donations presents a collective action problem. The electorate as a whole benefits from the non-excludable public goods that parties produce. Yet, since no individual donation is likely to be sufficiently large to ensure the continued provision of public goods (the efficacy function), it is non-rational to donate, since the benefits of the production of public goods are non-excludable. Faced with this dilemma, state funding is a rational response to the collective action problem.

A second argument in favour of state funding concerns equality of opportunity for political competitors. Politics costs money, and some claim that money distorts political equality and work from the premise that greater financial means will lead to greater political influence (Adamany and Agree 1975, 2-3; Ewing 1992). It is argued that since all citizens have an equal right to political participation, so all interests should receive financial support in proportion to their adherents. The reality is, however, that wealthy groups are often represented beyond the proportion of their number. As a result, inequalities in money are greater than any other inequalities of the resources that go into political life, because money can buy virtually any of the resources that are given directly by citizens (Adamany and Agree 1975; Paltiel 1981). From this perspective, parties that cannot avail themselves of large sources of private income should not be disadvantaged. Importantly, it may not be parties of the left that are primarily disadvantaged. In Britain, for example, whereas the Conservative Party has traditionally been the primary recipient of corporate donations, Labour has enjoyed the significant financial support of some trade unions throughout its history. Thus, state funding may be endorsed as a means of supporting new entrants into the party system, as a means of supporting existing parties that do not enjoy regular support from established interests, and as a means to generate a more even political playing field when the income disparities between parties become too marked.

A third argument in favour of state funding is a desire to limit the influence of private money on politics and to limit its potential for distorting the democratic process. Thus, state funding is designed to limit or eliminate the potential for corruption and, importantly, the fear of corruption through the practice of voluntary donations (Gidlund 1991a; Pierre and Svåsand 1992; Nassmacher 1993). The point about the fear of corruption, rather than necessarily the actuality, is of key importance here. As Lösche (1993) has observed in Germany, even the *appearance* of corruption leads to negative feelings about parties and the ways those parties finance their organizations. As a result, if the state has an interest in maintaining the role of parties in a democracy, then it is legitimate to support parties financially in an effort to reduce or eliminate parties' reliance on private money. By doing this, fears about corruption, which can lead to a decline of public confidence in the probity of parties and public life, are removed. Birch (2008), for example, shows in a twenty-eight-country comparative analysis that the presence of state funding does tend to be associated with greater public confidence in the conduct of elections. That said, repeated comparative evidence points to continued problems of corruption and loophole seeking in spite of the existence of comprehensive state funding.

As a related point, state funding can be advanced as a means of protecting parties from the competition inherent in fundraising, thus allowing them both to pursue policies that serve the public good, rather than having any necessary concern for the impact of such policies on those that primarily fund them, and to spend time on drafting policy for the public good, rather than raising funds to assist party organization. Equally, as Hopkin (2004, 644) notes, a stronger emphasis on public rather than private money, distributed perhaps on the basis of electoral performance, exposes parties to greater competition than if they are traditionally shielded by wealthy contributors. For example, the review by Sir Hayden Phillips, a retired civil servant charged with leading an inquiry into British party finance, proposed an increase in state subventions based on votes received not only at Westminster level but also at devolved and European levels. If implemented, this would expose parties to greater competition, since the inclusion of non-Westminster parties would diminish the share enjoyed by the larger parties, in part because of the use of proportional electoral systems used in non-Westminster elections (Fisher 2009, 311).

The Cases Against
The theoretical cases against state funding are also numerous and include the idea of the cartel party. In the first instance, the idea of state funding can be seen as the threat to the historical role of parties as voluntaristic organizations and to the notion of parties as agents of participation and representation (Pierre, Svåsand, and Widfeldt 2000, 1). State funding challenges the notion of parties being agents of civil society, acting as intermediaries between citizens and the state, and instead makes parties, in effect, part of the state. Parties funded by the state rather than through voluntary effort, it is suggested, lose their independent role. Pierre, Svåsand, and Widfeldt (2000, 2-3) summarize this argument neatly: "Public financial support to the parties cannot guarantee the supremacy of the parties in the democracy, but may well jeopardise the representative and voluntaristic nature of the parties by effectively placing parties under state control."

In support of these broad arguments are theoretical claims about the detrimental impact of state funding – the claims are theoretical because, as Pierre, Svåsand, and Widfeldt (2000) illustrate, they are rarely subject to rigorous empirical investigation, yet enjoy almost mythical status. The first claim is that state funding affects the internal organization of political parties. In particular, it is argued that once in receipt of state money, parties will be disinclined to sustain or increase party membership. State funding therefore leads to a reduction in parties' dependence on membership dues and other voluntary membership donations. Not only that, state funded parties are able to replace voluntary labour (by members) with paid professionals, meaning that leaders need to take little or no heed of members' policy demands, since members effectively lose any sanction they enjoyed – either exiting the party or suspending campaigning activities. In sum, state funding creates parties that are non-responsive to party members because there is no incentive to exercise internal democracy. This leads to alienation of members and contributes to increasing centralization of party organization. Voters too become alienated because their participation has little impact on the operation of parties – the parties are funded regardless of how they perform. To take this argument to its logical conclusion, parties become more concerned with their relationship with the state, rather than with voters (ibid., 3).

A second claim made against systems of state financial support is that it petrifies the established party system. The virtue of voluntary funding is that parties survive or decline on account of their responsiveness to the electorate. Parties that are non-responsive, it is argued, will lose support and income, and new parties will emerge to replace them. State support, however, protects non-responsive parties and effectively prevents or slows down party decline. This not only maintains party positions artificially but also prevents declining parties being replaced by new entrants. This argument finds support from a free market position inasmuch as the state should not intervene in the marketplace of politics, since this distorts competition and is therefore not a legitimate means by which the state should utilize taxation. In addition, established parties have an interest in maintaining their advantaged position and therefore impose thresholds for state support, which are unattainable for new entrants. This has the effect of slowing or even preventing new entrants into the party system, since, like all parties, they need money to flourish.

A third argument in opposition to state funding is that the taxpayer should not be forced to financially support a party of which he or she does not approve. State funding, it is argued, forces citizens to support not only liberal democracy and the established party system but also political positions to which they themselves may be strongly opposed. A classic example used by proponents of this argument is the state support of extremist parties that may qualify under party funding rules but which a large majority of the electorate finds repugnant. Equally, however, supporters of one party may argue that it is unpalatable that they should indirectly support a competitor.

What Explains Decisions on State Funding?

Such arguments against state funding find their most accomplished theoretical representation in the idea of the cartel party. Katz and Mair (1995) outline how the cartel party has emerged and offer a somewhat pessimistic view of the effects of comprehensive state funding. Their analysis is based on the premise that state funding has grown significantly in many democracies but that the effects of state funding are ones that are controlled by dominant parties. To use their words, the "environmental change [of the growth of state funding] is far from exogenous to the parties" (ibid., 15). Thus, since parties also play the role of governors, it is they who are responsible for laying out the conditions under which parties are supported by the state and, indeed, how much they receive. For Katz and Mair (1995, 16), parties effectively "invade" the state and determine the resources to be distributed. By doing this, they seek to ensure their own survival and enhance their ability to resist the rise of alternative parties. Parties become "semi-state agencies" (ibid., 16).

Critically, parties collude in this process. This is a rational and predictable response in a game of coordination. For example, let us say there are two dominant parties. If Party A acts alone and seeks only to protect itself, there is a risk that when Party B returns to power, it will act in a punitive manner toward Party A. Party B faces the same dilemma. As a consequence, since both parties have an incentive to resist increased competition, the optimal outcome is coordination. This ensures that new entrants are disadvantaged, while reducing the risk of punitive action by the other party when it enters power.

For Katz and Mair (1995), the emergence of this cartel system leads to many of the problems identified by other opponents of state funding. For example, they suggest that campaigns run by cartel parties are almost exclusively capital-intensive, professional, and centralized, and that cartel parties rely increasingly for their resources on state subventions (as well as other state privileges afforded by their status) (ibid., 20). This, they argue, affects the status of members within parties, even makes the distinction between members and non-members potentially more blurred, with non-members invited to participate in party activities and decisions (20-21). In sum, state subventions create a cartel party system that is in almost every respect undesirable.

Cartel parties limit the possibility of intra-organizational dissent, minimize the consequences of competition within the cartel, protect themselves from the consequences of electoral dissatisfaction (since they will be funded anyway), and effectively prevent elections from performing a feedback function (23).

The arguments Katz and Mair advance have enjoyed mythical and perhaps even legendary status and are cited in supportive ways by commentators and academics alike. But more recent work casts doubt upon both the theoretical justifications of their position and the empirical evidence to support their assertions. For example, at the most basic level, we would expect some of the phenomena attributed to the introduction of extensive state funding of parties not to occur in countries where voluntary funding dominates. Yet, in Britain, where there is comparatively little in the way of state subventions, there is not only increasing party centralization (Fisher and Denver 2008, 808-11) but also an increasing blurring between members and supporters of parties (Fisher 2008, 261). One case does not, of course, tell the whole story, but this simple example highlights that a number of the effects associated with extensive state funding may actually be a function of other explanations.

The first alternative theoretical perspective is outlined by Scarrow (2004). She questions the assumption that the rational position for a party in state funding debates is always one of revenue maximization. A revenue-maximizing party is primarily interested in increasing its income, even beyond its immediate needs. This assumption lies at the heart of the cartel thesis, since it provides an incentive for parties to collude and shields them, to an extent, from the potentially damaging consequences of competition. Scarrow, however, posits an alternative incentive for parties. She suggests that rather than revenue maximization, parties may have short-term electoral success as their primary aim, and that they will evaluate revenue primarily in these terms. She calls this the "electoral economy" view (2004, 656). From this perspective, parties will seek only those funds that satisfy their needs and, once achieved, will not continue to devote energy to fundraising. Nonetheless, these two priorities are not mutually exclusive. Clearly, parties taking this view still require money to operate and campaign and, equally, revenue-maximizing parties will still seek electoral success. The principal difference between the revenue-maximizing party and the electoral economy party is the degree to which their differing views are prioritized.

Scarrow's insight suggests alternative outcomes to those predicted by the cartel model. First, the coordination and collusion predicted by the cartel thesis no longer holds. Scarrow suggests that from the revenue maximization perspective, parties will favour any scheme to increase their own income, regardless of whether this also assists their opponents. However, from an electoral economy perspective, we move from a game of coordination to one of conflict. Parties not only seek funds sufficient for their own needs, they also consider the effects of state subventions on their political competitors. For Scarrow (2004, 656), this helps explain why parties in receipt of individual and institutional donations, who have less need for state aid, have often been among the fiercest critics of state subventions. Of course, parties may have principled ideological objections to state support – particularly if they are supporters of laissez-faire economics. But Scarrow's explanation is nevertheless persuasive, since it allows for circumstances to change and parties to change their position – perhaps when private funds become less plentiful.

A second consequence of the electoral economy model is that parties may take into account public opinion on issues of state subventions and take a position accordingly, which may not be financially advantageous to them. With regard to public opinion, it is worth making two points. First, additional public expenditure on party funding is rarely likely to be popular. Second, public ignorance (not to mention media ignorance) about party funding is often substantial (vanHeerde-Hudson and Fisher forthcoming), or informed by broader (and not necessarily directly relevant) attitudes toward government (Persily and Lammie 2004; Rosenson 2009). For example, a 2003 survey conducted by MORI for the British Electoral Commission revealed that only 27 percent felt well informed about party funding (United Kingdom, Electoral Commission 2004, 14). Nevertheless, when there are party finance episodes ("scandal" is an overused and potentially spurious term), the salience of the issue rises significantly and can lead to significant changes in public opinion. For example, in 2004, ICM Research surveyed the British public about the principle of state funding as a means by which parties' dependency on donations could be reduced. Some 62 percent favoured state subventions (Joseph Rowntree Reform Trust 2004, 7). By 2006, following a significant episode in British party funding, ICM found only 20 percent favoured state subventions (ICM Research 2006).[1]

Scarrow (2004, 657) suggests that two likely outcomes flow from such patterns. First, when the public is "inattentive," the political costs of introducing additional public expenditure in the form of state funding are likely to be relatively low. However, and second, the costs rise considerably when there is negative publicity pertaining to party finance (and probably to parties in general). The result is that parties are less likely to support increases in state subventions in such circumstances. But more critically, electoral economy parties may seek to gain competitive political advantage by actively opposing increases in subventions, even if this is potentially financially damaging to their own party. Scarrow (2004, 659) therefore concludes that an assessment of which incentives – revenue maximization or electoral economy – are paramount, depends on political context, and indeed may help explain why different regulatory outcomes occur.

Scarrow's theory (2004) is tested in both the (West) German and British cases. In the German case, she shows that both the revenue-maximization and electoral economy theories are supported at different times, depending on the context. In Germany, she argues, there is more likely to be evidence of electoral economy parties, since there is a longer tradition of competition in party finance. Scarrow's evidence suggests, therefore, that the predictions of the revenue-maximization model do not always bear empirical scrutiny. Although they are apparent in Germany, they are not always so at all times, and in Britain there is far more support for the electoral economy model. Indeed, more recent research on the British case continues to confirm the fragility of the cartel approach for similar reasons (Fisher 2009).

A second alternative perspective is put forward by Clift and Fisher (2004), who examine party finance reform from a new institutionalist perspective. Using normative and historical institutionalism, they suggest that party funding reforms, including state funding, are likely to be a function of the constraints imposed by institutions rather than the intentional actions of strategic agents, as the cartel theory would suggest.

Normative institutionalism explicitly focuses on and takes account of the way in which institutions embody values. Although there is recognition of the interaction of institutions and individuals, and indeed of ideas, institutions, and interests (Thelen and Steinmo 1992, 14, 23), normative institutionalism assumes that political institutions influence behaviour by shaping "values, norms, interests, identities and beliefs" (March and Olsen 1989, 17). It is normative in the sense that it sees norms and values as explanatory variables.

The means by which values impact on behaviour is through the generation of norms, rules, understandings, and routines that "define appropriate actions" (March and Olsen 1984, 741; 1989, 21-26). This logic of appropriateness can constrain and shape the behaviour of actors. Actors consider whether behaviour is consistent with the internal norms or value structure of the institution. Thus, choices are constrained by what Peters (1999, 29) refers to as "the parameters established by the dominant institutional values." Institutions shape their own participants by supplying "systems of meaning," enabling institutions to express a logic of appropriateness. Thus, an "institution defines a set of behavioural expectations for individuals in positions within the institution and then reinforces behaviour that is appropriate for the role and sanctions behaviour that is inappropriate" (30). By such means can normative institutions "enforce" values and shape decisions. Decision makers, for example, may come to share particular values regarding the roles of political parties and their relationship to the state. As Young and Jansen show in this volume (Chapter 1), the party funding reforms introduced in Canada formed part of a broader ethics package following several scandals. Through the lens of normative institutionalism, the behaviour was no longer consistent with the norms and value structures within Canadian life, and the reforms could be seen as being shaped by a desire to restore appropriate behaviour. Critically for this approach, what constitutes a breach of the logic of appropriateness in one society may not represent a breach in another.

Clift and Fisher (2004) apply their hypotheses to the cases of France and Britain and find empirical support for their models. In the French case, they argue that normative institutional approaches have the most explanatory purchase over the introduction of state funding after 1988. They show that the voluntarist tradition of party finance had demonstrated its inability to "deliver" corruption-free political finance and, as a result, public confidence in the political system had been undermined. The response was the introduction of more comprehensive state funding, reflecting a continuation of the normative French model of party democracy: that parties are central to a functional French democracy and the normative goal was to deliver freely competitive political parties.

By way of contrast, normative institutionalism helps explain why Britain has resisted comprehensive state funding. Despite an overhaul of party funding legislation in 2000, the values of voluntarism in party finance were maintained. State funding was rejected by the main parties, reflecting a logic of appropriateness in terms of the most politically acceptable means of funding political parties. A further example of this came following the Phillips review of party finance. The review advocated an increase in state subventions (alongside the introduction of a cap on contributions), and the extension was not at the time opposed by any of the major parties. However, the subsequent government response rejected enhanced state funding, thereby maintaining the traditions of voluntarism (Fisher 2009, 315).

Clift and Fisher (2004) also utilize historical institutionalism, the key aspect of which is that choices are made early in the history of any policy or system, and these initial policy choices determine subsequent decisions. These choices may be normative, of course. Yet, although some initial choices will be based on normative values, others will not. A policy choice may, for example, originate as a result of expediency. The point remains, however, that regardless of subsequent structural choices, initial choices in a policy field will have an enduring impact – they will shape both the strategies and goals pursued by political actors (Thelen and Steinmo 1992, 8). This may be referred to as path dependency. Policy evolution can occur, but developments are constrained by the formative period of the institution (Peters 1999, 65). These constraints will also be influenced by historical preferences for certain ideas or core values. Here, institutions produce sets of ready solutions for policy problems, based on enduring ideas. These contribute to limits on what are acceptable actions by governments or institutions. Thus, attempts at institutional redesign are carried out against a backdrop of a set of past practices, which brings with it its own peculiar set or constraints and possibilities (Goodin 1996, 30). In sum, it is these perspectives that largely determine the course of party finance reform, including state funding. Both normative and historical institutions constrain policy choices, thus making it either more or less likely that state funding will occur.

Clift and Fisher's examination (2004) of the British approach to party funding suggests the utility of these historical approaches. For example, the introduction of national spending ceilings in 2000 as a means of reducing excessive spending and alleviating concerns about the ability of wealthy candidates to gain political advantage represented an echo of legislation first introduced in 1883. Spending limits were adopted rather than other means of equalizing electoral contests, such as state funding. Thus, historical precedent provided a constraint on other possible policy options on the basis that it has been seen to work relatively well at the local level. This approach was repeated in the government's response to the Phillips review, with emphasis again placed on limiting campaign spending as a means of equalizing electoral contests (Fisher 2009, 312-15). In Canada, too, Young and Jansen in this volume (Chapter 1) show how the regulatory tools employed in the reforms frequently reflected tried and tested policy instruments.

A further variant on these themes is advanced by Koss (2008). He draws on actor-centred institutionalism, which argues that decisions on state subventions and party finance reform more generally are a function of the desires of intentional actors (as per Katz and Mair 1995, and Scarrow 2004), but that the actors' interactions are "structured, and the outcomes shaped by the characteristics of the institutional settings in which they occur" (Scharpf 1997, 1, as quoted in Koss 2008, 285). This approach claims to reject normative institutionalism as an explanation (as advanced by Clift and Fisher) and instead focuses on the interaction between the institutional context, the actors' orientations, and the context of specific situations in which decisions take place (Koss 2008, 285). Arguably, however, the "context of specific situations" is actually a component of the normative institutionalism advanced by Clift and Fisher (2004), since it focuses on such things as dominant discourses on political corruption in shaping parties' goals. This is akin to the logic of appropriateness, as it appears in normative institutionalism.

Nevertheless, the key contribution of Koss's approach is to highlight the institutional setting as a further explanation for why reforms such as state funding are introduced. He highlights the veto points that different institutional arrangements produce. For example, using Germany as a case study, he suggests that the electoral law in Germany led parties to be reluctant to adopt confrontational strategies on party finance. Rather, the institutional setting led them to prefer cooperation on this issue through a desire to retain influence in coalition arrangements (Koss 2008, 294).

Empirical Evidence

Both Scarrow's and Clift and Fisher's analyses arrive at similar conclusions, despite using different theoretical paradigms. Neither finds consistent evidence of the kind of collusion predicted by the cartel model. Moreover, Fisher's subsequent study (2009) of proposed British reforms arrives at similar conclusions. In the Belgian case, Weekers and colleagues (2009, 45) also find that, rather than active party cooperation, fear of corruption and the increases in campaign expenses were of decisive importance in the adoption of party funding reforms, which included state subventions. Koss, too, although finding evidence of cooperation between parties, suggests that the basis of cooperation is less to do with cartel-like behaviour and more to do with institutional arrangements and their related veto points. In short, the "legend" of the cartel model is open to challenge on theoretical grounds.

However, this work, as well as that of others, indicates that many of the claims about state funding are also questionable on wider empirical grounds. Pierre, Svåsand, and Widfeldt (2000) test numerous assumptions about the outcomes of state funding – particularly those advanced by the cartel thesis. What they find is very limited support for the claims made about the effects of state funding. First, they show that, far from as predicted, there is no continuous pattern of increasing financial dependency on the state. Moreover, far from helping to exclude new party entrants, state funding regimes appear to help consolidate the position of smaller parties following an electoral breakthrough. Second, they challenge the assumption that state funding leads to membership decline and is welcomed by party elites in order to provide stable income and reduce incentives for membership involvement (ibid., 16-19). They suggest that trends in party membership decline are not exacerbated by the introduction of state subsidies, as critics predicted. Rather, patterns of membership decline (and in some cases expansion) continue much as they were, regardless of the introduction of subventions. Third, they test assumptions about party system petrification (20-21) and again they show that the assumptions do not bear up to empirical scrutiny. Party systems are not petrified by the introduction of state subventions.

Other comparative research (Nassmacher 1989; Gidlund 1991b) also suggests that the purported negative impacts of state funding have been overstated. On the one hand, the claim that state funding is a tool to fight corruption where it exists is not supported. It has not wholly eliminated corruption or loophole seeking. In addition, it suggests that party bureaucratization and professionalism has grown, as have party resources and costs. However, these studies do show that state funding is just one of many factors that lead to party centralization. Finally, and on a more positive note, it is the case that state funding has produced an increase in party activities and a greater ability to maintain activities between elections.

Overall, then, many of the assumptions associated with the cartel thesis, both in terms of an explanation for the introduction of extensive state subventions and the consequences of their adoption, are evidently open to challenge. Indeed, what perhaps hinders the broader explanatory power of this model and related works on party funding is a particular normative conception of the state (Fisher 2009, 315). Katz and Mair present a fairly grim picture of cartel parties, suggesting that their behaviour and the state funding that follows produces outcomes that are almost universally negative. Equally, van Biezen and Kopecký (2007) exaggerate what they describe as party dependence on the state by using only a binary measure to indicate the availability of state funds. As Fisher (2009, 302-4) shows, this fails to differentiate appropriately between the wide range of subvention levels that are available and therefore potentially distorts the picture. In a similar vein, Fisher criticizes van Biezen and Kopecký's assertion that any form of party regulation represents state management (ibid. 304). The use of such misleading language again betrays the normative basis of their claims, which may potentially diminish their otherwise significant empirical contribution.

None of this, of course, is to challenge the wisdom of using comparative politics to help explain phenomena and inform about the potential impacts of reforms. As Fisher (2009, 315) notes, one of the least helpful criticisms of comparative analysis is pedantic claims about models not fitting all cases equally well. The arguments presented here represent a desire, rather, to also present comparative models that apply different variables and make different assumptions about actors' rational motivations. Legends should not be the only model in town, particularly when there are very credible alternatives.

Conclusions

Until recently, the study of party funding in general, and state funding in particular, has suffered from a lack of conceptual and comparative work. The result was that several "truths" were established. These so-called truths were neither systematically tested nor subject to theoretical rigour. As a result, arguments surrounding state funding, both positive and negative, were often based on myths and untested "truths." Katz and Mair's (1995) analysis represented a sophisticated attempt to address this lacuna – a legend was born that was theoretically informed and offered a plausible interpretation of the motivations of parties and the effects of state funding.

Yet, more recent work has cast doubt upon both the early myths and the insights of Katz and Mair. From a theoretical perspective, the work of Scarrow (2004), Clift and Fisher (2004), and Koss (2008) suggests that different explanations from that of revenue maximizing parties may drive party finance reforms, which include state funding. Scarrow's insights, like those of Katz and Mair, are informed by rational choice theory but argue that parties may have different goals than those assumed by Katz and Mair. Clift and Fisher base their analysis in new institutionalism, and suggest that this is a more convincing model to explain changes in party finance regulations – at least in France and Britain. And Koss reminds us that the broader institutional environment may influence decisions. Empirically, too, there are reasons to question the applicability of Katz and Mair's cartel model. Pierre, Svåsand, and Widfeldt (2000), for example, demonstrate that many of the effects of state funding claimed by Katz and Mair are not supported in their comparative analysis.

Yet, despite all this work, some commentators and political scientists remain loyal to the myths and legends. In Britain, for example, commentators appear to cling to the idea that either state funding is a "cure" for apparent corruption or that an imminent return to the mass party is realistic. Neither view is credible. Equally, the cartel model generates loyalty. Jonathan Hopkin (2004, 635), for example, although acknowledging the critics of the cartel model, still essentially endorses the thesis.

In sum, although the comparative approach is to be strongly endorsed, the work of Clift and Fisher, Scarrow, and Koss suggest that such models should have the capacity to evaluate individual national conditions rather more fully. Clift and Fisher's analysis of France and Britain, for example, shows that the same comparative framework can be used but that different results may emerge in each country on account of differing institutions and preferences. As a consequence, it is arguably better to employ such methods as competing explanations to untested "truths" and myths, and the legend of the cartel model.

NOTE

1 This was the so-called loans-for-peerages episode, where it was alleged that those who had made financial loans to political parties were nominated for peerages in return. The allegations prompted a lengthy police enquiry, which resulted in no charges being brought. However, despite the lack of any evidence of wrongdoing, press coverage of the episode was overwhelmingly negative.

WORKS CITED

Adamany, David W., and George E. Agree. 1975. *Political Money*. Baltimore: Johns Hopkins University Press.
Birch, Sarah. 2008. Electoral Institutions and Popular Confidence in Electoral Processes: A Cross-National Analysis. *Electoral Studies* 27(2): 305-20.
Clift, Ben, and Justin Fisher. 2004. Comparative Party Finance Reform: The Cases of France and Britain. *Party Politics* 10(6): 677-99.
Ewing, Keith. 1992. *Money, Politics and Law*. Oxford: Clarendon Press.
Fisher, Justin. 2002. Next Step: State Funding for the Parties? *Political Quarterly* 73(4): 392-99.
–. 2008. Whither the Parties? In *Constitutional Futures Revisited*, ed. Robert Hazell, 249-66. Basingstoke: Palgrave.
–. 2009. Hayden Phillips and Jack Straw: The Continuation of British Exceptionalism in Party Finance? *Parliamentary Affairs* 62(2): 298-317.
Fisher, Justin, and David Denver. 2008. From Foot-Slogging to Call Centres and Direct Mail: A Framework for Analysing the Development of District-Level Campaigning. *European Journal of Political Research* 47(6): 794-826.
Gidlund, Gullan. 1991a. Public Investments in Swedish Democracy. In Wiberg 1991, 13-54.

—. 1991b. The Nature of Public Financing in Nordic States. In Wiberg 1991, 173-85.
Goodin, Robert. 1996. Institutions and Their Design. In *The Theory of Institutional Design*, ed. Robert Goodin, 1-53. Cambridge: Cambridge University Press.
Gunlicks, Arthur B. 1993. *Campaign and Party Finance in North America and Western Europe*. Boulder, CO: Westview Press.
Hopkin, Jonathan. 2004. The Problem with Party Finance: Theoretical Perspectives on the Funding of Political Parties. *Party Politics* 10(6): 627-51.
ICM Research 2006. Guardian Poll: Fieldwork Dates 21-23rd April 2003. London: ICM Research.
Joseph Rowntree Reform Trust. 2004. *State of the Nation Poll 2004: Summary of Main Findings*. London: Joseph Rowntree Reform Trust.
Katz, Richard, and Peter Mair. 1995. Changing Models of Party Organization and Party Democracy: The Emergence of the Cartel Party. *Party Politics* 1(1): 5-28.
Koss, Michael. 2008. Party Goals, Institutional Veto Points and the Discourse on Political Corruption: The Evolution of the German Party Funding Regime. *Journal of Elections, Public Opinion and Parties* 18(3): 283-301.
Lösche, Peter. 1993. Problems of Party and Campaign Financing in Germany and the United States – Some Comparative Reflections. In Gunlicks 1993, 219-30.
March, James G., and Johan P. Olsen. 1984. The New Institutionalism: Organizational Factors in Political Life. *American Political Science Review* 78(3): 734-49.
—. 1989. *Rediscovering Institutions*. New York: Free Press.
McKenzie, Robert T. 1955. *British Political Parties*. London: Heinemann.
Nassmacher, Karl-Heinz. 1993. Comparing Party and Campaign Finance in Western Democracies. In Gunlicks 1993, 233-67.
Paltiel, Khayyam Z. 1981. Campaign Finance: Contrasting Practices and Reforms. In *Democracy at the Polls*, ed. David Butler, Howard R. Penniman, and Austin Ranney, 138-73. Washington, DC: American Enterprise Institute.
Persily, Nathaniel, and Kelli Lammie. 2004. Perceptions of Corruption and Campaign Finance: When Public Opinion Determines Constitutional Law. *University of Pennsylvania Law Review* 153(1): 119-81.
Peters, B. Guy. 1999. *Institutional Theory in Political Science*. London: Continuum.
Pierre, Jon, and Lars Svåsand. 1992. *The Parties and the State: Money, Members and Managers*. Paper presented at the European Consortium for Political Research conference, Limerick, Ireland.
Pierre, Jon, Lars Svåsand, and Anders Widfeldt. 2000. State Subsidies to Political Parties: Confronting Rhetoric with Reality. *West European Politics* 23(3): 1-24.
Rosenson, Beth Ann. 2009. The Effect of Political Reform Measures on Perceptions of Corruption. *Election Law Journal* 8(1): 31-46.
Scarrow, Susan. 2004. Explaining Party Finance Reforms: Competition and Context. *Party Politics* 10(6): 653-75.
Scharpf, Fritz W. 1997. *Games Real Actors Play: Actor-Centred Institutionalism in Policy-Research*. Boulder, CO: Westview Press.

Thelen, Kathleen, and Sven Steinmo. 1992. Historical Institutionalism in Comparative Politics. In *Structuring Politics,* ed. Sven Steinmo, Kathleen Thelen, and Frank Longstreth, 1-32. Cambridge: Cambridge University Press.

United Kingdom. Electoral Commission. 2004. *The Funding of Political Parties.* London: Electoral Commission.

van Biezen, Ingrid. 2004. Political Parties as Public Utilities. *Party Politics* 10(6): 701-22.

van Biezen, Ingrid, and Petr Kopecký. 2007. The State and the Parties: Public Funding, Public Regulation and Rent-Seeking in Contemporary Democracies. *Party Politics* 13(2): 235-54.

vanHeerde-Hudson, Jennifer, and Justin Fisher. 2011. Parties Heed (with caution): Public Knowledge of and Attitudes towards Party Finance in Britain. *Party Politics* (forthcoming).

Weekers, Karolien, Bart Maddens, and Jo Noppe. 2009. Explaining the Evolution of the Party Finance Regime in Belgium. *Journal of Elections, Public Opinion and Parties* 19(1): 25-48.

Wiberg, Matti, ed. 1991. *The Public Purse and Political Parties,* ed., 13-54. Helsinki: Finnish Political Science Association.

3

Public Funding of Political Parties
The Case for Further Reform

F. LESLIE SEIDLE

A 2005 study of the state of Canadian political parties concluded they do not have strong roots in the community, do not empower their members to act politically, and are not the vehicles for "bold new policy ideas" (Fox 2005, 4). In some respects, this was old news. After all, public opinion research has shown for some time that many Canadians are critical of political parties, including the degree to which they are responsive to citizens and can be trusted to keep their promises.[1]

Even if this critique was not new, it should be of concern to Canadians – even more so because of the extent to which taxpayers now fund federal political parties. Public funding of parties is, of course, not unique to Canada and, as discussed in the first section of this chapter, can be justified on a number of grounds. The main elements of the Canadian regime – reimbursements to parties and candidates, and tax credits for donations – date from 1974. As described in the second section, the level of public funding increased markedly as a result of legislative changes that took effect in 2004, notably the introduction of new annual allowances to parties. The latter were intended to compensate for the expected loss of revenue from the new contribution limits that were central to the 2004 reform. The debates on that occasion underlined how the evolution of public funding has evolved with little reference to concerns about parties' inter-election activities and overall role within the democratic process. The third section addresses further reforms intended to make the public funding regime more accessible to emerging parties, provide incentives to elect more women, and enhance public policy development. The chapter concludes by suggesting that when Parliament reviews the political finance reforms of the last decade, changes to promote these objectives should be on the agenda.

The Rationale for Public Funding of Political Parties

The International Institute for Democracy and Electoral Assistance (IDEA) reported in 2003 that 65 of the 111 countries that participated in its study provided direct public funding to political parties (International IDEA 2003, 182-83).[2] The roots of public funding in these countries vary considerably. In certain cases, as in Canada, the groundwork for reform may have been laid by an independent commission or a legislative committee. In other situations, the introduction of public funding has come about in a more ad hoc manner – sometimes following inter-party agreement. As for the objectives of such measures, the academic literature and reports by election management bodies identify numerous benefits often associated with the public funding of political parties.[3]

Reducing Undue Influence from Large Private Donations

Political parties face considerable pressure to fund increasingly costly election campaigns. In countries that limit the election spending of parties and/or candidates, the clamour of fundraising may not be as intense, but in an era of citizen indifference it is rare for any party to be significantly in the black following a general election. Where spending limits do not apply or are not very stringent, the need for significant private money can lead fundraisers to seek out large donations and, in some cases, to reach understandings with donors about future government projects, grants, and so on. Replacing some private money with public money is thus seen as a way of reducing undue influence. In some cases, public funding has been introduced as a response to scandals about money from suspect sources (Pinto-Duschinsky 2002, 74).

Strengthening Parties through a More Stable Financial Base

Even in political systems with fairly extensive regulation, such as election spending limits, costs cannot be accurately predicted; nor can revenues. A party's coffers may suffer not only because fundraising efforts flag but also because of fluctuations in its popularity. Public funding for parties is most often based on performance at the previous election (for example, votes received, members elected). Each party can thus count on a certain amount of money from the state each year. The financing of parties is sometimes linked to their fundamental role within democratic systems. For example, in its 1991 report, Canada's Royal Commission on Electoral Reform and Party Financing (the Lortie Commission) devoted an entire chapter to public funding and other reforms reflecting parties' role as primary political organizations. In a similar vein, one of the other authors in this volume has written that "there is a strong case to be made that more comprehensive state funding should be introduced to ensure that parliamentary democracy is properly funded" (Fisher 2002, 398).

Fostering Fairness and Equity for Political Parties

As with election spending limits, it is argued that public funding helps level the playing field: the measures can narrow the gap between the larger, well-established (and often richer) parties and smaller or new parties, which often have lower revenues from private sources. The degree to which this objective is met depends in part on how difficult it is for smaller parties to gain access to public funding. For example, with a fairly low vote threshold, a greater number of parties will qualify (even if the amounts they receive may not be very high).

Promoting Research, Policy Development, and Political Education within Parties

In a considerable number of countries – particularly in western Europe – public funding is intended to sustain parties' inter-election activities, including research, policy development, and political education. The Netherlands provides an interesting example of belief in such objectives. In the International IDEA survey referred to above, the response of the Dutch government to the question "What is the purpose of the direct public funding?" was as follows:

> 1. Socio-political education. 2. To provide information to political party members. 3. To keep in touch with political sister organizations in other countries. 4. To support socio-political education for the benefit of political sister organizations in other countries. 5. Research activities developed by political parties. 6. Activities promoting the political participation of youth. (International IDEA 2003, 214)

All but the third and fourth of these elements reflect a vision of political parties as organizations that devote considerable resources to important inter-election activities such as research and policy development, and to informing, educating, and mobilizing present and potential party members (particularly youth).

In some countries, notably the United States, there is strong resistance to the public funding of parties and/or candidates. The limited public funding of presidential campaigns – based on an income tax check-off – has survived from the 1974 campaign finance reforms,[4] but various attempts to institute more robust measures to diminish the need for contributions from individuals and political action committees have failed. However, public funding of parties faces criticism even in countries where the principle is well established.[5] The following are some of the concerns expressed:

- Taxpayers should not be obliged to fund parties (including extremist ones) and/or candidates with whom they disagree.
- Public funding will entrench the existing parties and make it more difficult for new ones to enter the political arena.[6]
- Parties will devote less effort to local and member-based fundraising, thus diminishing member involvement and grassroots activity in general.
- Parties will become less able to act independently of government. According to Richard Katz and Peter Mair (1995, 16-17), state subvention has led to the emergence of cartel parties, which depend on public resources rather than volunteers, leading to "the interpenetration of party and state."[7]

With regard to the last claim, Leon Epstein introduced the label "public utility" to describe the transformation of parties resulting from several developments, including the introduction of party labels on ballots and the spread of state-administered direct primaries. As a result, parties became "agenc[ies] performing a service in which the public has a special interest sufficient to justify governmental regulatory control" (Epstein 1986, 157).

As for other countries, Epstein (1986, 156) wrote that "generally ... parties outside of the United States do not purchase the privilege of ballot access by surrendering control of their label bestowal to a government-conducted election or even to an election or other process closely supervised by governmental authority." He clearly had not examined the Canadian case. Even at the time his book was published it was already justifiable, as we shall see in the next section, to apply the label "public utility" to Canadian federal political parties (see van Biezen 2004).

The Evolution and Impact of Public Funding of Canadian Political Parties

The 1970 introduction of party labels on ballots for Canadian federal elections was an important initial step in the regulation of parties' election spending and finance (Courtney 1978). In fact, more comprehensive regulation of these matters began to be studied a few years earlier. Although outright corruption was less a factor than in some other countries, certain financial scandals in the early 1960s were part of the reason the Liberal government established the House of Commons Committee on Election Expenses (Barbeau Committee) in 1964 (Seidle 1985, 114). Other factors were the rising costs of elections and the example provided by Quebec's 1963 reform.[8] The committee's principal recommendations (Canada, Committee on Election Expenses, 1966) were to institute spending limits for candidates (but not parties), reimbursement of part of candidates' media advertising costs, disclosure of parties' and candidates' revenue and spending, and a tax credit for contributions to parties and candidates.

Although continued escalation of election costs, particularly television advertising, was the main reason the Trudeau Liberal government finally introduced political finance legislation, controversy about the sources of party funds (the Liberal Party was often criticized as being too reliant on contributions from big business) and spillover from the Watergate scandal in the United States were also factors (Seidle and Paltiel 1981, 229, 232). A key objective of the reforms was to promote greater fairness in electoral competition. A further objective was to encourage participation in public life. David Lewis, then leader of the New Democratic Party (NDP), referred to the principle of public funding as "one of the best ways of making certain the relatively poor person can be a candidate, and the relatively poor political party can do a job for the people of Canada" (Hansard, 12 July 1973).

The Election Expenses Act, which came into effect in 1974, introduced what was then the most comprehensive political finance regulatory framework in Canada. This included spending limits for registered political parties and candidates; annual reporting of registered parties' revenue and expenses; and reporting of parties' and candidates' election expenses and contributions. As for public funding, the rules were as follows:

- To qualify for public funding, political parties had to be registered, which meant they either had to have twelve MPs when Parliament was dissolved or have nominated fifty candidates for the election. All registered parties could claim reimbursement of 50 percent of their radio and television advertising expenses.

- Registered parties had the right, during and between elections, to issue receipts allowing donors to claim an income tax deduction; and they were allowed (a practice that predates the 1974 reform) to sponsor "free time" radio and television broadcasts between and during elections.
- Candidates also benefited from public funding: those who obtained at least 15 percent of the votes in an electoral district qualified for reimbursement of 50 percent of their election expenses; during election campaigns, all candidates had the right to issue income tax receipts.

Evolution of the Public Funding Regime
The public funding regime evolved in the 1980s and 1990s through a number of changes. In 1983, the law was amended to stipulate that, to qualify for reimbursement, a party had to spend at least 10 percent of its election expenses limit. The rationale for this amendment is unclear. If there was a concern that fringe parties would cash in on the public purse, this was largely unfounded. Parties other than the three represented in the House of Commons together received only $2,017 in reimbursements following the 1980 election. The same bill also led to a new basis for calculating the reimbursement: qualifying parties were subsequently reimbursed for 50 percent of their total election expenses.

In 1996, the 10 percent spending rule was replaced with the following provision: a registered party has to win at least 2 percent of the valid votes cast nationwide or 3 percent of the votes in electoral districts in which it had candidates to qualify for reimbursement. This came about through a private member's bill sponsored by Ian McClelland of the Reform Party. His action was apparently triggered by the Natural Law Party of Canada, following the 1993 general election, receiving a reimbursement of $712,722. (One of the party's election advertisements, which featured a yogic flyer who promised to use magic to make the federal government's debt disappear, did not amuse everyone.) In the debate on McClelland's bill, MPs and senators repeatedly claimed they did not wish to block the way for new parties but said a line had to be drawn somewhere. As shown in Figure 3.1, the number of parties qualifying for reimbursement dropped from the high of eight reached in 1993 to five in 1997, where it has remained for the four subsequent elections.

Parties' access to public funding was also affected by a 1993 amendment that raised the candidate's deposit from $200 to $1,000. The candidates of a new party seeking registration thus have to raise a total of $50,000 just for deposits. However, it has since become considerably easier for a party to

FIGURE 3.1

Registered parties and parties that qualified for reimbursement, 1979-2008 federal general elections

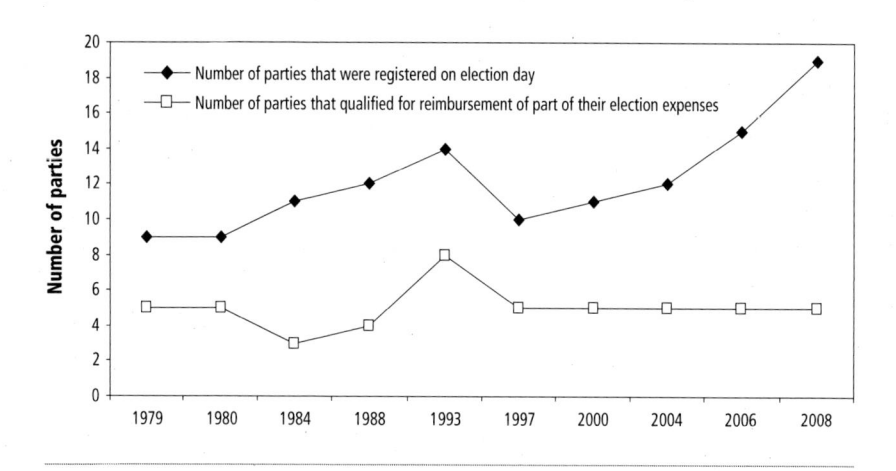

```
                    Number of parties that were registered on election day
                    Number of parties that qualified for reimbursement of part of their election expenses
```

[Line graph showing number of parties on y-axis (0-20) versus election years on x-axis (1979, 1980, 1984, 1988, 1993, 1997, 2000, 2004, 2006, 2008). Registered parties line: 9, 9, 11, 12, 14, 10, 11, 12, 15, 19. Qualified for reimbursement line: 5, 5, 3, 4, 8, 5, 5, 5, 5, 5.]

become registered. Shortly before the 2004 election, legislation (Bill C-3) that responded to the Supreme Court's 2003 decision in the *Figueroa* case came into effect.[9] As a result, a party now becomes registered (or remains registered) if it fields at least one candidate at a general election.

As illustrated in Figure 3.1, the number of parties that met the registration requirements rose in the 1980s, reaching fourteen in 1993. In 1997, the number dropped to ten, and then rose to eleven in 2000. Although the number of registered political parties has risen since passage of Bill C-3, the increase has not been as large as some MPs feared: in the 2004 election, twelve parties were registered; in 2006, there were fifteen; and in 2008 nineteen.

Khayyam Paltiel described some of the initial amendments to the 1974 reform as "testimony to the institutionalization of the major parties" (Paltiel 1996, 418). Some thirty-five years after that reform, this has not been the case. New parties have not only been able to register, but some of them have elected significant numbers of MPs. In the 1993 election, in which the governing Progressive Conservative (PC) Party was reduced to two members, two parties formed only a few years before won more than one-third of the seats: the Bloc Québécois (BQ), a sovereignist party created in 1990 after the death of the Meech Lake constitutional accord, elected fifty-four MPs and became the official opposition; and the Reform Party, a "true" conservative party based in western Canada that was registered for the 1988 election (but elected no MPs), won fifty-two seats. The BQ has continued to hold the largest share of Quebec's seats. After a series of intermediate steps, the Alliance Party merged with the remnants of the PC Party in 2004 to form the Conservative Party of Canada (CPC); in 2006, the CPC formed a minority government. Thus, although the major parties may have colluded to try to ensure the registration and reimbursement rules were not overly welcoming to new parties (Young 1998, 357-58), the result has not been petrification or cartelization of the federal party system.

Bill C-24 and Bill C-2

With minor exceptions, the other relevant elements of the Canada Elections Act remained unchanged until the amendments introduced through Bill C-24 came into effect on 1 January 2004. Its principal objective, according to government statements, was to counter perceptions of undue influence on the part of major donors to the Liberal Party – some of whom, as it was later shown, benefited from generous government contracts (this is discussed further in Chapter 1).[10] Bill C-24, which led to the most extensive reform of federal party and election finance since 1974, included limits on political contributions, regulations of nomination contestants and leadership contestants, an increase in the rate of reimbursement for political parties, a new quarterly allowance for parties, and an increase in the value of the income tax credit (for details, see Table 1.1).

Reflecting his personal commitment to the reforms, Prime Minister Chrétien – rather than the sponsoring minister, Don Boudria (Government House Leader) – moved second reading of Bill C-24 on 11 February 2003. Chrétien made it clear that the primary purpose of the increase in public funding was to make up for the parties' loss of revenue from business and trade unions:

> The increase in the individual tax credit, the increase in the rebate and the direct subsidy to the party will make up for the loss of corporate and trade union contributions and it will do so through public financing, the only way to remove the perception that big money influences decisions of government. We can do this at a cost of about 65¢ per Canadian in non-election years and a bit more than $1 per Canadian in an election year. This is a very small price to pay for helping to improve our democracy. It is a very good investment of public funds. (Hansard, 11 February 2003)

When Boudria appeared before the House of Commons Standing Committee on Procedure and House Affairs, he explained how the amount per vote used to calculate each party's allowance had been determined: "We took into account contributions received by parties over the last electoral cycle, and we estimated the amount of contributions that would have been lost to parties as a result of the prohibition on corporate and union donations. The resulting ... allowance would ensure that no party would lose from this restriction." Boudria did make a nod to parties' roles between elections: "Political parties ... incur expenses outside election periods. They carry out responsibilities, and public funding or funding of some sort is essential to their effectiveness" (Canada, House of Commons, Standing Committee on Procedure and House Affairs). This recalls one of the objectives of public funding that Justin Fisher identifies in his chapter in this volume: recognizing that parties are a fundamental part of a modern democracy and that the state has a legitimate interest in providing an alternative source of income if there is an imbalance in their revenue and expenditure needs. Boudria had no more to say about the policy objectives of this very significant increase in public funding, and during the remainder of the committee proceedings the debate focused on the issue of compensating the parties for the projected loss of revenue they would suffer as a result of banning business and union donations. There was also some discussion of the amount of the allowances, and the committee recommended that the amount per vote per year, originally set at $1.50, be increased to $1.75. During report stage, the bill was amended to this effect.

In late 2006, Parliament adopted Bill C-2, the Accountability Act, which the Harper government introduced in response to the report of the Gomery Commission (discussed in further detail in Chapter 1). This led to significant changes to the contribution limits that had come into effect only at the start of 2004. As of 1 January 2007, individuals could give a maximum of $1,000 to a registered party each year. At the constituency level, businesses, unions, and other organizations could no longer make political contributions, and the amount of an individual's contributions was limited to an aggregate of $1,000 a year to the local entities of a registered party (candidates, electoral district associations, and nomination contestants). In addition, an individual could give a maximum of $1,000 to a candidate or candidates in a party leadership contest (adjusted for inflation).

These two sets of amendments have had a significant impact on the funding of national parties. For some parties, public funding is now several times greater than their revenue from donations. The BQ is the most notable case in point. As shown in Table 3.1, its total direct public funding in 2004 was 6.3 times the total contributions it received from individuals; this figure rose to 9.8 in 2006 and dropped to 7.7 in 2008. The ratio for the Liberal Party in 2004, 4.1, was the second highest. In 2006, the NDP had the second-highest ratio, and in 2008 the Liberals were again in second position. The contrast with the pattern prior to the 2004 amendments is very striking: in 2000, the ratio of public funding to donations to the BQ was 0.18; the ratios for the other parties that qualified for reimbursement were: Progressive Conservative – 0.16, NDP – 0.16, Liberals – 0.14, and Alliance – 0.11 (for additional discussion of these trends, see Chapter 5).

Looking at the pattern of non-public contributions (from all sources in 2000 and from individuals only in 2004), additional contrasts emerge. The Liberals, who were returned as a minority government at the 2004 election, received only $4.7 million in contributions (from individuals) that year – equal to 24 percent of the party's total donations in 2000 (not counting inflation). In 2006, the year it lost power to the Conservatives, the Liberal Party's fundraising improved somewhat, but by 2008 donations fell back to slightly less than $6 million. The second-greatest difference in 2004 was for the BQ: its total contributions equalled 38 percent of the donations it received in 2000. By 2006, contributions to the BQ amounted to only 23 percent of its 2000 donations. On a proportional basis, the BQ has clearly benefited the most from the 2004 public funding measures. That said, the data suggest it may be devoting less energy to fundraising than it did prior to the introduction of the annual allowances: in 2007, the BQ received only $430,061 from private contributions. The Green Party has also been a clear beneficiary. Based on the expectation that it would qualify for a reimbursement and the annual allowance, it was able to borrow money and conduct more professional campaigns in 2004 and 2006. Moreover, the party's move from the fringes of national politics, assisted partly by public funding, meant that by the 2006 election it was receiving more extensive media coverage (Young, Sayers, and Jansen 2007, 345). In addition, it has increased its support from individuals: in 2007, the Greens received $984,605 from contributions – more than it did in election year 2006 (and 2.3 times the value of contributions to the BQ in 2007). It remains to be seen whether the next step for the Green Party is to enter the House of Commons. In the meantime, it is fair to say that public funding has helped raise the party's profile.

The Liberals, traditionally heavily dependent on business, have had considerable difficulty adapting to the C-24 rules. The party was also hampered by the absence of a national membership list (the provincial and territorial wings kept separate lists). Following a rule change adopted at the Liberals'

TABLE 3.1

Public funding of Canadian federal political parties, 2000-08 election years

Political party	Total non-public contributions* ($)	Post-election reimbursements ($)	Annual allowances** ($)	Public funding as proportion of non-public contributions (%)
2008				
Liberal	5,811,492	7,259,963	8,701,264	275
Conservative	21,179,483	9,709,290	10,439,132	95
NDP	5,412,940	8,377,235	5,030,293	248
Bloc Québécois	713,085	2,438,060	3,017,093	765
Green	1,621,532	1,397,900	1,289,952	166
2006				
Liberal	9,063,126	8,719,845	8,572,965	191
Conservative	18,641,306	9,009,590	9,388,357	99
NDP	3,972,763	6,735,433	4,611,140	286
Bloc Québécois	529,513	2,261,702	2,950,984	984
Green	832,631	455,489	1,199,287	199
2004				
Liberal	4,719,388	9,962,717	9,141,408	405
Conservative	10,910,320	10,370,554	7,913,242	168
NDP	5,194,170	7,211,359	2,883,919	194
Bloc Québécois	858,746	2,704,519	2,733,868	633
Green	351,031	298,908	523,694	234
2000				
Liberal	20,067,820	2,809,219	N/A	14
Alliance***	19,641,006	2,167,520	N/A	11
NDP	8,978,136	1,423,516	N/A	16
Progressive Conservative	5,621,694	875,701	N/A	16
Bloc Québécois	2,259,752	404,402	N/A	18
Green	137,171	N/A	N/A	0

* Excluding intra-party transfers and loans.
** Annual allowances, which are paid in quarterly instalments, began in 2004.
*** The party's official name was Canadian Reform Conservative Alliance.
Source: Various reports on the Elections Canada website (www.elections.ca).

2006 convention, the party began developing a national membership list and hired two professional fundraisers (Taber 2007). In contrast, the Conservative Party's extensive experience with direct mail solicitation and telemarketing meant that it did not really suffer from the introduction of the contribution limits (the rise in the Conservatives' popular support leading to the 2006 election was no doubt also a factor). In 2006, contributions to the Conservatives were double the total sum given to the Liberals. In 2007, the ratio approached four to one: the Conservatives received $16.9 million in contributions, compared with $4.5 million for the Liberals.

What are the implications of the post-2004 regime for the role and activities of political parties? Although it is too early to offer a firm answer, there have been some preliminary assessments. The Public Policy Forum (PPF) study mentioned at the outset of this chapter concluded that the new law "remains fundamentally controversial." A "sizable minority" of those interviewed "believe the principle of public financing to be noble and necessary." However, the study also found significant concerns: "In the words of one participant, "C-24 causes parties to not need people." Others argue public financing was creating a culture of dependency (Fox 2005, 12-13; see also Cross 2004, 156-57).

In November 2008, the Harper government took many by surprise by announcing in its Economic and Fiscal Statement that it planned to eliminate the annual allowances to political parties. In the words of Finance Minister Jim Flaherty: "There will be no free ride for political parties. There never was. The freight was being paid by the taxpayer" (Canada, Department of Finance 2008, 9). Although the move was probably aimed at the cash-strapped Liberals, all three opposition parties were outraged (they also reacted badly to some other elements in the economic statement – see Valpy [2009]). In the days that followed, they agreed on the terms of an alternative coalition government. Even though Flaherty backed down on the plan to eliminate the party subsidies, the parties threatened to defeat the government. Prime Minister Harper defused the situation with a controversial move to have Parliament be prorogued.[11] The issue was not buried, however: just weeks after the government's reversal, Harper indicated the Conservative Party's next election platform would include a commitment to abolish the allowances (Whyte 2009). Since 1974, the public funding of federal parties has evolved in several fairly important respects. Amendments adopted in 1983 and 1996 were intended to make it somewhat more difficult for parties to qualify for reimbursement. In 2004, registration of political parties was made considerably easier with the adoption of the one-candidate rule. As noted above, the stated objective of the increased public funding that resulted from Bill C-24, notably the new allowances, was to fill the gap parties would face once donations from business and labour were banned. The other parties' reaction to the Harper government's 2008 attempt to eliminate the allowances underlines – as do the data – how extensively they have come to rely on public funding. The episode also suggests that this part of the 2004 reforms cannot be considered a permanent element of the federal political finance regime.

Further Reform of the Public Funding Regime

Although the debate that arose in late 2008 focused on whether the annual allowances should continue, some proposals to *modify* the public funding regime have been put forward. These have variously been intended to make public funding somewhat more accessible to new and smaller parties, to encourage the election of more MPs from under-represented groups (notably women), and to strengthen parties' policy-development capacity.

As noted above, the Lortie Commission conceived political parties as primary political organizations. The commission could have employed the term "public utility." After all, it rejected the view, then still shared by numerous political activists, that parties were largely private organizations, and it recommended regulation of several activities that were not then within the ambit of the law, notably the financing of constituency associations, party leadership candidates, and nomination contestants. At the same time, the commission had what Jane Jenson (who wrote two research studies for the commission) has described as "a more 'European' notion of parties as ongoing institutions of democratic representation." This entailed the following: "Not only are parties the institutions through which governments are selected, but also they provide the means by which society represents itself to itself, defining political community" (Jenson 1995, 226-27).

In this context, the Lortie Commission attached considerable weight to the objective of accessibility. For example, on reimbursements it rejected the rules then in place because, in its view, the 10 percent spending threshold for parties and the 15 percent vote threshold for candidates "send a clear message to smaller parties and their candidates as well as to independent candidates: their participation is not welcome" (Canada, RCERPF 1991, vol. 1, 365). Accordingly, the commission recommended that registered parties with at least 1 percent of the national vote qualify for reimbursement, and that the threshold for candidates be 1 percent of the votes in a constituency (ibid., vol. 1, 372).

Although the 1996 amendments to the Canada Elections Act introduced a vote-based rule for access to party reimbursements, consideration could be given to lowering the current threshold of 2 percent of the national votes to 1 percent. In principle, this would slightly broaden access to public funding for new parties (the same threshold is used to determine which parties qualify for annual allowances). At least in some cases, this could in turn help put new ideas on the public agenda – as has occurred with the growth of the Green Party. The amount of money involved would not be great. Indeed, for the 2006 general election, no additional party would have qualified for reimbursement if the rule had been 1 percent of the national vote. It has also been suggested that, consistent with the "norms of Canadian federalism," party thresholds should be modified to require that a party receive a certain level of voter support in more than one province or region (Stark 2009).

It is possible that, as occurred with the registration threshold, change to the criteria to qualify for the annual allowance could result from a judicial decision. A group of seven smaller political parties has launched a challenge to the threshold for the allowance. In an October 2006 decision, Mr. Justice J. Matlow of the Ontario Superior Court declared the provision unconstitutional on the basis of section 3 of the *Canadian Charter of Rights and Freedoms* (right to vote and be a candidate). The decision stated that the public funding was intended to encourage individuals to participate in elections but that as a result of the threshold, "the quality and vigour of Canadian democracy suffers because such a threshold effectively discourage[s] individuals who do not support one of the larger parties from participating in the electoral process" (*Longley v. Canada (Attorney General)* 2006, 6). The Supreme Court did not agree to hear the appeal, so this ruling stands.

The Lortie Commission's focus on access to elected office also led it to propose additional public funding measures intended to correct the "representational deficits" of women, visible minorities, and Aboriginal people. To redress the representational deficit of women, it recommended that any registered party electing at least 20 percent women to its parliamentary group receive an increased reimbursement equivalent to the percentage of its women MPs, up to a maximum of 150 percent; the measure would automatically be eliminated once the overall percentage of women in the House of Commons reached 40 percent; if it were still in place after two general elections, Parliament would have to decide whether to retain or adjust it (RCERPF 1991, vol. 1, 273; see also Arscott 1995).

Despite the continuing low representation of women in the House of Commons (following the 2006 election, 21 percent of MPs were women), the Lortie recommendation has remained on the shelf. However, in two provinces, similar proposals have been put on the public agenda. In Quebec, the draft Election Act tabled in December 2004, which would have introduced a semi-proportional mixed electoral system (Seidle 2007, 316-20), included provisions for an increased annual allowance for any party with at least 30 percent women candidates and increased reimbursements for those candidates.[12] In New Brunswick, the Commission on Legislative Democracy recommended in its January 2005 report that any party with at least 35 percent women candidates receive an increase to its annual allowance (New Brunswick, Commission on Legislative Democracy 2004, 101).

Although hearings were held on Quebec's draft legislation, neither of the reform proposals has proceeded.[13] It was nevertheless interesting that, more than a decade after the Lortie Commission, its proposal to promote the election of more women was picked up in policy debates in the two provinces. Although none of the three measures just reviewed may be the ideal means to help raise the proportion of women in the House of Commons, the possibility of providing political parties with financial incentives in this regard merits consideration, along with some of the non-legislative initiatives certain parties have taken (Young 2002).

As for policy development within political parties, the Lortie Commission presented a fairly bold set of recommendations centred on the establishment of publicly funded party foundations. The commission had visited Germany early in its mandate, and Lortie was impressed with the scale of the country's party foundations and their impact on the policies of the parties with which they are affiliated.[14] Based in part on comparative research it sponsored (Chandler and Siaroff 1991), the commission recommended the establishment of party foundations and that they be funded as follows:

- an initial allowance to the parties represented in the legislature equal to 25 percent of their current annual allowance or $25,000, whichever is greater;
- in subsequent years, an annual allowance to all registered parties equal to $0.25 for each vote received in the previous general election; and
- extension of the province's political contributions tax credit to cover contributions to the foundations.

Launching a foundation with an initial allowance of $25,000 would require considerable ingenuity, to say the least. Although the commission hoped that private funding would follow from the extension of the tax credit, this too would probably be modest (the commission recommended that, consistent with the limits for political financing generally, contributions to the party policy foundations be limited to $3,000). Nevertheless, this proposal constituted a reasoned response to the growing concern about the policy development capacities (or lack thereof) of political parties. The link to declining youth involvement is an interesting additional argument that should be included in any future policy debates on public funding measures to support party policy development.

Bill Cross and Lisa Young have advocated the creation of what they refer to as policy foundations. As they see it, such foundations would be a vehicle for grassroots supporters and "substantive experts" to participate in the development of policy options. For Cross and Young, parties that were more active in "policy study" would do a better job of "brokering ... various parochial concerns and forging national interests" (Cross and Young 2006, 24). As for financing the foundations, they suggest that a portion of the parties' current public funding be directed to policy foundations and that the political contribution tax credit be extended to cover donations to the foundations. Robin Sears, a former national campaign director for the NDP, has also called for separate public funding for party think tanks or "permanent policy forums" in order to create "serious thinking opportunities in each of the political families." He added, however, that this will happen only if parties are pushed to spend money between campaigns on party building by what he calls a tough-love approach (Sears 2005, 15). Unfortunately, Sears did not explain how to overcome the expected objections of some party activists. Irvin Studin has made a slightly different case for publicly funded party think tanks. He sees their work in creating and advancing "rigorous policy" as an instrument to help ministers counter the influence the bureaucracy exercises over policy making, even in cases when parties assume office with fairly clear ideas (Studin 2008, 66).

As noted above, the parliamentary debates on Bill C-24 did not address the possibility of assigning part of the public funding for federal political parties to policy development activities. If federal political parties hope to continue to merit the label "primary political organizations" that the Lortie Commission developed for them, they – with the active involvement of their members – need to play a larger role in the development of innovative, inclusive policies. Various options for public funding to further this objective could be considered.

The most ambitious route would be to legislate a set of provisions to govern the establishment, funding, and ongoing activities of party foundations.

The recommendations of the Lortie and New Brunswick commissions would be a good start for those charged with developing the foundations' mandate, governance structure, and so on. As for financing, it is clear that foundations could not be run on a shoestring. The Lortie Commission estimated in late 1991 that its model would cost $3.04 million a year. Although it might be possible to fund policy foundations for a somewhat lower amount, it is not evident that the government and most Canadians would be in favour of yet another significant increase in the public funding of federal parties. An alternative would be to subtract a portion of each party's annual allowance and allocate that to the funding of policy foundations, perhaps enriched by a supplement of new public funding. However, senior party officials could be expected to resist reducing the unrestricted annual allowance.

Yet another option would be to provide each registered party that qualified for an annual allowance with a yearly policy development grant. Such payments were introduced in the United Kingdom in 2002, and each year a total of £2 million is divided among the parties with at least two MPs. The fund is administered by the Electoral Commission and seems to be working reasonably well. In part because this avenue would not entail funding entirely new organizations, a Canadian variant of this program would be less costly and thus probably more acceptable to politicians and taxpayers. To discourage parties from diverting the funds to other purposes, they would need to be required to submit a report each year detailing how the policy development grant was spent. Although some party organizers could call this an intrusion in internal affairs, bearing in mind the extent to which parties now receive public funding that can be spent on any purpose whatsoever, their plea would be rather hollow.

Conclusion

This chapter began with a discussion of the public policy objectives that can be served by the public funding of political parties. These range from reducing the likelihood of undue influence from well-heeled donors by diminishing parties' reliance on private money to promoting research, policy development, and political education. Public funding has its critics, even in countries where such arrangements are well established. For example, there are fears that existing parties will become dependent on public resources and devote less effort to member-based fundraising and grassroots activity in general.

In Canada, as elsewhere, public funding has become part of a fairly extensive legislative framework that governs the financial and other activities of political parties, both during and between elections. Although the term is not widely used outside the academic literature, Epstein's label "public utility" is appropriate because, in his words, parties perform "a service in which the public has a special interest sufficient to justify governmental regulatory control" (Epstein 1986, 157). That said, governments do not regulate party activity just for the sake of regulation; policy objectives should underpin the measures enacted by legislatures. What have these been in the Canadian case?

As recounted above, the 1974 Election Expenses Act was intended above all to put a brake on the escalating costs of elections, particularly for parties. The spending limits placed a cap on what parties and candidates could spend. At the same time, reimbursements reduced somewhat their reliance on donations from private sources. In addition, donations from private sources (for parties, now confined to individuals) are facilitated by a quite generous income tax credit.

In the parliamentary debates of the early 1970s, there were some references to another policy objective – accessibility. If election spending is limited and public funding diminishes somewhat the reliance on private money, it should be easier for those who do not have a large bank account, or are not connected to those who do, to compete for elected office. This includes both candidates and parties. As we have seen, however, the evolution of the public funding rules has not generally been in the direction of making the electoral process more accessible to new and emerging parties. In fact, hurdles have been placed in their way, usually weakly justified by a concern for protecting the public purse. Party registration, a condition for accessing public funding, is now considerably easier, but this came about only because the Supreme Court of Canada struck down the long-standing fifty-candidate rule. If the House of Commons is to become more truly representative of Canada's diversity – both of people and ideas – a premium should be placed on removing hurdles and providing incentives so that Canadians from many backgrounds run for office and a wide range of the voices is heard.

Public funding of parties can serve another important objective: promoting policy development. In light of the very significant increase in public funding that came about through Bill C-24, there was an opportunity to consider this. However, the sponsoring minister and other MPs focused almost exclusively on compensating for the drop in party funds that would result from the ban on business and union donations. Despite continuing concern about the weaknesses of political parties – including the growing tendency for policy to emerge from an internal elite, with limited member involvement – the possibility of targeting some public funding to policy development was not on the agenda. As with the accessibility objective, belief in the merits of directing some public funding to support these inter-election activities continues to be confined to academic circles (with the notable exception of the New Brunswick Commission on Legislative Democracy).

The House of Commons Standing Committee on Procedure and House Affairs has a mandate to review the political financing provisions of the Canada Elections Act (section 536.1) that were amended in 2004 and 2007. If such a review eventually takes place, it is to be hoped that MPs and others will take a serious look at some of the reform proposals reviewed in this chapter. These measures would (with one exception) make it somewhat easier for parties to access public funding; encourage more women to run for Parliament; and support the research, policy development, and member engagement activities of political parties through the establishment of foundations or grants to parties specifically for those purposes. The various measures that have been proposed, and others that will come forward, constitute a future agenda for a richer examination of public funding of the federal electoral and political processes. It is to be hoped that, this time, the debate will actively address the important policy objectives of enhancing access to election and strengthening policy development within political parties.

NOTES

The author wishes to thank Hugh Meighen, Grant Holly, and Jean-Simon Farrah for their research assistance during the preparation of this chapter.

1 For example, in the 2000 Canadian Election Study (CES), 30 percent of respondents agreed that political parties don't care what ordinary people think, and 40 percent agreed that political parties hardly ever keep their election promises. For discussions of CES and other survey data on attitudes toward parties, see Carty, Cross, and Young (2000, 27-29) and Gidengil et al. (2002, 77-78).

2 Based on research carried out almost at the same time as the International IDEA survey, Michael Pinto-Duschinsky (2002, 78) found that 84 of 143 countries (59 percent) classified as "free" or "partly free" by Freedom House had laws providing for some direct public funding for parties and candidates (Freedom House is a Washington-based independent watchdog organization that supports the expansion of freedom around the world).

3 The following discussion of the benefits of public funding for political parties draws on United Kingdom, Electoral Commission 2003, 20-22. See also Justin Fisher's chapter in this volume and International IDEA (2003, 8).

4 Only presidential candidates who agree to have their campaigns subject to spending limits qualify for public funding.
5 On arguments against public funding, see Justin Fisher (this volume); United Kingdom, Electoral Commission (2003, 22-24); and Nassmacher (2003, 8).
6 Khayyam Paltiel (1981, 170) suggested public funding provisions were prompted by "the desire of legislators to stabilize the party system and entrench the electoral position of established groups." Twenty years later, empirical research on western European countries "suggest[ed] that the introduction of public subsidies to the parties in and of itself cannot delay the emergence of new parties" (Pierre, Svåsand, and Widfeldt 2000, 21).
7 In his chapter in this volume, Katz carries the argument further. He suggests that, as part of the "price" for state funding, parties have accepted a large body of regulations that limit their activities; they have, as a result, become institutions of the state.
8 Quebec was the first jurisdiction in Canada to introduce spending limits (for parties and candidates) and direct public funding through reimbursements to candidates; see Angell (1966).
9 The *Figueroa* case resulted from the deregistration of the Communist Party of Canada during the 1993 general election for failing to nominate at least fifty candidates (which it had done in all general elections since 1970). Its leader, Miguel Figueroa, launched a challenge under several provisions of the Canadian Charter of Rights and Freedoms. After a lengthy legal battle, the Supreme Court of Canada ruled, in *Figueroa v. Canada (Attorney General)*, that the fifty-candidate rule was unconstitutional because it infringed s. 3 of the charter (right to vote and be a candidate) "by decreasing the capacity of the members and supporters of the disadvantaged parties to introduce ideas and opinions into the open dialogue and debate that the electoral process engenders." MacIvor (2004) provides a full account of Figueroa's campaign and the Supreme Court decision. For a description of the present registration rules, see Elections Canada (2005).
10 According to a press report, "the Prime Minister, fed up with a long string of opposition charges that generous Liberal donors have been rewarded with government contracts, decided the dramatic measures were necessary to restore public confidence in the political system" (Bryden 2002).
11 See the articles by a group of senior political scientists and legal scholars in Russell and Sossin (2009).
12 Any party whose candidates were between 30 and 34 percent women would receive a 5 percent "top up" of its annual allowance; in addition, the women candidates of parties that met that threshold would receive a reimbursement equal to 60 (rather than 50) percent of their election expenses; and the party's women candidates who were elected would receive a 65 percent reimbursement. The supplementary public funding in all three cases would increase further if the party had between 35 and 39 percent women candidates and again if it had 40 percent or more women candidates. The measure would expire once 50 percent of the members of the National Assembly were women (Quebec, Secrétariat à la réforme des institutions démocratiques 2004).

13 Some women's groups called for a change to the measure in the draft bill that would have linked the supplementary public funding to the proportion of women *elected*, rather than a party's share of women candidates.
14 For the commission's evaluation of the role of the German foundations, see RCERPF (1991, 297-98); also Chandler and Siaroff (1991, 248-49). According to a German authority, in 2000 public funding of the six foundations amounted to approximately 400 million Euros. However, in part because of their extensive international activities, research and analysis account for only about 15 to 20 percent of each foundation's budget (Thunert 2004).

WORKS CITED

Angell, Howard M. 1966. The Evolution and Application of Quebec Election Expense Legislation 1960-66. In Canada, Committee on Election Expenses 1966, 279-319.

Arscott, Jane. 1995. A Job Well Begun ... Representation, Electoral Reform and Women. In *Gender and Politics in Contemporary Canada*, ed. François-Pierre Gingras, 56-84. Toronto: Oxford University Press.

Bryden, Joan. 2002. PM Seeks Ban on Corporate, Union Donations. *National Post*, 29 November.

Canada. Committee on Election Expenses. 1966. *Report*. Ottawa: Queen's Printer.

–. Department of Finance. 2009. Economic and Fiscal Statement. http://www.fin.gc.ca/ec2008/Speech/speech-eng.html.

–. Elections Canada. 2005. Registration of Federal Political Parties. http://www.elections.ca/.

–. House of Commons, Standing Committee on Procedure and House Affairs, 2003. Evidence, 3 April. http://www.parl.gc.ca/committee/CommitteePublication.aspx?SourceId=27480.

–. RCERPF (Royal Commission on Electoral Reform and Party Financing). 1991. *Final Report*. 4 vols. Ottawa: Ministry of Supply and Services.

Carty, R. Kenneth, William Cross, and Lisa Young. 2000. *Rebuilding Canadian Party Politics*. Vancouver: UBC Press.

Chandler, William M., and Alan Siaroff. 1991. Parties and Party Government in Advanced Democracies. In *Canadian Political Parties: Leaders, Candidates and Organization*, vol. 13 of the Research Studies for the Royal Commission on Electoral Reform and Party Financing, ed. Herman Bakvis, 191-263. Toronto: Dundurn Press.

Courtney, John C. 1978. Recognition of Canadian Political Parties in Parliament and in Law. *Canadian Journal of Political Science* 11(1): 33-60.

Cross, William. 2002. *Political Parties, Representation, and Electoral Democracy in Canada*. Don Mills, ON: Oxford University Press.

–. 2004. *Political Parties*. Vancouver: UBC Press.

Cross, William, and Lisa Young. 2006. Are Canadian Political Parties Empty Vessels? Membership, Engagement and Policy Capacity. IRPP (Institute for Research on Public Policy) *Choices* 12.

Epstein, Leon. 1986. *Political Parties in the American Mold.* Madison: University of Wisconsin Press.

Fisher, Justin. 2002. Next Step: State Funding for the Parties? *Political Quarterly* 73: 392-99.

Fox, Graham. 2005. Rethinking Political Parties: Discussion Paper. Ottawa: Public Policy Forum. http://www.ppforum.ca/sites/default/files/rethinking_political_parties.pdf.

Gagnon, Alain-G., and A. Brian Tanguay. 2007. *Canadian Parties in Transition,* 3rd ed. Peterborough, ON: Broadview Press.

Gidengil, Elisabeth, André Blais, Richard Nadeau, and Neil Nevitte. 2002. Changes in the Party System and Anti-Party Sentiment. In Cross 2002, 68-86.

International IDEA (Institute for Democracy and Electoral Assistance). 2003. *Funding of Political Parties and Election Campaigns.* Stockholm: International IDEA.

Jenson, Jane. 1995. The Costs of Political Elitism. In *Canada's Century: Governance in a Maturing Society,* ed. C.E.S. Franks, J.E. Hodgetts, O.P. Dwivedi, Doug Williams, and V. Seymour Wilson, 217-37. Montreal and Kingston: McGill-Queen's University Press.

Katz, Richard, and Peter Mair. 1995. Changing Models of Party Organization and Party Democracy. *Party Politics* 1: 5-28.

Lambert, Lisa A., and Harold J. Jansen. 2007. Party Building by a State Dependent Party: The Case of the Green Party of Canada. Paper presented at the annual meeting of the Canadian Political Science Association, Saskatoon, 30 May-1 June.

Longley v. Canada (Attorney General), 2006 CanLII 36358 (ON S.C.).

MacIvor, Heather. 2004. The Charter of Rights and Party Politics: The Impact of the Supreme Court Ruling in *Figueroa v. Canada (Attorney General).* IRPP (Institute for Research on Public Policy) *Choices* 10.

Nassmacher, Karl-Heinz. 2003. Introduction: Political Parties, Funding and Democracy. In International IDEA 2003, 1-19.

New Brunswick. Commission on Legislative Democracy. 2004. *Final Report and Recommendations.* Fredericton, NB: Commission on Legislative Democracy.

Paltiel, Khayyam Z. 1981. Campaign Finance: Contrasting Practices and Reforms. In *Democracy at the Polls: A Comparative Study of Competitive National Elections,* ed. David Butler, Howard R. Penniman, and Austin Ranney, 138-72. Washington, DC: American Enterprise Institute.

–. 1996. Political Marketing, Party Finance, and the Decline of Canadian Parties. In *Canadian Parties in Transition,* 2nd. ed., ed. A. Brian Tanguay and Alain-G. Gagnon, 403-22. Scarborough, ON: Nelson.

Pierre, Jon, Lars Svåsand, and Anders Widfeldt. 2000. State Subsidies to Political Parties: Confronting Rhetoric with Reality. *West European Politics* 23: 1-24.

Pinto-Duschinsky, Michael. 2002. Financing Politics: A Global View. *Journal of Democracy* 13: 69-86.

Quebec. Secrétariat à la réforme des institutions démocratiques. 2004. La représentation équitable des femmes à l'Assemblée nationale. http://www.institutions-democratiques.gouv.qc.ca/publications/fiche_4_femmes.pdf.

Russell, Peter H., and Lorne Sossin. 2009. *Parliamentary Democracy in Crisis.* Toronto: University of Toronto Press.

Sears, Robin V. 2005. The Decline and Irrelevance of Canada's Political Parties. *Policy Options* 26 (May): 9-16.

Seidle, F. Leslie. 1985. The Election Expenses Act: The House of Commons and the Parties. In *The Canadian House of Commons: Essays in Honour of Norman Ward*, ed. John C. Courtney, 113-34. Calgary: University of Calgary Press.

—. 2007. Provincial Electoral Systems in Question: Changing Views of Party Representation and Governance. In Gagnon and Tanguay 2007, 303-34.

Seidle, F. Leslie, and Khayyam Z. Paltiel. 1981. Party Finance, the Election Expenses Act, and Campaign Spending in 1979 and 1980. In *Canada at the Polls, 1979 and 1980*, ed. Howard R. Penniman, 226-79. Washington, DC: American Enterprise Institute.

Stark, Andrew. 2009. Knock a Chip Off the Old Bloc. *Globe and Mail*, 5 August.

Studin, Irwin. 2008. Revisiting the Democratic Deficit: The Case for Political Party Think Tanks. *Policy Options* 29 (February): 62-67.

Taber, Jane. 2007. Liberals Face Huge Fundraising Deficit. *Globe and Mail*, 3 July.

Thunert, Martin. 2004. The Development and Significance of Think Tanks in Germany. In *Think Tank Traditions: Policy Research and the Politics of Ideas*, ed. Diane Stone and Andrew Denham, 71-88. Manchester: Manchester University Press.

United Kingdom. Electoral Commission. 2003. *The Funding Of Political Parties: Background Paper.*

Valpy, Michael. 2009. The "Crisis": A Narrative. In Russell and Sossin 2009, 3-18.

van Biezen, Ingrid. 2004. Political Parties as Public Utilities. *Party Politics* 10: 701-22.

Whyte, Ken. 2009. Maclean's Interview: Stephen Harper. *Maclean's* 19 January, 20-22. http://www2.macleans.ca/2009/01/08/macleans-interview-stephen-harper-2/.

Young, Lisa. 1998. Party, State and Political Competition in Canada: The Cartel Model Reconsidered. *Canadian Journal of Political Science* 31: 339-58.

—. 2002. Representation of Women in the New Canadian Party System. In Cross 2002, 181-200.

Young, Lisa, Anthony Sayers, and Harold Jansen. 2007. Altering the Political Landscape: State Funding and Party Finance. In Gagnon and Tanguay 2007, 335-54.

4 Finance Reform and the Cartel Party Model in Canada

RICHARD S. KATZ

This chapter explores the applicability of the cartel model (Katz and Mair 1995) to Canada, with particular reference (but not limited) to the changes in party finance regulation that took effect in 2004. First, however, it will be useful both to recapitulate the original cartel argument and further developments of it (Katz and Mair 2002; Blyth and Katz 2005), and to make some general observations about the model that will frame the Canadian discussion and further clarify the expectations that should be attributed to the cartel party hypothesis.

The Cartel Party Hypothesis

The cartel party hypothesis emerged inductively from a data collection effort that had been designed to document party organizational forms and adaptation to social and political change in a cross-nationally comparable way. Rather than designing the project to test a particular theoretical model or set of hypotheses, we deliberately tried to include data that would be appropriate to the testing of a wide range of hypotheses derived from a wide range of theoretical perspectives employed not only by ourselves but also by unknown future researchers. Although the theory that we advanced to account for the trends that we believed were emerging certainly was intended to be applicable beyond the thirty-year period for which we collected data, and beyond the eleven western European countries plus the United States from which the data came, the terms of reference for expectations such as a "weakening of ties between parties and civil society" remained predominantly west European. In this case, for example, the "weakening of ties" was understood to be relative to the expectations of the model of the mass party of integration; whether one should expect ties also to weaken in cases in which they had never been particularly strong remains to be seen.[1]

Similarly, although the theory was intended to be about the gestalt of party organizations in general, the choice of the specific aspects of party development that we emphasized in the original papers was driven as much by the availability of data in our project as it was by any a priori assessment of their relative importance. Of particular relevance to this chapter is, of course, the emphasis that we put on the increasing dependence of parties in many countries on public financial subventions. Although we certainly saw this to be one of the expected reactions to the conditions that we speculated were underlying the process of cartelization, both later analysts (for example, Pierre, Svåsand, and Widfeldt 2000) and we ourselves probably went too far in giving this a pre-eminent position as *the* indicator of cartelization. Beyond the question of data availability, this overemphasis on party funding was also reflective of our initial concern with the individual party as the unit of analysis, and with the dynamics of organization and balance of influence among what we had earlier identified as "the three faces of party organization" (Katz and Mair 1993) within those individual parties as the principal *explanandum*.

The denomination "cartel" also implies attention to inter-party or system-level dynamics, and in particular to a distinction between those players that are "within" the cartel and those that are excluded from it. Indeed, part of the original argument was that participation in a cartel-like pattern of constrained competition with other parties would both facilitate and, at least to a certain extent, require many of the changes in internal party arrangements that we identified with the cartel party as an organizational form. Thus, even if analytically separable, the idea of a party cartel as a system-level characteristic and the idea of a cartel party as a type analogous to the mass party or the catch-all party are closely intertwined (Katz and Mair 1996).

Attention to the system-level or inter-party side of the argument requires that two points be clarified. On one hand, the set of parties that are expected to be "in" the cartel must be specified. We have sometimes identified this as the set of "governing parties" (Katz 2002, 2003). Unfortunately, in practice this phrase has proven to be slightly ambiguous, but what it clearly does *not* denote is simply those parties that are in government (holding ministerial portfolios, or the equivalent) at any particular time. Although it does not necessarily extend to all parties that are theoretically coalitionable (that is, that are not excluded from government on a priori grounds) or that play a governing role in *any* subnational government, it does extend to all parties that have a reasonable expectation that they *might* be included in a national governing coalition or in a significant share (defined jointly by number, size, and range of competences) of subnational governments within the reasonably foreseeable future.[2] Although a cartel does imply constrained competition within the cartel, this refers to the nature of the competition, not to an absence of electoral turnover, and to the question of whether it makes any difference who wins, not to the frequency with which different parties win – and, indeed, absence of an expectation of turnover would be a factor strongly militating against the formation of a cartel. Thus, that the American Republicans in the House of Representatives appeared in the early 1990s to be condemned to permanent opposition status was a major contributor to Newt Gingrich's "Contract with America" as a way to fracture a cartel that arguably included both Democrats and Republicans in the Senate and in presidential politics. Conversely, the replacement of the Martin Liberal minority government with the Harper Conservative minority government after the 2006 election may ultimately support cartelization, rather than indicating an increase in competition, which would be contrary to the cartel model.

On the other hand, although the idea of a cartel implies concerted action, when translated into the cartel party model, the term was not intended to imply or depend on an actual conspiracy, and it is particularly in this respect that the choice of denomination may have been less than perfect. Rather, as anyone involved with legislation concerning anti-competitive practices in the economy is well aware, it is possible to produce the *effects* of collusion without any illicit communication or covert coordination. In an oligopolistic market, which an electoral market with only a handful of parties receiving nearly all of the votes certainly approximates, overt signalling can produce virtually the same result as covert conspiracy.

With those preliminaries, the relevant aspects of the cartel party argument can be summarized relatively briefly. At least by the 1970s, the dominant form of party organization in most democratic countries approximated what Kirchheimer (1966) had identified as the catch-all party. Although there were still obvious connections, both in terms of formal organization and affective ties, between particular parties and particular social groupings, these had noticeably weakened. Increasingly, parties were seen – and saw themselves – as brokers among social groups and between social groups and the state, rather than as the political arms of specific groups. Ideological conflicts had been transformed into amorphous differences in general left-right orientation. A significant component of electoral competition involved the provision of public services, with parties in effect bidding for support from voters by promising more services (especially on the left) and lower taxes (especially on the right), and for support from potential contributors by offering specially tailored legislation that often resulted in the weakening of otherwise desirable regulation or the collection of less revenue.

This situation confronted the parties with three interrelated classes of problems. First, the moderation of class and other subcultural conflicts, and the increasing homogeneity of experiences and expectations of the vast majority of citizens associated with the rise of mass society and the welfare state (mass media and mass culture; mass education; near universal provision for health care, unemployment, and old age) reduced the value of appeals to class or cultural solidarity. Concurrently, there was a general decline in affective attachment to parties per se as part of a process of partisan de-alignment (Dalton and Wattenberg 2000). Not only party psychological identification but also formal party membership declined (Mair and van Biezen 2001; Cross and Young 2004). As two sides of the same coin, electoral supporters (party members, party voters, organizational contributors) became less reliable and demanded more in return for their support.

Second, with the increasing reliance on mass media in campaigning, and with the attendant increase in the need for professional expertise (pollsters, advertising consultants, marketers, and direct-mail fundraisers), the economic costs of remaining competitive were rising more rapidly than the ability or willingness of the party on the ground to pay. The initial response of turning to a range of interest organizations (primarily unions) and corporations also began to reach the limits of willingness to pay, at least without quid pro quos bordering on, or entering, the realm of the corrupt. These changes also meant that the resources that the party on the ground could bring to the table (for example, volunteer labour for campaigning, knowledge of local opinion) were becoming relatively less valuable to the party in public office (in comparison to mass media space or information gathered by professional pollsters).

Third, the governments of many welfare states appeared to have backed themselves into a corner from which the only escape without, and potentially even with, untenable tax increases was equally untenable service cuts. Moreover, the public debts accumulated, while deferring addressing this dilemma threatened to convert tax regimes that originally had been intended to redistribute income from the rich to the poor into devices that instead transfer wealth from the productive elements of society to the bond holders.

Although of a different type, one additional development can be added to this list. As politics has become an increasingly specialized profession, the potential personal costs of electoral defeat or organizational contraction have increased. Further, the separation of parties from ancillary and other interest organizations that is characteristic of the catch-all party has reduced the availability of jobs in those organizations for politicians who are "resting" between engagements. Simply, when politics is a person's primary source of income, the stakes are higher (Borchert 2000). Complementing the decline in ideological differences among mainstream parties, this reinforces the truth of de Jouvenel's observation that *"Il y a moins de différence entre deux députés dont l'un est révolutionnaire et l'autre ne l'est pas, qu'entre deux révolutionnaires, dont l'un est député et l'autre ne l'est pas."* (There is less difference between two deputies, one of whom is a revolutionary and the other is not, than between two revolutionaries, one of whom is a deputy and the other is not.)

These problems are shared by all governing parties and set up the conditions for the formation of what is effectively a cartel, in which participating parties serve their joint interest in providing for their own security and survival. In terms of relations among parties, this has two primary aspects. The first is restriction of policy competition, with policy promises effectively playing the role of quantity offers in an economic cartel. This is evident in the increasingly common moves to take issues out of the realm of party competition by delegating them to "non-political" agencies such as independent central banks, courts, or the EU Commission; by privatizing previously public functions (for example, pension reform or health care reform); and by the increasingly common acceptance of various models of governance (Pierre 2000), new public management (Osborne and Gaebler 1992; Kettl 2000), the regulatory state (Majone 1994), and consensus democracy (Lijphart 1999), all of which privilege questions of technical and managerial expertise over those of values or political preference. Even in case of issues that have not explicitly been departisanified, cartel parties limit the degree to which they attempt to out-bid one another: many issues are simply avoided by the mainstream parties as demagogic, and the range of proposals offered for those issues that remain are often highly limited in the name of realism or responsibility.[3]

The second aspect, and the one of most direct concern here, involves attempting to solve the problem that internally generated funds prove inadequate to the exigencies of modern politics, and to mitigate the risks of electoral misfortune by reducing the disparity of resources available to those in and out of government at any particular moment, in both respects by turning to the coffers of the state. In the first respect, state subventions become significant – in some cases helping to fill the gap between traditional sources of party income and perceived needs, and in others largely replacing private contributions. In the second respect, a system in which the parties of the ruling coalition enjoyed the resources of the state (the power to appoint to office, and perhaps to "tax" the appointees, the research capacities of the civil service, and so on) while the other parties were left to their own devices is supplanted by arrangements that allow all of the cartel parties to share in the bounty and thus to reduce the pecuniary difference between being in office and out of office.

Cartels face two potential threats. One, as Kitschelt (2000) has pointed out, is defection.[4] The other is challenge from new entrants. Thus, an additional aspect of the cartel is the structuring of institutions such as the financial subvention regime, ballot access requirements, and media access in ways that disadvantage challengers from outside.

Parties are not unitary actors. As a result, the leaders of the party in public office (from whose perspective this model has been developed) face not only the threat of defection or challenge by new party entrants but also pressures or threats from within their own party. It is in responding to these challenges that parties tend to become cartel parties with respect to their internal structures. One aspect of this has already been mentioned: by turning to state subventions, parties and their leaders become less dependent on members and other contributors. A second aspect is the disempowering of the activists in the party on the ground, as they are the ones most likely to make policy demands inconsistent with the "restraint of trade" in policy that is implied by the cartel model. Although the objective is a kind of party oligarchy, the means ironically (or not, depending on one's reading of Michels (1962/1911) and the iron law of oligarchy) may be the apparent democratization of the party through the introduction of devices such as postal membership ballots or mass membership meetings at which large numbers of marginally committed members can be expected, with their silence, lack of capacity for prior independent (of the leadership) organization, and tendency to be oriented more toward particular leaders rather than to underlying policies, to "drown out" the activists. A third aspect is the centralization and professionalization (in particular emphasizing the cash nexus of an employment contract instead of partisan loyalty or ideology as the basis for commitment), or ultimately even the outsourcing, of campaigning and of the other functions of the party central office and traditional party on the ground, again with the result of freeing the leadership from constraints from below.[5]

One more aspect of the cartel party model is that it affects the nature of the relationship between parties and the state. In the traditional models of party democracy, parties are seen as agents of groups within civil society, or perhaps of society as a whole. Although the winning parties may temporarily take control of the main policy-making structures of the state, they remain separate from it, and firmly rooted in society. The processes of cartel formation and maintenance, however, imply a dramatic weakening of whatever sense there was of parties as agents of society. With significant policy competition largely precluded, whether as part of cartelization or simply because of fiscal and political constraints (themselves hypothesized to be among the underlying stimuli to cartelization in the first place), party spokespeople tend to become apologists for and defenders of policies that have become more generically "policies of the state" than they are policies of any particular party or coalition. As part of the price for state funding (see below), parties have accepted a growing body of regulations limiting both their activities and their structures. Parties move beyond the public utility model (Epstein 1986; van Biezen 2004) of regulation to become, in effect, institutions of the state.

Finally, even with the use of qualifying words such as "tend," the cartel party remains an ideal type, to be approximated or approached but not achieved – just as there never were any parties that fully met the ideal type definitions of "mass party" or "catch-all party." Even with that said, however, two forces restraining the cartelization of parties must be recognized. The first is that the process of cartelization is profoundly undemocratic, and yet parties, even in the cartel model – or perhaps particularly in the cartel model – justify their own existence and their claim on state resources on the basis of their contribution to democracy. On one hand, cartelization has contributed to the rise of "anti-party-system-parties" that appeal directly to public perceptions that the mainstream parties are indifferent to the desires of ordinary citizens, and in doing so underline the dangers to cartel parties of excessive(ly overt) cartelization. On the other hand, cartel parties also have to be attentive to the potential backlash of being perceived to have excessively violated norms of democratic fairness. Although one would expect a certain level of disingenuous rhetoric attempting to justify regulations that are in the parties' interest as actually being in the public interest, particularly with an aggressive free press there will be real limits to the degree to which parties can construct institutional biases in their favour without incurring even greater political costs.

The second restraining factor is that although parties through their parliamentary majorities make the rules that govern their own behaviour and structures, govern entry to the political marketplace, and allocate state resources, they do not do so with complete autonomy. Most obviously, they are bound by constitutional restrictions. Thus, although the basic logic of a cartel might lead one to expect the ruling parties to restrict access to public finance to themselves (as for all intents and purposes they have done in American presidential elections), German parties were forced by the Bundesverfassungsgericht (Federal Constitutional Court) not just to provide public funding to parties that clear the 5 percent threshold for representation in the Bundestag but to all parties that achieve one-tenth of that result. Similarly, in *Figueroa v. Canada (Attorney General)*, the Supreme Court of Canada overturned the provision of the Canada Elections Act that required a party to have candidates in at least fifty ridings, a requirement that would either have denied the benefits of party registration to most small parties or forced them to bear the burden of nominating candidates in many ridings that they did not intend seriously to contest.

Cartels, Party Finance, and the 2004 Reforms

Between 1974 and the end of 2003, Canadian national parties relied on private individual, corporate, and associational donations. The government encouraged individual donations with a very generous tax credit for small donors. It also made the money go further by reimbursing both parties and their candidates for a substantial portion of their electoral expenses, though only after the election. As Young (1998) observes, although these forms of subsidy may have made individual fundraising easier and more effective, they did not alter the fundamental financial dependence of the parties on cultivating a substantial donor base.

The 2004 amendments to the Canada Elections Act made a number of profound changes to the regulations concerning the financing of Canadian elections and, because they are the fundamental contestants of those elections, to the financing of Canadian parties.[6] The main provisions of the legislation can be found in Chapter 1.

From the perspective of the cartel party hypothesis, these changes pose two questions. First, does their enactment provide evidence for or against the relevance of the cartel model for Canadian parties at that time? Second, should the new political finance regime be expected to further or retard the development of cartel parties in Canada in the future?

Were the 2004 Reforms Evidence of a Cartel?
Intentions are notoriously difficult to prove. In the absence of the kind of smoking gun that rarely if ever appears, it would be impossible to find concrete evidence that the 2004 reforms were introduced or enacted as a direct result of a cartel-like calculation or conspiracy. On the one hand, the model itself does not require actual collusion, and on the other hand the cartel model has associated with it a conception of democracy that would allow even conspiring parties to justify their actions in terms that appear to be public spirited.[7] As a result, one must instead ask whether the new regime is consistent with the expectations raised by the model concerning what a cartel party would do, unfortunately always tempered by the fact that parties in models generally have perfect information and simple motives, whereas parties in the real world have neither.

That said, the first question must be *cui bono* – who benefited, or should have been expected to benefit, from the new regime? Using this information to assess the consistency of the 2004 amendments with the cartel model requires that three classes of parties be distinguished: (1) the Liberals themselves as the party holding a majority in the House, (2) the other parties that might reasonably be considered cartel members if there is a cartel (the Conservatives and the NDP), and (3) all other parties, including in particular the Bloc Québécois and the Greens. Although benefit to the Liberals is relevant in the sense that a reform that specifically advantaged the party in power over all other parties would be inconsistent with the model, the real question is whether the reform benefited parties in the second group over those in the third. And the immediate and short-run answer appears to be that it did not.

As is evident from the data presented in Chapter 5 (see Figure 5.3), there were two obvious winners from the 2004 reforms. The first was the Bloc. Having voluntarily adhered to the much stricter Quebec provincial party funding rules, the Bloc's individual fundraising lagged far behind the other parliamentary parties, and its corporate/association fundraising (for loss of which the party subventions in C-24 were explicitly intended to compensate the parties) was practically non-existent – but it does, of course, share in the per-vote subvention nonetheless. That the Bloc would be a primary beneficiary was well recognized in advance, as Bloc MP Antoine Dubé's description in the House of Commons of the bill as "almost a gift to us Quebeckers" reflects. Moreover, because the Bloc has candidates only in Quebec – with the first order effect that its campaign spending ceiling is far lower than that of the other parliamentary parties, and the second order effect that its per-vote subvention covers a far larger proportion of its allowable campaign spending – it has been able to redirect some of the funds it would otherwise have solicited for itself to sovereignist candidates or parties at the provincial level.[8] Unless one assumes that the Bloc is somehow part of the cartel (an assumption that may become plausible depending on relations between the Bloc and the minority Harper government but that at the moment seems highly implausible), this must count as evidence against C-24 being an example of cartel-based legislation.

The other big winner from the 2004 amendments, and also clearly outside whatever cartel there may be, was the Green Party. Recognizing that they could win even while losing the election, in 2004 the Greens deliberately nominated candidates in every riding (to make it easier to surpass the 2 percent national threshold for subvention) and appealed to electors on the grounds that their votes would help fund the party even though they might not contribute to parliamentary representation. Aided by this strategy, and borrowing in anticipation of clearing the 2 percent threshold, the Greens were able to spend just over $498,000 (in contrast to less than $18,000 in 2000), increased their share of the vote from less than 0.5 percent to 4.3 percent, and as a result became eligible for just over $1 million per year in federal subsidies (and almost $300,000 in reimbursement).[9] Although this appears to contradict Jim Abbott's claim in the third reading debate on the bill that it would further a "closed shop situation" in which a new party – like his own (Reform) had been fifteen years before – would be unable to compete effectively against well-financed ("out of the taxpayers' pockets" [*Hansard Parliamentary Debates* no. 115, 10 June 2003, 1230]) major parties, this public subsidy did not allow the Greens to expand their vote significantly in 2006, when it rose only to about 4.5 percent. Again, this bit of evidence appears to point against the cartel hypothesis, though with somewhat less force if (for reasons discussed below) the amount of the subvention to the Greens, permanent office, and a few staff members to the contrary notwithstanding, prove inadequate to support a further substantial increase in votes, let alone a breakthrough to parliamentary representation.

The Greens are, moreover, in a unique position among minor parties in that they have international name recognition and thus some domestic standing even with electoral support that for other parties might be described as derisory. In this respect, Jim Abbott's observation about the consequences for the Reform Party had the current system been in place in the 1980s, or the claim of Kevin Peck, chief agent of the Canadian Action Party (CAP), in his affidavit in the *Canadian Action Party et al. v. Attorney General of Canada* case, that "prior to the 2004 election, CAP survived financially due to receipt of donations from individual donors of amount significantly higher than the $5000.00 limit" (Ontario Superior Court of Justice, court file 05-CV-291729PD2, para. 17), suggest that the 2004 reforms may in most cases indeed serve to protect the established parties by preventing upstarts – regardless of the popularity they might enjoy if they had the opportunity to get their message out in the first place – from establishing themselves by drawing on large donations from a few committed supporters.

The costs of campaigning are largely independent of the size of the party, though not necessarily independent of the nature of the target audience. (A campaign limited to Quebec or to French-speaking Canadians, for example, by the Bloc, would be less costly than one aimed at the entire country, for example, by the Greens.) Moreover, it is unreasonable to suppose that the payoff from, or effectiveness of, campaign spending is a straight line function of the amount spent. If a fixed increment in spending is likely to have less effect for a campaign that is near the bottom of the spending distribution than the same increment would have for a party that was already spending more (as hypothetically illustrated in Figure 4.1, in which the impact of a marginal increase in spending is represented by the slope of the curve at the point at which the increase occurs), then what appears to be equal per-vote subsidy may actually be quite unequal per-vote impact, even for a party such as the Greens that manages to clear the 2 percent (or 5 percent) threshold and qualify for subsidy. If, in concrete terms, five ads will be more than five times as effective as one – the basic premise of saturation advertising – the Greens may simply be getting enough support to mount an *in*effective campaign.

What then of the other three parliamentary parties? In purely financial terms, and looking only at the national party, the NDP appears also to have been a winner, though to a far lesser extent than the Bloc. Although their state subsidy in 2004 and beyond (the gain) is less than their union (and other corporate or organizational) contributions in 2003 (the loss), the 2003

FIGURE 4.1

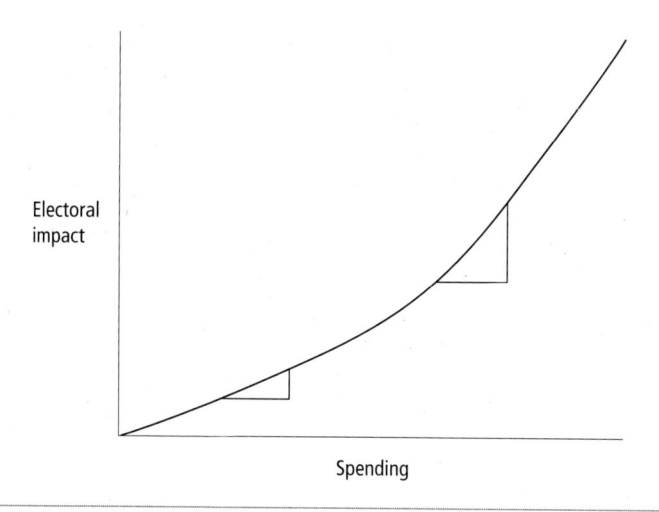

Hypothetical relationship between campaign spending and electoral impact

figures were dramatically inflated by a special union fundraising campaign conducted in anticipation of the new rules coming into effect. The average of union contributions to the NDP in 2001 and 2002 was only a bit over $1.25 million, in contrast to state payments in 2004 and 2005 of almost $3 million and almost $4 million respectively. On the other hand, the NDP suffered two losses that are not accounted here: by counting all affiliates of a national union as part of the same organization, the legislation effectively bars union contributions to the constituency associations in a way that it does not bar contributions from independent businesses; and the secondment of union staff for election campaigns was prohibited. At the same time, one use to which the specially raised funds were put was to buy the building in which NDP headquarters are located. In purely financial terms, and aside from freeing the party of the need to pay rent, this partially compensates the NDP for the new inability of the unions to co-sign bank loans to the party: instead, they can use the building as collateral. More significantly from the perspective of the cartel party model, in political terms, this weakens the potential blackmail power of the unions: every time a union co-signed a loan, it was making a new decision that, presumably, it could decline to make at some point in the future were the party to stray too far from the unions' preferences. As the owners of their own building, however, the NDP does not need union approval before using that building to secure a loan. The replacement of resources for the provision of which the party was dependent on the unions with funds that come automatically from the state certainly is a cartel-consistent development.

The Conservatives also appear to be winners. Most directly, their 2005 state subvention is more than 2.5 times their 2003 corporate contributions plus individual contributions over $5,000 (even counting all of those contributions, not just the portion over $5,000). This is especially significant in terms of the cartel hypothesis because, prior to 1993, corporate contributions to the Progressive Conservative Party appeared to be relatively independent of whether or not the party was in power. It is impossible to tell whether the collapse of corporate contributions to the PCs (from $6.8 million in off-year 1992 and $13.2 million in election-year 1993 to $2 million in 1994 and thereafter to never more than $3.1 million in an off year or $6.5 million in an election year), and the failure of the lost contributors to move to the Reform Party or the Canadian Alliance reflected a fundamental change in corporate donations such that they would in the future go overwhelmingly to the party in power at the time (between 2001 and 2003, the division of corporate contributions between the governing Liberals and all other parties ran between 69:31 and 82:18, in contrast to Paltiel's earlier estimates [1970, 10] of 60:40 in favour of the governing party), or simply reflect corporate disenchantment with the PCs and the Reform's and Alliance's failure to appeal. In either case, however, the new legislation appeared in the short run both to level the playing field between Conservatives and Liberals (roughly equal corporate contributions, at roughly zero; roughly equal state subventions so long as the parties' vote shares remained roughly equal) and, in particular, to replace a source of funds that could be won (or lost) on the basis of electoral victory or defeat (which in 2004 may have appeared to be the Conservatives' long-term prospect), with a source of funds that depends only on maintaining their numbers of votes. Somewhat less directly, but by 2005 far more dramatically, the Conservatives also won in another way. Between the grassroots insurgency of Reform and rebuilding efforts within the PCs, the Conservatives had developed a vastly superior (to the Liberals) capacity to raise money from small individual donations, with far more donors and a far smaller proportion of the money raised coming from contributions over the newly legislated limit. Whether, or how soon, the Liberals will be able to approximate Conservative success in this respect remains to be seen.

As this implies, particularly in relative terms, the Liberals themselves were the losers. They did provide themselves with some insulation from the potential loss of corporate support were they to lose office (as they did in 2006), but at some financial cost in that their subvention in 2005 was considerably less than their prior corporate contributions. This, of course, raises the question of why the Liberals would propose a system that cost them money, while apparently being at worst neutral and more generally beneficial for their competitors. One possible explanation is that the Liberals anticipated the fallout of the Gomery investigation (although the Commission of Inquiry was not established until 2004, one can only presume that the Liberals had some sense of what their Quebec branch had been doing, and in any case there were already reports of questionable practices in the media) and decided that something like C-24 was the least they could do without suffering even greater consequences later on. A second, and related, explanation is that they hoped partially to insulate themselves from the financial consequences of their declining popularity and even more from those of an anticipated election defeat at some point in the reasonably near future. A third explanation is that they had a desire to free themselves from the need to satisfy large donors, whether corporate or individual. Although the first two of these do not directly support a cartel explanation, in that either could equally be attributed to simple and narrow self-interest, neither are they incompatible with it; the third explanation is directly derivable from the cartel model. Moreover, with regard to *cui bono*, the unanswerable question is what corporate and large individual donations to the Liberals would have been in the face of a Conservative minority (or less plausibly, majority) government. But not having to find out is part of the point of cartelization.

The cartel model leads to several expectations (not all of them unique to the cartel model, however) of the expected nature of a party finance regime:

- *There should be generous state subventions to compensate for the failure of existing financial arrangements to keep up with rising costs and to protect against the vagaries of private member/corporate donations.* Particularly if one assumes the Liberals could anticipate a dramatic drop in corporate support in the face of impending scandals, this appears largely to have been satisfied. (Alternatively, the failure of the Liberals to raise the spending limit more than they did even though they were raising in 2003 nearly twice as much money as the Conservatives could also be interpreted as evidence in favour of cartelization over maximization.)
- *The financial regime should reduce the difference in resources between the*

party or parties that are in office at the moment and those (cartel) parties that are out of office. The Conservatives' superior financial position beginning in 2004 appears to be the result of superior fundraising ability rather than the Conservatives' assent to power, which it predates. Although the conclusion must rest on speculation about the likely pattern of corporate donations with the Conservatives in power, it is likely that beginning in 2006 the disparity in favour of the governing party would have been much larger in the absence of the reforms. To the extent that this would have been so, this expectation is met.

- *The financial regime should help insulate the central leadership of the parties from the influence of the organized party on the ground and external big or organized contributors who would be able to impose constraints in exchange for their support.* In the absence of data concerning the financial independence of the riding associations, and the full financial relationship between them and the central parties, one cannot reach a judgment on the first part of this proposition. The elimination of union and very large individual contributions, and the dramatic limitation of corporate contributions, appear to support the second part.
- *The financial regime should be skewed in favour of the cartel parties and against those outside the cartel.* Within the constraint imposed (or reasonably expected to be imposed) by the Supreme Court, there is some reason to believe that this is satisfied with respect to most of the small and potential upstart parties. Its truth is seriously questionable with regard to the Greens, and it appears to be flatly contradicted by the Bloc.

Although not directly related to the legislative changes, another indicator of cartel-like behaviour is the expansion of resources available to non-government parties in the House of Commons. The Leader of the Opposition has been paid a special salary (now equal to that of a cabinet minister) since 1905 (plus a car allowance since 1931 and has been given an official residence in Ottawa since 1950). Since the 1970s, and continuing into the 1980s and 1990s, however, there has been an explosion in the number of non-government-party MPs receiving special salaries and allowances to include in 2006 the Leader of the Opposition, the leaders of all other parties, the Opposition House Leader, the House leaders and deputy House leaders of all other parties, and the whips (both chief and deputies) of all parties. Although of course justifiable in terms of the importance of these offices to the smooth functioning of Parliament, these salaries also serve, as the cartel model would predict, to mitigate the costs of electoral defeat (leaders and whips may expect to go to the somewhat lower supplementary salaries paid to the Opposition or other party rather than to the simple base MP's salary). At the same time, by limiting these benefits to parties with at least twelve MPs, what appears to be a general benefit is in fact restricted only to parties that have already broken into the system and thus would not be available to the Greens (or other minor parties) even if they were to win a few seats.

Overall, then, the picture is mixed (and incomplete) but is for the most part not inconsistent with the expectations raised by the cartel party model.

Expectations for the Future

Opponents of public subsidies to parties often argue that these will undercut the links between society in general, and party membership organizations in particular, on the one hand, and the parties in public office that claim to represent them, on the other. Although the cartel hypothesis in part reversed the order of causation (making public finance a response to, rather than a cause of, disengagement between citizens and parties), it also in part directly supports it (making freedom from the constraints of satisfying financial contributors one of the reasons for introducing public subsidies).

More generally, in speculating about the significance of the 2004 reforms for the future development (as opposed to the prior existence) of a cartel-party-like system in Canada, there are three subjects that might be considered: the relations between the central parties and the organized party on the ground; the relations between the central parties and civil society; and the nature of electoral competition (again, not the likelihood of electoral turnover, but the substance of the choices available to voters).

It is beyond the scope of this chapter to predict the future nature of Canadian electoral competition – although it might be suggested that the elimination of significant corporate contributions may make it easier for the Liberals to move toward the left, as some have suggested.[10] Ironically, this would be a non-cartel-party-model result (widening the gap between the parties) based on a cartel-party-model mechanism (freedom from the constraints of major contributors).

With regard to ties between parties and civil society, the new regulatory regime clearly puts a premium on increasing the number of individuals who make financial contributions. The questions are whether, or to what extent, "fundraising based on many small contributions from individuals fosters connections between [a] party and its social base," as Young and colleagues (2005) suggest, and whether the loss of contributions from organizations of civil society entails a weakening of links to civil society. With regard to the latter, the strongest links clearly were between the unions and the NDP. Although it may be imprudent to attribute everything to C-24, the decision of the Ontario NDP to suspend Canadian Auto Workers (CAW) union president Buzz Hargrove, and then the CAW executive's retaliatory advice to its members to stop supporting the NDP both provincially and federally, certainly is suggestive of weakening ties (Ha 2006). It remains to be seen whether the NDP's relations with other unions will deteriorate over time as well.

Young and colleagues (2005) also point to changes in the nature of relations between corporate Canada and the Liberal Party, with, for example, corporate tables at large fundraising dinners being replaced by more intimate (if one can use that word for a dinner with thirty to fifty people) $5,000-a-plate affairs with the prime minister. Whether this practice will continue for the Liberals (or be adapted by the Conservatives now that they are in power) remains to be seen, as does the question of whether bigger donations or some face time with the prime minister ultimately reflect a closer tie. Young and colleagues also report a drop (from well over half in 2000 to less than one-third in 2004) in the share of donations to Liberal candidates coming from corporate or business sources. As with the NDP, although the ban on union contributions "has not dealt a death blow to ongoing connections," it does appear to have been associated with a weakening of those ties.

With regard to fundraising from many small contributors, the question is whether this kind of chequebook democracy represents meaningful participation by citizens or meaningful engagement with civil society by parties. Ultimately this is a philosophical question, but an appropriate analogy may be to chain stores. Clearly, if a store becomes excessively detached from its customers (that is, fails to offer them anything they want to buy), it is in danger of going out of business. But at the same time, customers are in no way part of management in the way that democratic citizens might be expected to be part of the management of their government or party members might be expected to control their party. And like customers, who have no way to express demands except by taking their business elsewhere, contributors have no way to express demands except by ceasing to contribute – and these actions allow only expression of general dissatisfaction, not any particular demand. If none of the four stores in town chooses to carry what a consumer wants (analogously, if none of the parties address the issues the citizen wants addressed), he or she is simply out of luck. Although dependence on small individual donors involves more connection to civil society than would total state funding, its atomized and anonymous nature still provides very weak connection. Moreover, because it is a form of connection that is not amenable to the making of concrete demands, it is fundamentally consistent with the idea that the leaders of cartel parties want or need to free themselves from popular constraints.

Looking instead at connections between the central party and the party on the ground, the direct subsidies provided by the state clearly should help make the central party more independent. The real question, however, is whether adaptation to the new rules will result in the channelling of individual contributions directly to the central party or, alternatively, whether contributions to electoral district associations that are transferred to the centre at the discretion of the local parties are important. The second possibility, which is inconsistent with the cartel hypothesis, cannot be ruled out, yet the exigencies of direct mail fundraising strongly suggest that the first is likely to predominate. In this case, we might expect growing detachment and independence of the central party, as suggested by the cartel party model.

There is, however, one additional way in which the new rules might contribute to a cartel-party-like pattern of central party-local party relations that at least deserves mention. The cartel thesis suggests an increasing concentration of control in a central office that is increasingly professionalized and/or outsourced. One aspect of the new regime that seems to favour this trend is the inclusion of polling as an election expense subject to the spending caps. According to Liberal pollster Michael Marzolini, this reform is likely to preclude commercial polling by candidates, for whom the spending limits are low relative to the cost of a poll, while still allowing polling by the national parties (with larger, and increased, spending limits and lower amortized costs for a poll) (Francoli 2003). To the extent that polling is valuable to local candidates, this would represent an additional dependence on the central party – in the sense that access to polling data conceivably could be withheld, but more significantly in the sense that the substantive content of the polls (the questions asked) will be determined by the agenda of the central leadership.

Conclusion

In one respect, Canada should not be terribly fertile ground for cartelization of the party system. Looking at Britain, for example, Katz and Mair (1995) suggested that the winner-take-all nature of the electoral system should militate against the formation of cartel parties. On the other hand, although Canada continues to hold first-past-the-post elections, and to cling to the Westminster model of single-party governments, one might expect that what now looks like it is becoming the norm – minority governments – would create pressure toward a regularized modus vivendi among the parties. If the end result is a bipolar system capable of resulting in alternating majority governments, whether single party or coalition, one would expect cartelization to be inhibited.

If, however, the result is a series of minority governments that can survive only with the acquiescence of their erstwhile electoral opponents, the situation will be quite different. Under this scenario, a voter might well ask what is the point of elections: either nothing changes at all, or else changes proposed by governments that have majorities neither in the electorate nor in Parliament are enacted with a wink and a nod from the parties that shamelessly claim the title "opposition." Given this, it should be no surprise that the increase in turnout between 2004 (60.9 percent) and 2006 (64.7 percent) now appears to have been a temporary blip, with turnout in 2008 dropping to a record low of only 58.8 percent. Moreover, even if expectations are adjusted downward so that turnouts below 60 percent are accepted as tolerable, the apparent gutting of the meaning of elections might lead to a collapse in the numbers of citizens prepared to cross the much higher threshold of commitment required to send money.

Whether this would represent a true crisis of democracy may be largely in the eye of the beholder. For those who identify democracy with government for the people rather than of or by the people, it may not. If one regards roughly equal satisfaction between winners and losers as a desideratum, as, for example, Lijphart (1999, 286-87) apparently does, lesser citizen involvement may be an unintended consequence. On the other hand, a collapse of contributions almost certainly would represent a crisis for the parties. The question then would be how the governing parties react. They could re-energize politics, in effect dissolving what would have become a tacit cartel. On the other hand, they could – in the name of maintaining the vital-for-democracy strength of parties, and avoiding national disunity – circle the wagons and increase their subsidies, increasing cartelization. But as with the cartel model in general, this would not indicate (although it might be taken to indicate) a premeditated conspiracy but rather self-defence. Indeed, to conclude on a provocative note, it may be that the phenomena that we identified with the cartel party, both as causes and as effects, are more directly intertwined with the ideas of good government, consensus democracy, and new governance than the advocates of these ideas would like to admit. Although the notion of democracy (a positive valence term, implying attention to the common good) without politics (increasingly a negative valence term, implying attention to private interests) may be appealing to citizens and pundits, that does not make it possible. Cartelization may be the price one pays for attempting to remove politics from democracy.

NOTES

1 In part, what this says is that we did not explicitly address the question of whether the cartel hypothesis is a theory about uniform directionality of trends or a theory about convergence, in which case the directions of trends would depend on the starting points of the cases.
2 Indeed, one of the hypothesized characteristics of a cartel system is to minimize the importance of the distinction between being in and being out of office at any particular time.
3 This is not to deny that, at least within the terms of current neo-liberal conventional wisdom, to exceed these limitations would be seen as unrealistic or irresponsible.
4 Although Kitschelt is correct that cartels are always threatened by defection, he is wrong in identifying this problem with the prisoner's dilemma, at least as it relates to the cartel party argument. Rather, the problem is more akin to the tragedy of the commons, in which it is foreseeable that short-term maximization by each would lead to ruin for all. In this respect, devolution of responsibility to non-party agencies should be interpreted as the kind of external constraint that rational egoists would accept on themselves because it also credibly constrains other players (see, for example, Olson 1965). For more on why the prisoner's dilemma is an inapt analogy, see Blyth and Katz (2005).
5 One implication of all this is that although it may be appropriate to attribute functions to parties – for example, to provide a linkage between citizens or social groups and the state – within the context of a theory about how democratic governments *should* work, it is not necessarily appropriate to assume that parties (or more accurately their leaders) give the performance of this function the highest, or even high, priority over such other potential goals as personal power or economic and job security. In particular with regard to party finance, the claim is not that state subvention makes it *more difficult* for parties to provide this linkage – for example, "extensive reliance on the state for funding contributes to an erosion of parties' capacity to link society and the state" (Young et al. 2005) – but rather that it reduces the parties' *need or desire* to do so, and thus is likely to reduce the degree to which parties actually provide linkage, even if their hypothetical capacity to do so were increased by access to additional funds.
6 As this phrasing suggests, there is no distinction in Canadian law analogous to the American distinction between hard money contributions to parties (funds donated and used to influence the outcome of an election specifically by supporting or opposing particular named candidates) and soft money contributions to parties for non-electoral functions such as maintaining party headquarters and facilities or registration drives and get-out-the-vote campaigns.
7 As Katz and Mair (1995, 22) put it, "The state provides contested elections. And

since democratically contested elections ... require political parties, the state also provides or guarantees the provision of, political parties." Thus, when Prime Minister Chrétien defended C-24 in the House of Commons, saying, "Political parties are essential to the democratic process. We all know that in this House. We all know that they need money to operate. That too is essential in a democracy" (House Debates, 11 February 2003), he was both justifying the bill in terms of the public interest and speaking in terms that are entirely consistent with the cartel thesis.

8 Payments to the Bloc were roughly 66 percent of its election expense limit for 2006, as opposed to roughly 40 percent for the Conservatives, 50 percent for the Liberals, and only 20 percent for the NDP (which had a slightly larger subvention but candidates to support throughout the country).

9 Green candidates in 2000 spent roughly $202,000 and received no reimbursement; in 2004, Green candidates spent just over $670,000 and were reimbursed for $74,000 of that.

10 For example, see Taber (2006) and *Globe and Mail* (2006).

WORKS CITED

Blyth, Mark, and Richard S. Katz. 2005. From Catch-All Politics to Cartelisation. *West European Politics* 28(1): 33-60.

Borchert, Jens. 2000. The Political Class and Its Self-Interested Theory of Democracy: Historical Developments and Institutional Consequences. Paper presented at the European Consortium for Political Research Joint Sessions of Workshops, Copenhagen.

Cross, William, and Lisa Young. 2004. The Contours of Party Membership in Canada. *Party Politics* 10(4): 427-44.

Dalton, Russell J., and Martin P. Wattenberg. 2000. *Parties without Partisans: Political Change in Advanced Industrial Democracies.* New York: Oxford University Press.

Epstein, Leon D. 1986. *Political Parties in the American Model.* Madison: University of Wisconsin Press.

Francoli, Paco. 2003. Grit Pollster Marzolini Takes Aim at Liberal's Campaign Bill. *The Hill Times,* 17 February.

Globe and Mail. 2006. The Liberals' True Place Is in the Political Centre. 12 April, A16.

Ha, T.T. 2006. CAW Leadership Urges Members to Abandon NDP. *Globe and Mail,* 25 March, A5.

Katz, Richard S. 2002. Whose Agent? Principles, Principals, and Party Politics. Prepared for the 2002 Meeting of the Council for European Studies, Chicago.

–. 2003. Cartels, Consensus Democracy, and Representation in the European Union. Paper presented at the European Consortium for Political Research Joint Sessions of Workshops, Edinburgh.

Katz, Richard S., and Peter Mair. 1993. The Evolution of Party Organizations in Europe: The Three Faces of Party Organization. *American Review of Politics* 14 (winter): 593-618.

–. 1995. Changing Models of Party Organization and Party Democracy: The Emer-

gence of the Cartel Party. *Party Politics* 1(1): 5-28.
—. 1996. Cadre, Catch-All, or Cartel? A Rejoinder. *Party Politics* 2(4): 525-34.
—. 2002. The Ascendancy of the Party in Public Office: Party Organizational Change in Twentieth-Century Democracies. In *Political Parties: Old Concepts and New Challenges*, ed. Richard Gunther, José Ramón Montero, and Juan J. Linz, 113-35. Oxford: Oxford University Press.
Kettl, Donald F. 2000. *The Global Public Management Revolution: A Report on the Transformation of Governance*. Washington, DC: Brookings Institute.
Kirchheimer, Otto. 1966. The Transformation of the Western European Party Systems. In *Political Parties and Political Development*, ed. Joseph LaPalombara and Myron Weiner, 177-200. Princeton, NJ: Princeton University Press.
Kitschelt, Herbert. 2000. Citizen, Politicians, and Party Cartelization. *European Journal of Political Research* 37(2): 149-79.
Lijphart, Arend. 1999. *Patterns of Democracy*. New Haven, CT: Yale University Press.
Mair, Peter, and Ingrid van Biezen. 2001. Party Membership in Twenty European Democracies, 1980-2000. *Party Politics* 7(1): 5-22.
Majone, Giandomenico. 1994. The Rise of the Regulatory State in Europe. *West European Politics* 17(3): 77-101.
Michels, Robert. 1962/1911. *Political Parties*. New York: Collier.
Olson, Mancur. 1965. *The Logic of Collective Action*. Cambridge, MA: Harvard University Press.
Osborne, David, and Ted Gaebler. 1992. *Reinventing Government: How the Entrepreneurial Spirit Is Transforming the Public Sector*. Reading, MA: Addison-Wesley.
Paltiel, Khayyam Z. 1970. *Political Party Financing in Canada*. Toronto: McGraw-Hill.
Pierre, Jon., ed. 2000. *Debating Governance*. Oxford: Oxford University Press.
Pierre, Jon, Lars Svåsand, and Anders Widfeldt. 2000. State Subsidies to Political Parties: Confronting Rhetoric with Reality. *West European Politics* 23(3): 1-24.
Taber, Jane. 2006. Liberals Contemplate Uniting the Left as a Way Back to Office. *Globe and Mail*, 13 April 2006, A4.
van Biezen, Ingrid. 2004. Political Parties as Public Utilities. *Party Politics* 10(6): 701-22.
Young, Lisa. 1998. Party, State and Political Competition in Canada: The Cartel Model Reconsidered. *Canadian Journal of Political Science* 31(2): 339-58.
Young, Lisa, Anthony Sayers, Harold Jansen, and Munroe Eagles. 2005. Implications of State Funding for Party Organization. Presented at the annual meeting of the American Political Science Association, Washington, DC.

5

Cartels, Syndicates, and Coalitions
Canada's Political Parties after the 2004 Reforms

HAROLD J. JANSEN AND LISA YOUNG

When Steven Harper's minority government almost fell in 2008 because of a dispute over public funding of political parties, it was tempting for observers to accept the idea that a "cartelization" of the Canadian party system had occurred. At that time, opposition parties were banding together in self-interest to preserve state subsidies, colluding in an arrangement that in many ways resembled Katz and Mair's cartel model. Upon closer examination, however, elements of the situation diverge significantly from the expectations of the cartel model. Most notably, the governing Conservative Party was not part of the colluding group, and has subsequently made clear its intention to make public funding for political parties an issue in the next federal election.

In this chapter, we examine the way in which Canadian parties have adapted to the very different political finance regime established through the 2004 and 2006 reforms, and frame these adaptations in the context of the dominant theoretical model proposed by Katz and Mair. Although discussions of party finance often rely on Katz and Mair's influential cartel model (1995), such models do not fit the Canadian case particularly well. We argue that instead of a cartel, it is useful to understand several of the major Canadian political parties as forming a syndicate to preserve the party finance regime. Four of the five parties (the Liberals, New Democrats, Bloc Québécois, and Greens) can be understood as members of this syndicate, content to rely on state funds for the bulk of their income and accepting the consequent equalization (in relative terms) of their incomes. But the Conservative Party, which did not support the reforms, has deviated from the behaviour anticipated by the drafters of the 2004 legislation by investing significantly in fundraising activities. As a result, the Conservative Party has financial resources that allow it to outspend the other parties by a significant margin during the period between elections. Even more significant, however, is the fundraising capacity the party has developed. This capacity would allow the party to maintain its national organization and contest elections successfully even in the absence of the quarterly allowance. During the five years in which the new election finance regime has been in place, the Conservative Party has explicitly rejected the core norm embodied in the regime (state dependence), thereby increasing its capacity to outspend its competitors. In December of 2008 it went one step further, seeking to dismantle the regime and thereby further increase its competitive advantage, at least in the short to medium term.

The Cartel Party in Canada

Katz and Mair's cartel party thesis (1995) remains the theoretical touchstone for examinations of the impact of extensive state subsidies on political parties. A core proposition in the model is the idea that parties' inability to access necessary resources (financial and volunteer) for political competition leads them to collude to extract resources from the state, typically in the form of increased state subsidies. Parties thus form a cartel, with constrained inter-party competition and increasingly tenuous links between parties and civil society. There are three elements of this model that we examine in the Canadian context: the formation of the cartel, the constrained competition, and the weakening of links between parties and civil society.

In Chapter 4, Richard Katz examines the 2004 reforms and finds only mixed evidence that they constitute the formation of a cartel. The problems with the model are rooted in the stances of the various parties. The most significant beneficiaries of the new party finance regime are the Greens, the Bloc Québécois, and the Conservatives. It is hard to imagine either of the first two as part of a cartel when the legislation was conceived and debated in 2003. The Greens were not in the House of Commons at the time and, as a separatist party, the Bloc Québécois was an unlikely candidate for collusion with the staunchly federalist Liberal government at the time. The Conservatives' predecessors opposed the new finance regime.

When it comes to a broader pattern of constrained competition and diminished ties between state and civil society, attempts to apply the cartel party thesis outside the context of continental European democracies have met with limited success, particularly in the case of Westminster/majoritarian democracies such as Canada. Young (1998) found that the model had limited applicability to the Canadian case, partly because the way state financing was delivered to parties required them to connect with individual, corporate, and union donors. The adoption of more extensive state subsidies in the 2004 party finance reform package, however, opened up the possibility of a move in the direction theorized by Katz and Mair. In particular, the quarterly allowance paid to Canadian parties does not require parties to solicit donations, as is the case with the political contribution tax credit. It is difficult, however, to argue that the move to more extensive state support for parties has coincided with a curtailment of competition. Since 2004, Canada's party system has become the most competitive it has been in the last two decades, with three consecutive minority governments, narrow margins of victory, and a change of government. In explaining the persistence of a competitive electoral environment despite the increased reliance on state money, Young, Sayers, and Jansen (2007, 336) highlight the significance of Canada's Westminster political heritage, with a winner-take-all electoral system and single-party governments limiting the extent to which Canada has gone down this path.

Despite these institutional limitations, the events in late 2008 provided evidence of four parties – the Bloc, Liberals, NDP, and Green Party – cooperating to maintain the 2004 party finance regime. The first three parties (with the support of the Greens) were poised to defeat the government and replace it with a coalition government. Could this be constituted as evidence of a cartel? The major problem with seeing this as an example of a Katz and Mair-style cartel is that it excluded the Conservatives, the party in government. Furthermore, it is hard to see how this coalition would work in the context of Canada's Westminster-style political system, particularly its adversarial electoral system.

Instead, we propose borrowing another concept from the language of corporate organization: the syndicate. A syndicate is defined as "a combination of capitalists or financiers entered into for the purpose of prosecuting a scheme requiring large resources of capital," especially "one having the object of obtaining control of the market in a particular commodity" (*Oxford English Dictionary*, 2nd ed.). What is attractive about the idea of a syndicate in the context of party competition is that it provides a model of limited cooperation to pursue a specific venture or shared interest. It does not imply a broader pattern of constraint of competition or the straining of ties between civil society and the state. Furthermore, it does not necessarily require the participation of the major competitors, as implied by the cartel model.

Parties' Responses to the 2004 Reforms

From this perspective, we have two distinct sets of parties in the Canadian system: those that belong to the syndicate, and the dissenting Conservative Party. The parties in the former group have responded in a fairly predictable manner to the advent of the 2004 and 2006 reforms: they began with an understanding that the new rules would allow them to shift the efforts of the extra-parliamentary party away from a focus on fundraising, and were content to rely to a considerable extent on public funds. Two developments have disrupted this approach. First, the unstable political situation producing three elections in four years has forced all parties to be on a permanent election footing, and to require more money than would otherwise have been the case. Second, the Conservative Party's rejection of the norm of state dependence, intensified by the permanent campaign, has forced most of the syndicate to focus on fundraising from individuals to a greater extent than would otherwise have been the case.

To understand the Conservatives' opposition to the party finance regime and the other parties' staunch defence of it, it is first necessary to examine how the parties have fared under the new regime. The new party finance regime significantly increased the amount of state money available to political parties in three ways. First, the legislation enriched the tax credit for political contributions. In particular, donations of up to $400 would now receive a 75 percent tax credit, up from the $200 in place before 2004. Although the amount of this subsidy is difficult to quantify, it does represent an indirect subsidy to Canada's parties. Second, the new legislation increased the election expenses reimbursements for federal parties from 22.5 percent to 50 percent (60 percent for the 2004 election only). The legislation also increased the spending limit and expanded the definition of eligible election expenses, allowing for more money to be reimbursed at the 50 percent level. Third, the legislation introduced the $1.75 per-year per-vote subsidy, the most significant break from the past.

After six years of experience with the new legislation and thanks to the more stringent reporting requirements under the law, we now have a significant body of data that allows us to understand better how parties have responded to the legislation. One important limitation of our analysis here is that we examine only the finances of the national party organizations. The new financing regime had some important implications for the financial relationship between national and local party organizations, as is discussed in Chapter 6. Table 5.1 reports the total income and income from state sources for Canada's largest parties. A few things quickly become clear from the table. First, most of the parties have experienced an increase in revenue since the new regime has come into effect. For some parties, such as the Bloc Québécois and the Green Party, the increase has been substantial. For others, the increase has been more modest. Second, all of the parties have become more dependent on state sources of income since 2004. Prior to 2004, in election years, the largest parties would typically derive 10 to 15 percent of their income from the election expenses reimbursement. In non-election years, the parties would receive no state support other than the indirect incentive of the tax credit. Between 2004 and 2009, over $250 million (in constant 2009 dollars) in state money has been given directly to the parties. In election years since 2004, we typically see the parties deriving approximately two-thirds of their income from state sources.

Although the legislation enriched other elements of the public financing of parties, the quarterly allowance was the most significant new element in party finance in 2004. Understanding the extent to which parties are dependent on the allowance has been difficult because of the enriched election reimbursement and the frequent elections Canada has experienced since 2004. Figure 5.1 reports the proportion of party income derived from the quarterly allowance with the election reimbursements removed from total party revenue. This allows us to isolate the significance of the allowance for Canada's parties. Figure 5.1 demonstrates that, although there have been changes over time, the most significant differences are those between the parties, differences that will be discussed later.

By eliminating donations from corporations and unions (to national parties in 2004 and completely with the passage of the Accountability Act), individual donations have become the only legal source of private financing for parties. The importance of these has been enhanced by the fact that the 2004 changes also made the tax credits for individual political contributions more generous. Figure 5.2 reports the revenue raised from individual donors in constant 2009 dollars. As with state dependence, the significant finding in Figure 5.2 is the variability between parties; some (such as the Conservatives) have experienced significant increases, others (like the Greens) modest increases, whereas yet others have seen their individual fundraising stagnate.

TABLE 5.1A

National party revenue and revenue from state sources, 1997-2001 (constant 2009 dollars)

	1997	1998	1999	2000	2001
BQ					
Total income	$3,183,162	$914,601	$1,588,782	$3,162,951	$674,050
Election reimbursement	$465,571 (14.6%)	–	–	$480,116	–
Quarterly allowance	–	–	–	–	–
State sources of income	$465,571 (14.6%)	$0 (0%)	$0 (0%)	$480,116	$0 (0%)
CPC					
Total income	$29,294,086	$14,566,572	$13,997,091	$33,605,510	$8,823,789
Election reimbursement	$4,174,344 (14.2%)	–	–	$3,612,989	–
Quarterly allowance	–	–	–	–	–
State sources of income	$4,174,344 (14.2%)	$0 (0%)	$0 (0%)	$3,612,989	$0 (0%)
GPC					
Total income	$79,777	$121,748	$125,004	$162,853	$84,237
Election reimbursement	$0 (0%)	–	–	$0 (0%)	–
Quarterly allowance	–	–	–	–	–
State sources of income	$0 (0%)	$0 (0%)	$0 (0%)	$0 (0%)	$0 (0%)
LPC					
Total income	$25,327,608	$25,327,608	$17,920,403	$27,160,203	$10,719,749
Election reimbursement	$3,129,870 (12.4%)	–	–	$3,335,176 (12.3%)	–
Quarterly allowance	–	–	–	–	–
State sources of income	$3,129,870 (12.4%)	$0 (0%)	$0 (0%)	$3,335,176 (12.3%)	$0 (0%)
NDP					
Total income	$19,500,630	$19,500,630	$7,868,277	$12,349,106	$5,945,138
Election reimbursement	$1,707,636 (8.8%)	–	–	$1,690,034 (13.7%)	–
Quarterly allowance	–	–	–	–	–
State sources of income	$1,707,636 (8.8%)	$0 (0%)	$0 (0%)	$1,690,034 (13.7%)	$0 (0%)

Notes: BQ – Bloc Québécois, CPC – Conservative Party of Canada, GPC – Green Party of Canada, LPC – Liberal Party of Canada, NDP – New Democratic Party.

Total income does not include transfers from other units of the party. Prior to 2004, Conservative totals are those for Reform/Canadian Alliance and the Progressive Conservatives combined.

Source: Elections Canada financial reports, adjusted for inflation according to Bank of Canada Consumer Price Index data at http://www.bankofcanada.ca/en/rates/inflation_calc.html.

TABLE 5.1B
National party revenue and revenue from state sources, 2002-05 (constant 2009 dollars)

	2002	2003	2004	2005
BQ				
Total income	$685,336	$597,604	$6,858,874	$4,053,764
Election reimbursement	–	–	$2,945,778 (42.9%)	–
Quarterly allowance	–	–	$2,977,745 (43.4%)	$3,269,886 (80.7%)
State sources of income	$0 (0%)	$0 (0%)	$5,923,523 (86.4%)	$3,269,886 (80.7%)
CPC				
Total income	$11,833,670	$12,469,003	$31,798,700	$26,862,929
Election reimbursement	–	–	$11,295,669 (35.5%)	–
Quarterly allowance	–	–	$8,619,445 (27.1%)	$7,821,585 (29.1%)
State sources of income	$0 (0%)	$0 (0%)	$19,915,114 (62.6%)	$7,821,585 (29.1%)
GPC				
Total income	$155,883	$260,865	$1,278,327	$1,569,681
Election reimbursement	–	–	$325,572 (25.5%)	–
Quarterly allowance	–	–	$570,411 (44.6%)	$1,132,940 (72.2%)
State sources of income	$0 (0%)	$0 (0%)	$895,983 (70.1%)	$1,132,940 (72.2%)
LPC				
Total income	$9,745,055	$19,513,369	$25,948,712	$18,597,562
Election reimbursement	–	–	$10,851,451 (41.8%)	–
Quarterly allowance	–	–	$9,956,876 (38.4%)	$9,695,224 (52.1%)
State sources of income	$0 (0%)	$0 (0%)	$20,808,327 (80.2%)	$9,695,224 (52.1%)
NDP				
Total income	$11,230,814	$11,230,814	$16,653,358	$9,602,735
Election reimbursement	–	–	$7,854,655 (47.2%)	–
Quarterly allowance	–	–	$3,141,182 (18.9%)	$4,139,355 (43.1%)
State sources of income	$0 (0%)	$0 (0%)	$10,995,837 (66.0%)	$4,139,355 (43.1%)

See Table 5.1A source and notes.

TABLE 5.1B

National party revenue and revenue from state sources, 2006-09 (constant 2009 dollars)

	2006	2007	2008	2009
BQ				
Total income	$6,025,393	$3,467,804	$6,250,114	*$3,363,341*
Election reimbursement	$2,373,245 (39.4%)	–	$2,470,423 (39.5%)	–
Quarterly allowance	$3,096,520 (51.4%)	$3,027,079 (87.3%)	$3,057,141 (48.9%)	$2,742,215 (81.5%)
State sources of income	$5,469,765 (90.8%)	$3,027,079 (87.3%)	$5,527,563 (88.4%)	$2,742,215 (81.5%)
CPC				
Total income	$38,865,952	$27,882,075	$41,876,487	*$28,053,272*
Election reimbursement	$9,453,924 (24.3%)	–	$9,838,170 (23.5%)	–
Quarterly allowance	$9,851,371 (25.3%)	$10,473,681 (37.6%)	$10,577,700 (25.3%)	$10,351,071 (36.9%)
State sources of income	$19,305,296 (49.7%)	$10,473,681 (37.6%)	$20,415,870 (48.8%)	$10,351,071 (36.9%)
GPC				
Total income	$2,610,081	$2,290,552	$4,366,586	*$2,986,250*
Election reimbursement	$477,953 (18.3%)	–	$1,416,456 (32.4%)	–
Quarterly allowance	$1,258,433 (48.2%)	$1,294,220 (56.5%)	$1,307,074 (29.9%)	$1,863,155 (62.4%)
State sources of income	$1,736,387 (66.5%)	$1,294,220 (56.5%)	$2,723,529 (62.4%)	$1,863,155 (62.4%)
LPC				
Total income	$27,655,757	$13,313,809	$22,061,726	*$16,280,509*
Election reimbursement	$9,149,890 (33.1%)	–	$7,356,332 (33.3%)	–
Quarterly allowance	$8,995,766 (32.5%)	$8,730,063 (65.6%)	$8,816,763 (40.0%)	$7,219,593 (44.3%)
State sources of income	$18,145,656 (65.6%)	$8,730,063 (65.6%)	$16,173,094 (73.3%)	$7,219,593 (44.3%)
NDP				
Total income	$16,074,854	$9,105,418	$19,070,288	*$9,006,713*
Election reimbursement	$7,067,611 (44.0%)	–	$8,488,433 (44.5%)	–
Quarterly allowance	$4,838,552 (30.1%)	$5,046,940 (55.4%)	$5,097,065 (26.7%)	$4,998,192 (55.5%)
State sources of income	$11,906,163 (74.1%)	$5,046,940 (55.4%)	$13,585,498 (71.2%)	$4,998,192 (55.5%)

See Table 5.1A source and notes.

FIGURE 5.1

Proportion of revenue derived from quarterly allowance

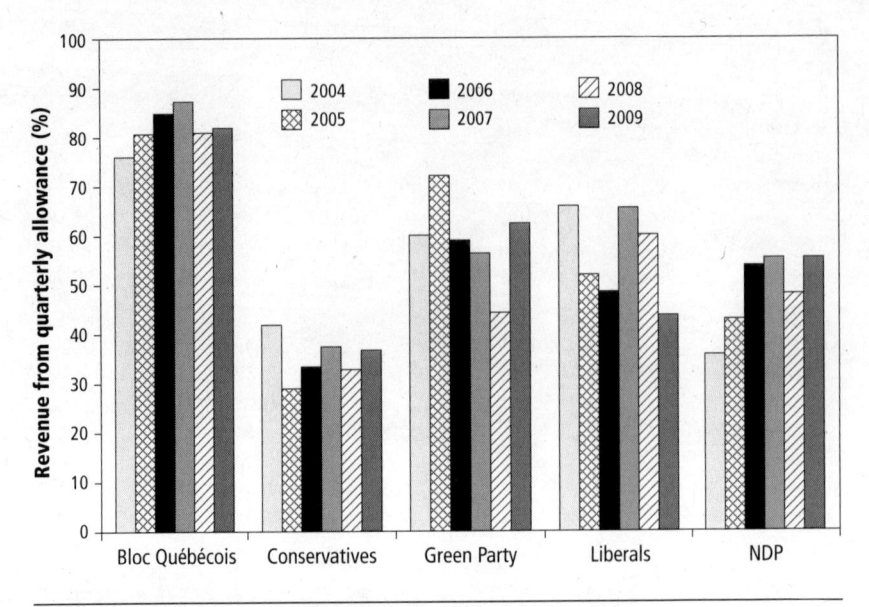

Note: Revenue does not include transfers or election expenses reimbursement.

Another way of understanding how parties are performing in individual fundraising is to use their electoral support as a baseline expectation for their individual fundraising. Stewart (2005) notes that a party's share of overall fundraising tended to follow its share of the popular vote, an analysis expanded upon by Lambert (2007, 50-55) in her study of the Green Party of Canada. Of course, Stewart's research looked at party fundraising prior to 2004, which also included corporate and union donations. Party strength in corporate or union fundraising could and did offset a party's weakness at fundraising among individuals (Jansen and Young 2008). Table 5.2 reports a party's share of the total number of individual contributors to political parties compared with its share of the vote in the preceding federal election.[1] Thus, a total above 100 percent indicates that a party is receiving donations from a number of contributors that exceeds what we would have expected based on its vote total; conversely, a total below 100 percent indicates the party's fundraising is performing less than what we might expect relative to the party's vote total. Table 5.3 reports the same information but based on a party's share of the total value of individual contributions.

FIGURE 5.2

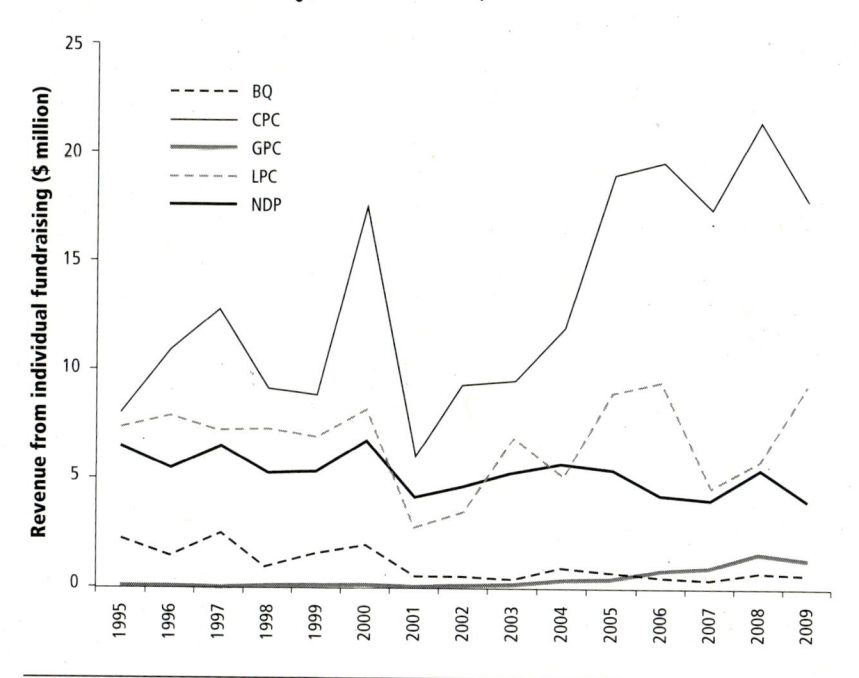

Revenue from individual fundraising (constant 2009 dollars)

Note: BQ – Bloc Québécois, CPC – Conservative Party of Canada, GPC – Green Party of Canada, LPC – Liberal Party of Canada, NDP – New Democratic Party.

TABLE 5.2

Fundraising performance based on share of the number of individual donors (percentages)

	2001	2002	2003	2004	2005	2006	2007	2008	2009
BQ	53.53	30.52	30.82	40.90	36.23	31.87	24.69	36.78	33.15
CPC	–	–	–	133.21	208.09	166.43	170.98	146.86	147.10
CA	189.71	227.34	204.33	–	–	–	–	–	–
PC	98.87	53.58	86.45	–	–	–	–	–	–
GPC	84.56	63.16	75.16	48.49	60.91	119.26	129.76	125.74	73.48
LPC	9.44	22.34	28.07	27.39	37.53	45.78	44.73	57.98	78.79
NDP	325.17	253.52	247.67	110.78	102.41	79.73	76.92	80.61	71.23

Notes: BQ – Bloc Québécois, CPC – Conservative Party of Canada, CA – Canadian Alliance, PC – Progressive Conservatives, GPC – Green Party of Canada, LPC – Liberal Party of Canada, NDP – New Democratic Party.

TABLE 5.3

Fundraising performance based on the value of individual donations (percentages)

	2001	2002	2003	2004	2005	2006	2007	2008	2009
BQ	37.54	27.92	20.35	20.95	17.92	14.57	14.84	19.93	33.15
CPC	–	–	–	111.26	182.00	148.28	169.39	156.82	147.10
CA	85.40	142.45	103.12	–	–	–	–	–	–
PC	157.21	113.27	126.92	–	–	–	–	–	–
GPC	75.75	101.85	103.30	24.71	28.82	53.60	78.46	66.70	73.48
LPC	51.01	46.69	74.40	38.83	68.65	86.49	53.51	61.69	78.79
NDP	362.78	296.36	272.71	100.08	98.66	65.58	81.95	83.00	71.23

Notes: BQ – Bloc Québécois, CPC – Conservative Party of Canada, CA – Canadian Alliance, PC – Progressive Conservatives, GPC – Green Party of Canada, LPC – Liberal Party of Canada, NDP – New Democratic Party.

Finally, Figure 5.3 reports the parties' election spending as a proportion of their maximum allowable spending. These results must be interpreted with the understanding that the data from 2004 onward are not strictly comparable with the data prior to 2004. In 2004, the maximum amounts that parties were permitted to spend were increased. Furthermore, certain expenses that were previously not included in the definition of election expenses (most notably public opinion polling) were included after 2004. Nevertheless, Figure 5.3 shows a more competitive electoral environment, with most parties spending more on their campaigns.

One thing is clear from these tables and figures: focusing on the aggregate obscures the fact that there is considerable variation between parties. To better understand how four parties came to band together to support the regime, while the governing party tried to dismantle it, it is important to examine the fundraising success and state dependence of each of the parties in turn.

The Bloc Québécois

Of the parties currently represented in the House of Commons, the Bloc Québécois most clearly fits the description of a cartelized party, as it is heavily reliant on state funding, and has in fact become less reliant on contributions from individuals since the quarterly allowance was instituted in 2004. The Bloc's situation is unique in that it contests federal elections only in Quebec. At a practical level, this means that the party has a much lower

FIGURE 5.3

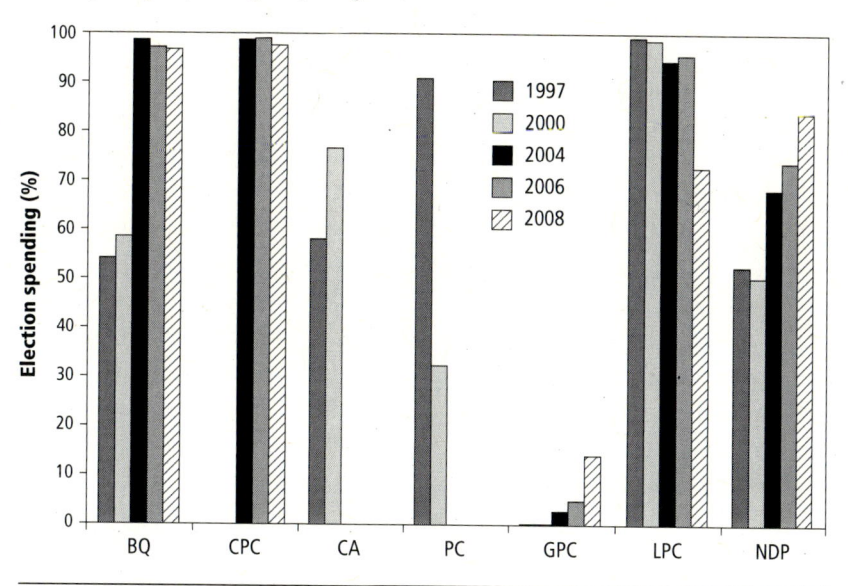

Election spending (as percentage of spending limit)

Note: Calculated from Elections Canada financial returns.
BQ – Bloc Québécois, CPC – Conservative Party of Canada, CA – Canadian Alliance, PC – Progressive Conservatives, GPC – Green Party of Canada, LPC – Liberal Party of Canada, NDP – New Democratic Party.

spending limit during the campaign than do other parties, but also that it must advertise in only one province, and generally in only one language. Whereas other parties must transport their leaders across a vast geographic area by chartered airplane, the Bloc needs only chartered busses to transport its leader around the province of Quebec. As Figure 5.3 illustrates, the advent of the quarterly allowance and the increase in the election expense reimbursement allowed the Bloc to start spending close to 100 percent of its election expense limit, a substantial increase from the 50 to 60 percent it had spent in elections prior to the change in the regulatory regime.

Moreover, the Bloc is formally independent from, but nonetheless supportive of, the provincial Parti Québécois. With its commitment to Quebec sovereignty, or at least a transfer of significant power from Ottawa to Quebec, the Bloc is necessarily subordinate to the Parti Québécois in political terms and has every incentive to assist its provincial counterpart by leaving the fundraising field clear for the provincial party, which cannot rely on state subsidies of comparable generosity. This helps to explain why the Bloc has raised relatively little money from individuals since the advent of the 2004 reforms. As Tables 5.2 and 5.3 demonstrate, the Bloc's fundraising efforts – both in terms of the number of individual donations and the value of those donations – substantially underperform relative to the party's vote share. Recall that scores above 100 percent indicate that the party is raising money or attracting donors above what would be expected according to its share of the popular vote; scores under 100 percent indicate that the party is underperforming. The Bloc's performance on these measures has declined since 2004. Examining its share of the number of donors, it has declined from 41 percent to 25 percent in 2007, rebounding in the election year of 2008; using the share of the value of individual donations, it has declined from 21 percent to 15 percent in 2007, increasing slightly in 2008. In short, the Bloc raises substantially less money from individuals than we would expect given its level of electoral support, and the overall trend is in a downward direction.

The Bloc's declining reliance on individual contributions has not had an adverse effect on its ability to contest elections, as public subsidies (both through the election expense reimbursement and the quarterly allowance) have provided a significant source of income for the party. The latter source has comprised more than three-quarters of the Bloc's revenue since 2004 (see Figure 5.1).

The almost entirely state-subsidized Bloc Québécois is one of the unintended consequences of the 2004 reforms, and an ironic legacy for Jean Chrétien, who spent much of his political career combating the Quebec sovereignty movement. From the perspective of the Conservative Party, the presence of the Bloc is doubly galling: first, the persistence of an almost entirely state-dependent party offends the Conservatives' notion that political parties are predominantly private entities that should be supported through private contributions from their supporters. Second, at a more pragmatic level, the Bloc's continued presence in Quebec has made it impossible for Stephen Harper to rebuild the Mulroney coalition, which relied on soft nationalist support from the province of Quebec as the third pillar of the coalition. In this respect, the Bloc's continued dominance in Quebec has made a majority government an elusive goal for Stephen Harper's Conservatives. The importance of the new regulatory regime to the Bloc Québécois in financial and perhaps electoral terms helps explain both the Conservatives' desire to end the state subsidy and the Bloc's decision to support a coalition government that would protect it.

The Green Party

The emergence of the Green Party as a significant political force has been a second unintended consequence of the new regulatory regime. On the surface, the new regime appeared to create significant barriers to entry for new political parties, thereby protecting the established parties that enacted the regime. To qualify for the quarterly allowance, a party has to win either 2 percent of the vote nationally or 5 percent of the vote in the ridings where it runs candidates. This threshold appeared designed to keep new entrants from enjoying the public subsidy intended for the parties with representation in Parliament.[2] But the leader of the Green Party at the time determined that if the party were to run candidates across the country, it might surpass the 2 percent threshold and gain access to public funding that would help establish the party as a more permanent and significant political force.

Ultimately, this calculation proved correct. The party surpassed the threshold in the 2004 election and began to benefit from the quarterly allowance. This has allowed the party to spend more on its election campaigns, culminating in the 2008 election, in which the party spent well over 10 percent of the national limit (see Figure 5.3) and won just under 7 percent of the popular vote. As the only party without a Member of Parliament but receiving public funds, the Green Party has also earned a unique status: it is not one of the major parties, but neither is it a minor party like the others. This was recognized when Green Party leader Elizabeth May was allowed to participate in the televised leaders' debates in the 2008 election.

Given that access to public funding has been critically important for the Green Party's emergence as a significant player, one might expect that the party would be similar to the Bloc in its heavy reliance on public funding. In fact, as Figure 5.1 demonstrates, this is not the case. In all but two years since 2004, the quarterly allowance has accounted for less than 60 percent of the Green Party's income.[3] Figure 5.2 shows that the party has been able to capitalize on its electoral success and new-found status to initiate a program of fundraising from individuals. In relative terms, this program has been very successful. Tables 5.2 and 5.3 demonstrate a consistent improvement in Green Party fundraising relative to the party's vote share. Although the party still underperforms in terms of the value of its donations, it has improved substantially from a score of 25 percent in 2004 to a score of 67 percent in 2008. With respect to the number of individual donors, the party has gone from underperforming in 2004 (48 percent) to overperforming in 2008 (126 percent). The proliferation of individual donors to the party speaks to a sustained effort to develop a widespread base of support for the party within the electorate, and contradicts the notion of the Green Party as a cartelized party with limited connection to society. The decline in fundraising performance in 2009, however, is an indication of the difficulty small parties can have in maintaining momentum.

Despite its success in individual fundraising, however, the Green Party remains dependent on the current regulatory regime both for a solid and predictable base of fundraising and for the status it affords the party. The Green Party's minor party status in 2003 means that it could not have been a founding member of any cartel. However, the decision of leader Elizabeth May to endorse the Liberal-NDP coalition in December 2008 is not at all surprising, given the party's reliance on state funding. The Green Party is thus a part of the syndicate protecting the party finance regime.

The New Democratic Party
Of the parties comprising the cartel, the NDP has been the least dependent on the state for funds. As Figure 5.2 shows, since 2004 the quarterly allowance has usually accounted for only half the party's income. The party's reluctance to lose the quarterly allowance, however, can perhaps be best understood by examining Figure 5.1. The party's fundraising from individuals has remained steady over the period in question, with little evidence that the party has the potential to significantly increase the number or size of its donations. In 2004, the party was able to solicit contributions from individuals in a magnitude consistent with its vote share, both in terms of size and source (see Tables 5.2 and 5.3). But the figures from 2005 to 2009 indicate an overall downward trend, suggesting that the party would be hard-pressed to further expand its donor base.

Unlike either the Bloc or the Greens, the New Democrats lost a significant portion of their income when union and corporate contributions were banned. The New Democrats had generally derived about one-quarter of their annual income from contributions from their affiliated unions (see Jansen and Young 2009), so the quarterly allowance is an important replacement for these lost funds. In this respect, the NDP had every incentive to work with the other parties in the syndicate to protect its state income, as the Conservatives' proposed measure did not seek to allow parties to solicit contributions from union or corporate sources.

Despite that the NDP's income from individual donors appears to have reached a plateau, the party has been able to steadily increase its spending during election campaigns, as indicated in Figure 5.3. Part of the increase between 2000 and 2004 is attributable to the fact that the party can now be reimbursed for public opinion polling, an expense that was previously excluded from the definition of election expenses, but even between 2004 and 2008 the party has become more competitive in national election campaigns, to the point where the NDP outspent the Liberals in the 2008 federal election. The party has reported that the annual allowance has made it easier to borrow money to finance the campaign (Jansen and Young 2009). The NDP's more competitive position in the Canadian party system is thus at least partly attributable to the new party finance regime, explaining the party's commitment to maintaining those rules and its willingness to be part of a coalition with the Liberals.

The Liberal Party
As the instigator of the new regulatory regime, and in this respect the leader of the syndicate, the Liberal Party found itself in a difficult position by 2008. The new regime has clearly benefited the Bloc Québécois, the Greens, and the NDP, allowing them to spend more during election campaigns than they had in the past (see Figure 5.3). The Liberal Party, however, has suffered considerably under these new rules. In part, this reflects a series of unforeseen events that conspired to harm the Liberals' situation. First, the merger of the Canadian Alliance and Progressive Conservative Party seemed unlikely at the time the legislation was conceived; had this not occurred, the Liberal Party would likely have continued to win substantially more votes than any other party, thereby cementing its financial lead. Second, not anticipating the merger of the two right-of-centre parties, the Liberals were in no position to imagine the consequences of the new party's dissent from the norms of the new regulatory regime. They did not conceive of the fundraising juggernaut that would emerge when the two parties joined forces. Third, once the Conservatives formed the government in 2006, they reduced the contribution limit from $5,000 to $1,000. This created a significant disadvantage for the Liberals, whose fundraising program was oriented toward fundraising events from members of the business and legal elite who could make contributions well in excess of $1,000. Finally, the Liberals suffered from being the only major party to hold a leadership contest under the new rules (see Chapter 8). The money raised by the many candidates for the party's leadership, and the subsequent fundraising to eliminate these candidates' debts, detracted from the party's fundraising efforts from 2006 until 2008.

As the authors of the syndicate, but also of their own misfortune, the Liberals now find themselves with little choice but to defend the arrangements at almost any cost, as was demonstrated in the December 2008 showdown. As Figure 5.2 shows, the Liberals lag far behind the Conservatives in individual fundraising. Under former leader Stéphane Dion, the party's fundraising was so poor that it was barely ahead of the NDP. Although the Liberals significantly improved their fundraising in 2009, the party's totals have basically recovered to what they were prior to the selection of Dion as leader and the implementation of the Accountability Act and are still well behind those of the Conservatives. In terms of both the number and the total value of their contributions from individuals, the Liberals have underperformed significantly since 2004. This is not inconsistent with the party's fundraising record prior to the 2004 reforms. The Liberals were the party most dependent on corporate finance for their revenues before 2004, with approximately 60 percent of their revenue coming from business donors between 2000 and 2003.

Whereas the Bloc and even the NDP have not faced an imperative to match the fundraising success of the Conservative Party, the Liberals have found themselves at a serious competitive disadvantage since the 2004 reforms came into effect. This disadvantage was exacerbated with the lowering of the contribution limit for individuals in 2006. As the Conservatives' main opponent in the elections of 2006 and 2008, the Liberals have been hard-pressed to mount campaigns that are as extensive and as effective as those of the Conservatives. Although the Liberals have been able to spend near the maximum allowed during the election itself, they have not been able to maintain the same level of election readiness as their Conservative counterparts. In a minority government situation, with the timing of elections very uncertain, this has been a strategic disadvantage for the party. Moreover, the Liberals' financial situation has likely contributed to the party's unwillingness (or inability) to run election-style advertisements outside the formal election period. This forms a sharp contrast to the Conservative Party, which ran a series of ads attacking the leadership of then-Liberal leader Stéphane Dion and another attacking current leader Michael Ignatieff's commitment to Canada. The strategic value of these advertisements is not self-evident; nonetheless, they illustrate the asymmetrical financial situation of the two main protagonists in Canadian elections.

Because they have not as of yet found a way to compete with the Conservatives' prowess in individual fundraising, the Liberals have been relatively more dependent on state funding than the NDP and the Conservatives. In fact, in 2004, 2007, and 2008, the Liberals were second only to the Bloc Québécois in the extent to which they relied on the quarterly allowance

(Figure 5.1). The sharp decline in reliance on state funds in 2009 is partly because of a recovery in the party's fundraising, but also because of the decline in the value of the quarterly allowance resulting from the party's relatively meagre share of the popular vote in the 2008 election. The quarterly allowance can be seen as having financially maintained the party through a bleak period under Dion's leadership. As bad as things were, the party would have been considerably poorer without the state funds. Until the Liberals can learn to compete with their main rival in fundraising, they will remain relatively more dependent on state funds and part of a syndicate to protect them.

The Conservatives

Unlike the parties forming the syndicate, the Conservative Party was formed after the legislation altering the regulatory regime was passed. As noted in Chapter 1, neither of the predecessor parties were wholly supportive of the legislation. The Canadian Alliance was amenable to banning corporate and union contributions but opposed the principle of public funding for parties between elections (Stephen Harper, Hansard, 11 February 2003). The Progressive Conservatives, more dependent on corporate sources of funding than the Alliance, wanted limits placed on corporate donations, not an outright ban (Gerstein 2003; Joe Clark, Hansard, 11 February 2003), and also argued that the subsidy forced citizens to subsidize parties with which they might not agree (Elsie Wayne, Hansard, 11 June 2003). In ideological terms, then, neither of the predecessor parties were as committed to the underlying logic of the new regime as were the parties on the centre and left of the political spectrum. Moreover, the dominant party in the merger (the Alliance) had not been particularly successful in soliciting contributions from corporate donors, so it had less to lose than some other parties when business contributions were banned. Corporate contributions had never exceeded one-third of the total value of contributions to the Canadian Alliance. Instead, the populist party tended to rely on contributions from grassroots supporters. Although the Progressive Conservatives had relied heavily on corporate contributions prior to 1993, once the party was marginalized in Parliament, its corporate contributions declined significantly. The party was more reliant on corporate contributions in relative terms than the Canadian Alliance, but in real terms tended to raise similar amounts from corporate contributors: less than $1.5 million in non-election years.

With the combined experience of the Canadian Alliance and PCs in direct mail and other grassroots forms of fundraising, the newly formed

Conservative Party was well positioned to dissent from the norms of the cartel and try to distinguish itself financially from its competitors. The party built on the grassroots fundraising tradition of the Alliance and has excelled at attracting individual donations, culminating in earning over $20 million from individual donors in the election year of 2008. The other parties have not managed to match the Conservatives' success. To put the Conservative lead in fundraising into perspective, in every year except for 2004, the Conservatives raised more money from individual donors than the *combined* fundraising total of all other parties. It is easy to overstate the lead, however. The kind of fundraising in which the Conservatives excel relies heavily on telephone solicitation and, hence, is labour and capital intensive. The amount of money the party is able to bank for future campaigns is thus significantly less than reported in their aggregate fundraising totals. Between 2005 and 2008, the party typically spent between 7 and 8 million dollars annually on fundraising costs, compared with around 2 million dollars for the Liberals and between 1 and 2 million dollars for the NDP (calculated from financial statements filed with Elections Canada). Still, the Conservatives have managed to build a "machine" to fundraise from individual donors that the other parties have yet to match (Flanagan 2007, 286-88; Flanagan and Jansen 2009). This has made them relatively less dependent on the state for revenue.

Figure 5.1 shows that since 2005, the Conservatives have been consistently less reliant on the quarterly allowance than any other party. This is a direct consequence of the party's ability to raise money from individual contributors. In effect, the Conservatives have rejected the unstated cartel norm of state dependence and thereby changed the competitive situation for all the parties competing nationally.

Under the current patterns of party revenue, the Conservatives would derive a competitive advantage from the elimination of the annual subsidy. The party faces a significant incentive to eliminate the subvention, even though in absolute terms the party is the biggest recipient of the subsidy. This is particularly true with respect to the party's competitive position when compared with the Liberals, the Conservatives' primary rival for power. The Conservatives' advantage over the Liberals in individual fundraising is significant: in the election year of 2008, they raised $3.64 for every dollar the Liberals raised. This is greater than the vote advantage the Conservatives enjoyed in the election that same year, where the Conservatives earned 1.43 votes for each Liberal vote. Even in 2009, when Liberal fundraising improved and Conservative fundraising declined slightly, the

Conservatives raised $1.85 for every Liberal dollar, still exceeding the vote advantage in the election. Because the annual subsidy is tied directly to vote totals, it helps the Liberals to narrow the gap in financial competitiveness with the Conservatives. Conversely, the elimination of the subsidy would extend the gap the Conservatives enjoy over the Liberals. Moreover, such a move would also be devastating to the Bloc Québécois, a significant rival for the Conservatives in Quebec. It is noteworthy that in the December 2008 budget update that almost precipitated the fall of their government, the Conservatives focused only on the quarterly subsidy, not on the election expenses reimbursement, which is also public money. Strategically, this also makes sense for the Conservatives. Compared with the other parties, the NDP is most reliant on the election expenses reimbursement. Keeping the NDP a viable competitor helps to divide the non-Conservative vote (Flanagan 2007, 275).

Although the parties that merged to form the Conservative Party objected to the 2004 reforms, these reforms have contributed significantly to the party's electoral viability. Because the Conservative Party has been able to benefit financially from the reforms without endorsing them in principle, and because the Conservative dissent from the reforms has launched the party into a program of fundraising that none of the members of the syndicate has been able to match, the Conservatives have found themselves in an advantageous financial situation. Had the Conservatives been able to eliminate the quarterly allowance, they would have enjoyed a remarkable financial advantage over their competitors.

Conclusion

As the Conservatives moved to disrupt the 2004 financing arrangement for parties, the opposition parties responded by proposing a coalition government to replace the Conservative government. This was an unprecedented development for the Canadian political system, which has had almost exclusively single-party governments, even in situations where no party earned a majority of the seats in Parliament. In keeping with the institutional incentives and tradition of the Westminster model, minority governments have typically survived with the support of a party that extracts policy concessions – not cabinet seats – as the price for its support. The proposed Liberal-NDP coalition was decidedly different from past practice.

The trigger for this development was not the result of the 2008 election but rather the move by the Conservatives to eliminate the annual subsidy. In forming the coalition, the Liberals and the NDP had the parliamentary support of the Bloc Québécois as well as the support of the Green Party. The four parties – all qualifying for the annual subsidy and all relatively more dependent on it than the Conservatives – acted together to preserve it. The four parties acted as a syndicate to preserve the party financing arrangements from which they benefited. They were able to do this because the minority government situation after 2008 gave the Liberals, NDP, and the Bloc a majority of the seats.

Although the proposed coalition government showed how far the syndicate was prepared to go to preserve the party finance regime, the proposal ran up against the institutionalized incentives toward competition inherent in Canada's political institutions. The coalition never had to face the issue of what the next election would have looked like. Would Liberal and NDP candidates have run against each other? Had the coalition government succeeded, the Liberals might have been tempted to bring the government down in order to try to get a single-party majority. The underlying competitive logic of Canada's political institutions limits the extent to which Canada can develop and sustain cartel parties. However, cooperation to sustain the laws in the face of a party with an incentive to overturn the regime was clearly necessary. Such cooperation is better described as a syndicate rather than as a cartel.

The events of December 2008 demonstrate the profound impact that the new electoral finance regime has had on Canadian political parties and party competition. Since Bill C-24 was adopted by Parliament in 2003, there have been a series of quite exceptional political developments at the federal level in Canada, including the merger of the two right-of-centre parties, three general elections producing three relatively unstable minority governments, two changes in the leadership of the Liberal Party, and the emergence of a formerly minor party as an electorally significant (if not winning) player. Although it would be inaccurate to argue that the new election finance regime caused these remarkable developments, it has nonetheless provided the backdrop against which they have taken place. Certainly, the extent to which changes to the Canada Elections Act have become weapons in the arsenal of political competition speaks to this. The Conservative Party's efforts to enhance its financial advantage by reducing the maximum size of contributions and eliminating the quarterly allowance are testament to this development.

NOTES

Financial support for this research was provided through a Standard Operating Grant from the Social Sciences and Humanities Research Council of Canada.

1 If there was an election that year, we use the vote shares for that election. Thus, the 2004 totals reflect the vote shares in 2004; the 2006 totals, the vote shares in 2006; and the 2008 totals reflect the vote shares earned in the 2008 federal election.
2 Most of the registered political parties without representation in Parliament shared this view. They challenged the constitutionality of the threshold in the Ontario Superior Court (*Longley v. Canada (Attorney General)*), but the challenge was not upheld. The Supreme Court declined to hear an appeal in the case.
3 In 2009, the increased state reliance is likely because of the increase in the quarterly allowance earned as a result of earning more votes in 2008; the party raised more money in 2009 from individual donors than in any year other than the election year of 2008.

WORKS CITED

Flanagan, Tom. 2007. *Harper's Team: Behind the Scenes in the Conservative Rise to Power*. Montreal and Kingston: McGill-Queen's University Press.

–. 2009. Only Voters Have the Right to Decide on the Coalition. *Globe and Mail*, 9 January, A13.

Flanagan, Tom, and Harold J. Jansen. 2009. Election Campaigns under Canada's Party Finance Laws. In *The Canadian Federal Election of 2008*, ed. Jon H. Pammett and Christopher Dornan, 194-216. Toronto: Dundurn Press.

Gerstein, Irvin. 2003. A Cure Worse than the Ailment. *Globe and Mail*, 21 April, A13.

Jansen, Harold J., and Lisa Young. 2008. The Impact of Changing Party Finance Laws on Canadian Political Party Competition. Paper presented at the annual meeting of the Prairie Provinces Political Science Association, Regina.

–. 2009. Solidarity Forever? The NDP, Organized Labour, and the Changing Face of Party Finance in Canada. *Canadian Journal of Political Science* 42: 657-58. TBD.

Katz, Richard S., and Peter Mair. 1995. Changing Models of Party Organization and Party Democracy: The Emergence of the Cartel Party. *Party Politics* 1: 5-28.

Lambert, Lisa. 2007. The Effects of State Subventions to Political Parties: A Case Study of the Green Party of Canada. MA thesis, University of Lethbridge.

Stewart, Ian. 2005. Bill C-24: Replacing the Market with the State? *Electoral Insight* 7(1): 32-26.

Young, Lisa. 1998. Party, State and Political Competition in Canada: The Cartel Party Reconsidered. *Canadian Journal of Political Science* 31: 339-58.

Young, Lisa, Anthony Sayers, and Harold Jansen. 2007. Altering the Political Landscape: State Funding and Party Finance. In *Canadian Parties in Transition*, 3rd. ed., ed. Alain-G. Gagnon and A. Brian Tanguay, 335-54. Peterborough, ON: Broadview.

6

The Impact of Election Finance Reforms on Local Party Organization

DAVID COLETTO AND MUNROE EAGLES

The passage into law of Bill C-24 in 2003 introduced sweeping changes to the financing of Canada's political parties, many of which profoundly alter the status and (potentially, at least) the importance of their electoral district associations (EDAs). Beginning in January 2004, the local organizations of all federal political parties were no longer private associations. Rather, these grassroots organizations were required by law to register with Elections Canada and to submit regular financial reports to this agency detailing their contributions and expenditures. In 2006, the Conservative government again amended the Canada Elections Act, further limiting the sources of funding available to EDAs. Along with the central parties and candidates, EDAs could not accept political contributions from corporations, trade unions, or other private associations. Therefore, both pieces of legislation raise three important consequences for party finance. First, financial contributions to local party organizations were limited for the first time. Prior to 2004, only national party organizations were required to submit annual financial reports to Elections Canada. Local organizations were not subject to reporting limits, nor were contributions to a party's EDAs constrained. After 2004, local party organizations were integrated in the overall regulatory apparatus that applies to all levels of party organization.

Second, local party finances are now transparent and open for scrutiny. The 2004 reforms therefore closed an important loophole in the regulation of election campaign financing. Before 2004, local party associations could amass sizable war chests (from private contributors or the reimbursement of election expenses). These funds could be transferred to their candidates for campaign purposes. This loophole made it impossible to trace the original sources of these transferred funds, thereby blunting the disclosure requirements of Canadian campaign finance regulation (Stanbury 1991, 419-21; Young 1991, 20-22; Geddes 2000). The extension of disclosure regulations governing contributions and expenditures to EDAs of Canada's parties have therefore tightened the regulatory regime.

Serendipitously, the 2004 reforms have opened up a valuable window for political scientists into the operation, activities, and vitality of these grassroots party organizations. It has been customary to discount the importance of EDAs. These organizations, along with other features of local political distinctiveness, have long been assumed to have been overtaken by the centralizing and modernizing forces associated with mass media markets and professionalism in the party's national campaign. These assumptions prevailed despite mounting evidence from various academic surveys of local party officials that gave evidence of the vitality of grassroots party organizations (Carty 1991). However, as valuable as these studies have undoubtedly been in demonstrating the continued vitality of political life at the grassroots level, the data collected are potentially subject to response bias (depending as they do on the voluntary compliance of local officials in completing and returning questionnaires), and they do not support longitudinal analyses. Beginning with 2004, the reporting provisions required by the 2004 legislation will generate a comprehensive (or at least reasonably so) supply of financial information regarding EDA activities that is growing in value with each passing year.

Of course, the advantages of comprehensiveness are offset somewhat by the necessarily narrow focus on financial records, and the validity of the data depends on the compliance of many hundreds of local party officials with the legal regulations. Nonetheless, along with volunteer labour, money is among the most important assets that these organizations deploy, both during and between campaigns (Stanbury 1991, 5). As such, financial records have the potential to offer concrete and important insights into the organizational vitality of party organizations. The source of contributions gives an indication of the structure of the local party's relationship to important components of their constituency. The level of expenditures serves as a reasonable proxy for the volume of party activity. For these reasons, a comprehensive financial portrait of Canada's local parties is a highly worthwhile undertaking.

Lacking detailed information on the pattern of contributions and expenditures of these grassroots units over the years prior to 2004, it is difficult to develop explicit hypotheses about if and how the 2004 and 2006 reforms are likely to impact upon EDAs. What follows in this chapter, then, is an exploration of putative "effects" of the new regulations, holding up what we know in the post-2004 period (thanks to the reporting requirements for EDAs) against what we understand from previous research to have been the situation in the period immediately preceding its implementation. Three dimensions organize the empirical analysis. First, we know from previous research that many dimensions of grassroots politics in Canada vary widely according to party. For example, in Duverger's (1964) terms the NDP is a mass party, whereas the Liberals and Conservatives are cadre parties. This distinction is important for understanding a variety of aspects of party organization and territorial integration, and as cross-party comparisons are prominent in this analysis. Second, we also know from previous research that local associations for incumbents tended to be larger and more vigorous than those for non-incumbents (Carty 1991, 39-46), so one prominent focus of our explorations will investigate differences in local associations that won the seat as compared with others that did not. We explore these dimensions in a discussion of the sources of revenue coming into EDAs and in patterns in the inter-election expenditure of funds. Finally, recognizing that Canada's parties are essentially vote-raising machines, a final section explores whether their success in this regard is attributable to the financial strength of their EDAs. The result of these empirical explorations is a benchmark portrait of grassroots party activity at the outset of the new regulatory regime. Before turning to this, however, some general comments on the potential impact of C-24 and Accountability Act reforms on EDAs are in order.

Some Possible Impacts of C-24 and Accountability Act Reforms on EDA Financial Life

As electoral machines, Canadian parties – at the federal, provincial, and local levels – tend to concentrate activity on the election campaign. Federal and provincial levels of the main parties maintain some organizational continuity between elections, but party life and vitality in the constituency trenches have traditionally been depicted as more closely tied to the electoral cycle. Here we encounter something of a paradox: EDAs themselves have only a tenuous relationship to this most important party activity. As Carty (1991, 156) has shown, local campaigning has traditionally been a candidate-centred affair, with official agents, campaign managers, and other key personnel often being appointed by the candidate rather than the local party organization (the exception is the NDP, where the party's local executive exercises relatively more control over candidate recruitment and the election campaign). This, coupled with the relative permeability of the major parties to insurgent or "outsider" candidates mobilizing large numbers of "instant members" through the nomination process, implies that there are potential divisions between local campaigns and parties. Until 2004, formal financial accounting was required only of the campaign team during the election period itself rather than of the local party organization, which was unregulated.

Research suggests that there may be considerable uncertainty and autonomy in the relationships between a party's campaign organization and its EDA, between EDA and higher levels of party organization, and between candidates' local campaign organizations and higher levels of the party. With successful campaigns often able to raise more money than required (after reimbursement of half their election expenses from Elections Canada), transferring this surplus to the party's EDA could provide the local organization with a significant war chest.[1] Perhaps for this reason the central offices appear to have come to regard their EDAs as a source of revenue. Carty's research (1991, 77) suggests that to the extent that funds are flowing across levels in a party at all, it seems as though the direction of flow is from the grassroots to the centre.

The centralizing nature of intra-party financial flows has a parallel in the relative lack of central party financing of local election campaigns. In contrast to the experience of several other countries (Carty and Eagles 2003), Canada's national or provincial party offices tend not to get heavily involved in the financing of candidates' campaigns. Rather, candidates and their campaign teams are expected to raise their campaign funds primarily from local sources. For example, a study of the transfers to candidates from registered parties in the context of the 1997 election campaign suggested that although between half and three-quarters of candidates received party money to help with their campaign, the amounts transferred accounted for less than a quarter of all the funds available to candidates (Carty and Eagles 2005, 89-90). In significant respects, then, Canada's federal parties "tax" their grassroots outside campaign period and do not compensate with transfers of funds at elections.

It seems likely that several of the reforms related to C-24 and the Accountability Act have the potential to impinge on several of these traditional patterns and relationships. In particular, elimination of corporate and union donations to all levels of the party organization has the potential to tighten the financial situation of some local associations by drying up a potential source of revenue. Now EDAs will need to compete with other levels of the party for these relatively modest amounts of legally permissible funds. The public funding that is designed to replace these sources of party money goes now to central parties and not to the EDAs (which nonetheless will remain responsible for mobilizing the votes upon which these subsidies are based and calculated). As such, it is possible that EDAs will grow more dependent on transfers from central party coffers. This may erode some of the traditional autonomy of grassroots party politics, perhaps making it easier for central party organizers to intervene in constituency election campaigns and target resources to marginal seats along the lines of parties in other settings (see the studies in Carty and Eagles 2003).

On the other hand, however, the C-24 reforms have the potential to invigorate and energize grassroots party politics. For example, requiring the formal and legal registration of EDAs as part of the regulatory apparatus governing party and campaign finance, and the requirement for regular financial record-keeping and reporting, may well help institutionalize and stabilize local associations. Compliance with the new regulatory regime will certainly call forth higher levels of expertise and more continuous and intense levels of commitment on the party of local volunteer activists. These developments have been shown elsewhere to have been associated with more institutionalized and stronger EDAs (Johnson 1991, 54-55). Although it will be some time before the full impact on EDAs of these reforms will be fully evident, we can begin to address these issues by inquiring about the state of EDA finances in the immediate period of the reforms' implementation.

The State of Local Party Finances Post C-24: Revenue, Expenses, and the Bottom Line

Perhaps the most basic and important question to ask regarding the state of local party organization in the post-2004 period concerns the financial health of local party organizations. Ken Carty's research (1991, 94-98) has shown that there is considerable variability in the financial circumstances of constituency associations, even within parties. In the past, the financial strength of an EDA has been closely associated with the ambitions and activities of a small core of local activists. Often these coalesce around a would-be candidate who works to invigorate the organization to support a future campaign (Stanbury 1991, 98). Carty's research based on surveys of local party officials suggests that relatively few local party organizations had amassed significant assets (only one in five overall reported more than

$10,000 in income for 1990; see Carty 1991, 79), and those which had managed to do so were in seats where they had won (ibid., 75).

How does this portrait stand up in light of the annual EDA financial reports required since 2004? Complete financial records, including sources and amounts of revenue and the nature and amount of expenditures, for all EDAs are available for 2004-2007. Including the opening balance that EDAs reported for 2004 as an indicator of the state of grassroots party finance immediately prior to the introduction of the C-24 reforms, we can identify the financial situation facing grassroots party organizations at four points in time – the beginning and end of 2004, the end of 2006, and the end of 2007. Table 6.1 presents information for the five major parties at these times.

The figures reported in Table 6.1 suggest that EDAs are generally solvent but far from wealthy. Liberal Party EDAs, coming off more than a decade as the party in government and the only one with electoral strength in all

TABLE 6.1

Mean EDA revenues, expenditures, and balance (assets and liabilities) by party, 2004-07

Year(s)		Conservatives	Liberals	NDP	Bloc Québécois	Greens
2004	$ Opening balance	14,944	25,761	5,620	5,044	346
	$ Income	23,546	38,256	12,492	39,291	4,038
	$ Expenditures	31,658	51,965	16,556	42,924	4,083
2006	$ Income	45,907	23,836	10,420	57,537	3,982
	$ Expenditures	22,388	25,219	9,118	42,270	2,824
2007	$ Income	40,316	23,433	7,347	30,292	4,745
	$ Expenditures	25,642	14,378	3,535	13,522	1,991
2004-06	% Change income	95%	-38%	-17%	46%	-1%
	% Change expenditures	-29%	-51%	-45%	-2%	-31%
2006-07	% Change income	-12%	-1.7%	-30%	-47%	19%
	% Change expenditures	15%	-43%	-61%	-68%	-30%
2004	$ Balance assets/liabilities	15,823	16,143	3,748	9,372	836
2005		20,140	29,113	5,792	6,786	277
2006		40,109	14,408	4,100	23,659	1,921
2007		53,794	23,224	8,061	39,175	3,799
2004-07	% Change balance	240%	44%	115%	318%	354%

regions, had significant advantages in terms of their average income and expenditures in 2004, and maintained a sizable advantage in terms of the bottom-line balance of assets and liabilities. At the end of 2004, Liberal Party EDAs averaged net assets of $16,143, compared with $15,823 for the Conservatives, $9,372 for the Bloc Québécois, and $3,748 for the NDP.

However, after 2005, the Liberal Party EDAs soon lost their advantage. During 2006, Conservative EDAs averaged income of $45,907 compared with $23,836 for the Liberals. Furthermore, at the end of 2006, Conservative EDAs were on average over $26,000 richer than their Liberal counterparts. Conservative EDAs had average net assets of $40,109, compared with $23,659 for the Bloc Québécois, $14,408 for the Liberals, and $4,100 for the NDP. It is, of course, too early to offer any definitive assessment of the putative impact of C-24 reforms on EDA vitality. However, it is interesting that over the 2004-07 period the average net assets of EDAs increased substantially for the Conservative and Bloc Québécois (BQ) EDAs, while increasing only slightly for Liberal and NDP EDAs.

Most striking is the balance growth for BQ EDAs. At the start of 2004, BQ EDAs averaged net assets of just over $5,000. At the end of 2007, they averaged over $39,000 in net assets, an increase of about 676 percent. Similarly, Green Party EDA finances have improved significantly from 2004. When financial reports became available in 2004, the average Green EDA had a balance of $346. At the end of 2007, thanks in large part to growing support across the country and the infusion of public subsidies to the central party, the net assets of Green EDAs averaged almost $3,800, representing an almost 1,000 percent increase. One of the most significant effects of the C-24 and Accountability Act reforms seems to be the growth of the Green Party's local organization and the persistence and viability of Bloc Québécois EDAs.

Overall, at the end of 2007, on average, the EDAs of all major Canadian political parties, except for the Liberal Party, were better off financially. This might appear promising for EDAs after 2004, but this was not an ordinary couple of years. Given that two elections transpired over this relatively short period, it is possible that a substantial portion of the revenues of the major parties resulted from the infusion of surplus campaign funds and expense reimbursements from Elections Canada. Equally, however, having to mount two election campaigns in relatively rapid succession may have depleted EDA treasuries to a greater extent than usual. Establishing the post-reform equilibrium in EDA finances will take time, and to understand how these forces balance out will require information from at least several more years of accumulated financial data. At this point, however, it is clear that there is no evidence to be found in this initial period of the reforms of an imminent crisis in grassroots party financing.

As was found in earlier studies of local party finances, there is considerable diversity of circumstance to be found within as well as between parties. At the end of 2007, several EDAs had been successful in amassing substantial war chests. Most of these EDAs were Conservative, with five having net assets over $200,000. These included Pontiac Conservative EDA ($286,650), Whitby-Oshawa Conservative EDA ($243,975), Calgary Southwest Conservative EDA ($241,826), Lanark-Frontenac-Lennox and Addington Conservative EDA ($219,921), and Calgary Southeast ($211,029). The wealthiest Liberal Party EDA was of the current Speaker of the House of Commons Peter Milliken in Kingston and the Islands ($134,344). New Westminster-Coquitlam NDP EDA ($70,438), de Bas-Richelieu-Nicolet-Béancour BQ EDA ($108,457), and Beaches-East York Green Party EDA ($20,236) were the wealthiest for their respective parties.

Outliers such as these extremely affluent EDAs have the potential to distort the party averages reported in Table 6.1. As Table 6.2 illustrates, the averages reported are in fact substantially inflated by the wealth of the most affluent outliers. However, even between 2004 and 2007, there does appear to be some significant changes in the distribution of EDA assets within political parties. In 2004, 35 percent of Conservative EDAs had less than $1,000 in assets, but by 2007, only 5 percent had such small asset reserves. In contrast, over three-fourths of Conservative EDAs had more than $10,000 in assets, a 44 percentage point increase from 2004.

The overall picture of EDA financial health that emerges from Tables 6.1 and 6.2 suggests that most EDAs have extremely modest assets – sufficiently modest compared to the average cost of fighting an election (for which the allowable limits range from roughly $60,000 to $100,000 per candidate) so as not to provide a serious inducement to assist in the recruitment of candidates who might be considering running for a local party's nomination.

Previous research on grassroots party organization in Canada has found sharp differences associated with the incumbency status of the local organization (Carty 1991, 94-95). The comparisons of the balance sheets of EDAs that won their seat in 2004 with those that did not dramatically confirm the persistence of this pattern in the 2004-06 period. The differences are quite striking in magnitude and not particularly concentrated in the NDP, the party where these differences were most evident in the past. These dramatic differences do not diminish over the three-year period we cover. In all

TABLE 6.2

EDAs and their assets by party, 2004, 2006, 2007 (N in parentheses)

	Conservative Party			Liberal Party			NDP			Bloc Québécois		
	2004	2006	2007	2004	2006	2007	2004	2006	2007	2004	2006	2007
< $1,000	35% (109)	7% (20)	5% (14)	28% (81)	14% (36)	10% (29)	51% (136)	42% (106)	30% (88)	13% (6)	4% (2)	2% (1)
$1,000-$4,999	17% (52)	15% (42)	10% (30)	21% (66)	26% (67)	15% (43)	30% (80)	30% (76)	29% (85)	35% (17)	6% (3)	7% (4)
$5,000-$10,000	14% (44)	9% (25)	8% (23)	13% (36)	15% (38)	17% (51)	10% (26)	10% (26)	17% (49)	21% (10)	8% (4)	9% (5)
> $10,000	33% (103)	69% (195)	77% (236)	36% (102)	45% (116)	58% (172)	10% (26)	18% (45)	24% (70)	31% (15)	83% (43)	83% (48)

Note: None of the eighty Green Party EDAs reporting to Elections Canada in 2004 registered any assets.

TABLE 6.3

Building local organizations – the importance of incumbency

		Assets/liabilities ($)		
		2004 balance	2005 balance	2006 balance
Conservatives	Won seat 2004	33,930	40,510	70,546
	Did not win 2004	7,175	10,397	22,834
Liberals	Won seat 2004	27,493	46,378	24,474
	Did not win 2004	7,775	15,640	5,931
NDP	Won seat 2004	17,825	32,098	19,106
	Did not win 2004	2,684	3,884	3,349
Bloc Québécois	Won seat 2004	9,605	7,322	23,404
	Did not win 2004	5,876	219	19,446

Note: No Green Party candidates were elected in 2004.

five parties, winning EDAs had bank balances that were at least three times (and in many cases many times more than this) higher than their counterparts that were electorally unsuccessful in 2004. Clearly, there is a close association between the ability of a party to raise money locally and the ability of their candidates to raise votes. We will return to explore the electoral connection and party financing in the final section.

Sources of EDA Revenue – Contributions and Intra-Party Transfers

In addition to the accumulated assets (or liabilities), the financial health of an EDA rests on its ability to attract financial contributions, according to the guidelines laid out by the Elections Act, and transfers of resources from other affiliated organizations within the party. Understanding how a local party organization raises its funds is revealing of a series of important relationships. First, patterns of financial contribution sources reveal something of the relationship between the local party and its (presumably primarily local) environment. Intra-party transfers are an unobtrusive indicator of the party's organization-building strategy and, depending on the net amount being transferred, could either be a source of revenue or a form of intra-party taxation on the EDA. The volume and direction of financial flows are therefore particularly revealing of a party's strategic orientation. On both of these dimensions, the motivation lying behind the decision to invest in an

EDA is likely to be responsive to whether the local MP is a member of the party. For this reason, we distinguish between seats held and not held by a party in the analysis that follows.

Of course, there are several financial strategies imaginable. A case in point is the recent controversy concerning the so-called in-out transfer of resources between the national and local Conservative Party campaigns in 2006. These transfers are suggestive of a logic other than simple party building or even "targeting the marginals." In this case, when the central Conservative campaign organization bumped up against its spending limit, the party transferred money into sixty-seven local campaigns to help them buy nationally focused advertising that is not counted toward the national party's legislated spending limit. Those candidates receiving these transfers then immediately returned the money to pay for ads that were almost identical to those being run by the national party. Not only did this allow "national" spending to exceed the legal limit but the recipient candidates were able to claim reimbursements for these election expenses from Elections Canada totalling approximately $1.3 million (CTV News 2008).[2]

Table 6.4 shows the sources and magnitude of contributions to local EDAs for each of the major parties for 2004. Since a federal election took place that year, it is important to remember that these funds are separate from, and in addition to, anything contributed to the official candidates of these parties. As such, the data speak rather generally but forcefully to one of the concerns raised by scholars of highly state funded party systems, namely, that the parties' reliance on state funding in such systems is likely to erode their ties to civil society (Katz and Mair 1995; van Biezen and Kopecký 2007). On the face of it, the evidence in Table 6.4 suggests that these concerns are misplaced – or perhaps premature – in the immediate aftermath of the 2004 reforms. Even in an election year, when candidates are hungry for political cash to fuel their campaigns, the EDAs at the base of the party system were able to secure significant amounts of money to fund their activities.

The results reveal interesting inter-party differences in the raising of party money. For example, in 2004, Liberal and BQ EDAs were greatly advantaged in terms of their ability to attract funds over the other parties. The total inflow of contributions to the EDAs of these two parties was almost twice that going to Conservative EDAs, and more than twice as much as that going to the NDP and the Greens. However, more recently, Conservative EDAs have outpaced all other parties except the BQ in fundraising. As expected, there are significant differences in each party between the amounts

TABLE 6.4

Contributions to EDAs, 2004 and 2006 (mean $)

	Conservatives			Liberals			NDP			Bloc Québécois			Greens
	Total	Seats won	Seats lost	Total	Seats won	Seats lost	Total	Seats won	Seats lost	Total	Seats won	Seats lost	Total
2004													
Individuals	7,950	9,680	7,123	12,027	16,698	8,189	7,203	19,200	6,288	16,131	16,672	8,018	2,502
Corporations	1,566	1,818	1,446	5,698	9,951	4,670	204	703	166	3,838	4,062	467	203
Trade unions	0	0	0	92	191	11	5	21	4	75	80	0	0
Registered associations	18	2	26	111	5	197	0	0	1	0	0	0	1
Total contributions	9,524	11,500	8,580	17,767	23,807	12,803	7,393	20,182	6,417	18,607	19,282	8,485	2,726
2006													
Total contributions	12,916	17,934	9,458	9,508	15,652	6,405	3,772	13,188	2,761	20,436	22,411	9,331	1,646
2007													
Total contributions	17,268	20,412	14,869	13,620	21,085	9,103	4,078	12,837	3,043	14,466	15,728	5,996	
Difference (2006-04)	3,392	6,434	878	-8,259	-8,155	-6,398	-3,621	-6,994	-3,656	1,829	3,129	846	-1,080
Difference (2007-06)	4,352	2,478	5,411	4,112	5,433	2,698	306	-351	282	-5,970	-6,683	-3,335	

raised by EDAs whose candidate won the races in 2004 and 2006 and those where they lost (though, of course, the Greens failed to win any seats, so there is no comparable comparison for that party). The gap is particularly large in the case of the NDP, confirming what we have long known about the sizable difference in vitality separating successful and unsuccessful local organizations in that party (Carty 1991, 241-42). The gap between NDP EDAs with and without a sitting MP exists whether an election is held during the year or not.

Given the constraints on union and corporate donations in place for the first time in 2004, it should not be surprising to find that all parties' EDAs raised substantially more money from individuals than from all other sources. Indeed, EDAs for the Liberals and the Bloc were the only ones with much success getting substantial corporate money over the year, and trade union contributions were negligible across the board (including even for the NDP). In every party, EDAs that experienced an election victory in June 2004 were more highly supported by contributions than others. Corporate donors to Liberal and Bloc EDAs were especially generous when the local party held the seat in 2004.

In addition to contributions, the other main source of revenue for EDAs comes in the form of financial transfers from unspent (or reimbursed) campaign funds from its candidates and from other parts of the party organization. Such transfers must now be recorded, but they are otherwise not constrained by the legal regime governing party financing. So parties are free to move resources as they see fit in accordance with their strategies of organization building. This may result in a net source of income for an EDA, but if the outflow of money to other levels of the party is not exceeded by the amount transferred in, such transfers will be a drain on EDA resources. If money flows from other (higher) levels of the party into the EDA, this reveals a relatively strong grassroots orientation for the party. However, if financial flows are from the EDAs outward to other levels of party organization, the party will have opted for a centralizing organization-building strategy. Given the enormous discrepancies we have seen in the financial situation of incumbent and non-incumbent EDAs, parties themselves are likely to distinguish between its winning and losing grassroots organizations when adopting a strategy of financing its operations. So it is important to continue with this distinction in our analysis of intra-party financial flows.

Based on the detailed financial records available from 2004 to 2007, Table 6.5 presents an overview of the parties' approach to organization building. Total transfers to the EDA includes transfers from the central party, from candidates, and from other registered EDAs. As noted earlier, parties can decide which level of the organization receives any surplus from the campaign funds of its candidates, and which result from any reimbursement of allowable expenses from Elections Canada. Since the electoral map was redrawn before the 2004 election, many local EDAs had to legally reconstitute themselves to accommodate the changes to their district boundaries. The act allows for the transfer of funds from the old associations to their replacements. Finally, the reforms extended contribution and spending limits to candidates seeking a party's nomination for the first time in 2004, and provided for the transfer of any surplus remaining for candidates to be transferred to the party (without stipulating which level of the party should receive this money).

Of course, political parties are free to move funds to any level of the organization they see fit. We have seen that EDAs are not without the means to raise their own money through contributions. As such, it is also possible that parties may decide to transfer money out of the local organization to fund the operations of higher levels of the party, or simply leave the EDA alone. Carty's analysis (1991, 77) of the situation in the late 1980s suggested that, except for the NDP, most parties opted for a policy of grassroots financial autonomy (no significant flows in or out of EDAs). Of those instances where money was transferred within the parties, however, it was almost always flowing out from EDAs to other, higher levels of the party organization. Inferences regarding party strategy, therefore, must incorporate both the inflow and outflow of money.

The data in Table 6.5 offer a contrast with previous scholarship in suggesting that there is considerable movement of money within Canada's parties. Much of the flow of money into EDAs comes from transfers from their general election (and to a much lesser extent, nomination) candidates. Of course, these sources will not be a factor in non-election years. However, it is also clear that EDAs – and particularly ones that won the local contest in 2004 – receive money from higher levels of the party organization. In every case, the total amounts transferred into the EDA from party coffers exceeded the totals transferred from their election candidates. And taken collectively, the totals transferred into EDAs provide a source of revenue that is generally comparable to the amounts we have shown that they raise through contributions. However, the third row of Table 6.5 shows that party strategies also involve taxing their local associations. In fact, the average amounts

TABLE 6.5

Party financial strategies for grassroots organization, 2004, 2006, 2007 (mean $)

		Total transfers to EDA	Transfers from EDA to party	Intra-party balance to EDA
Conservatives	2004	14,150	17,547	−3,397
	2006	23,507	8,512	14,995
	2007	15,957	2,969	12,988
Liberals	2004	11,020	29,002	−17,982
	2006	8,881	12,431	−3,550
	2007	7,430	2,852	4,578
New Democrats	2004	3,426	11,274	−7,848
	2006	5,232	5,769	−537
	2007	2,665	644	2,021
Bloc Québécois	2004	11,401	31,179	−19,778
	2006	20,960	26,171	−5,211
	2007	11,325	4,565	6,760
Greens	2004	608	2,303	−1,695
	2006	2,293	1,941	352
	2007	1,916	293	1,623

taken from EDAs by Canada's parties exceeded the total amounts transferred into grassroots organizing. This was the case with all parties, but the negative balances of Liberal, NDP, and BQ EDAs were especially large in 2004. The Liberals also tax their EDAs heavily, with average net outflows of money in 2004 representing over 100 percent of the net assets of their grassroots organizations.

In 2006, the situation appeared similar to 2004, with the exception of the Conservatives. In 2006, Conservative EDAs on average received more funds from other party units than they transferred out. This may be indicative of the Conservative Party's success at raising money, which has enabled it to transfer substantial amounts of money down to their EDAs, along with transferring the candidate's campaign surpluses to the EDAs.

In 2007, a non-election year, we see different financial flows than in 2004 or 2006. EDAs for all parties received more money from transfers than they sent to other party components. This makes sense, since money is not transferred to candidates when there is no election. However, there also seems to be some measure of local party building, particularly in the Conservative Party and Bloc Québécois. In both parties, EDAs averaged large net transfers to their EDAs. Although it is difficult to confirm, this may be an effect of the public funding the central parties receive. In this period, the Conservative Party and BQ were well financed and thus they may have transferred considerable funds to help support the development of local party organizations.

There is also the possibility that the national parties transfer funds down to EDAs in a strategic manner. Figure 6.1 examines the relationship between transfers from the national party to the EDA and the 2006 margin of victory for each province. As the scatter plots indicate, the relationship between national party transfers to the EDA and electoral margin is strongest for the NDP, and more modest for the Conservatives. It appears that the competitiveness of the local election is not a significant factor in transferring money to EDAs for the Liberals, the Bloc, or the Greens. Furthermore, as would be expected, availability of funds within the national party is an important factor in their ability to transfer money to EDAs. As Table 6.6 illustrates, the Bloc Québécois transferred the most money to EDAs on average in ridings where they ran a candidate, followed by the Conservatives, New Democrats, and Liberals. As a result, it appears that wealth at the national level can and is being transferred to the EDAs, and more significant to this study, the inclusion of public funding, particularly in the case of the Bloc Québécois, seems to aid local party organizations.

Although it is too early to make definitive conclusions on the impact of these reforms on party behaviour, there does seem to be some incentive for the national parties to adequately finance the EDAs and local campaigns. As one of the main instruments of voter mobilization, and in light of the relationship between votes and public funding (at an inflation-adjusted rate of $1.75 per vote), parties have an interest in maximizing votes even in non-competitive ridings. Therefore, it seems plausible that for the Liberals and Conservatives, who have traditionally had more financial resources than the NDP or Greens, supporting weaker EDAs or campaigns in non-competitive ridings with financial transfers makes some strategic sense.

In general, it appears from these data that intra-party finances involving EDAs have become significantly more integrated than was the case in the 1980s. Despite that the monetary allowances to Canada's parties provided by the C-24 reform package have flowed to the central party apparatuses, these organizations continue to extract significant resources from their

FIGURE 6.1

National party transfers to EDAs by electoral margin, 2006

Conservative Party
R^2 Linear = 0.132
R^2 Quadratic = 0.142

Liberal Party
R^2 Linear = 0.079
R^2 Quadratic = 0.09

NDP
R^2 Linear = 0.356
R^2 Quadratic = 0.381

Bloc Québécois
R^2 Linear = 0.047
R^2 Quadratic = 0.0

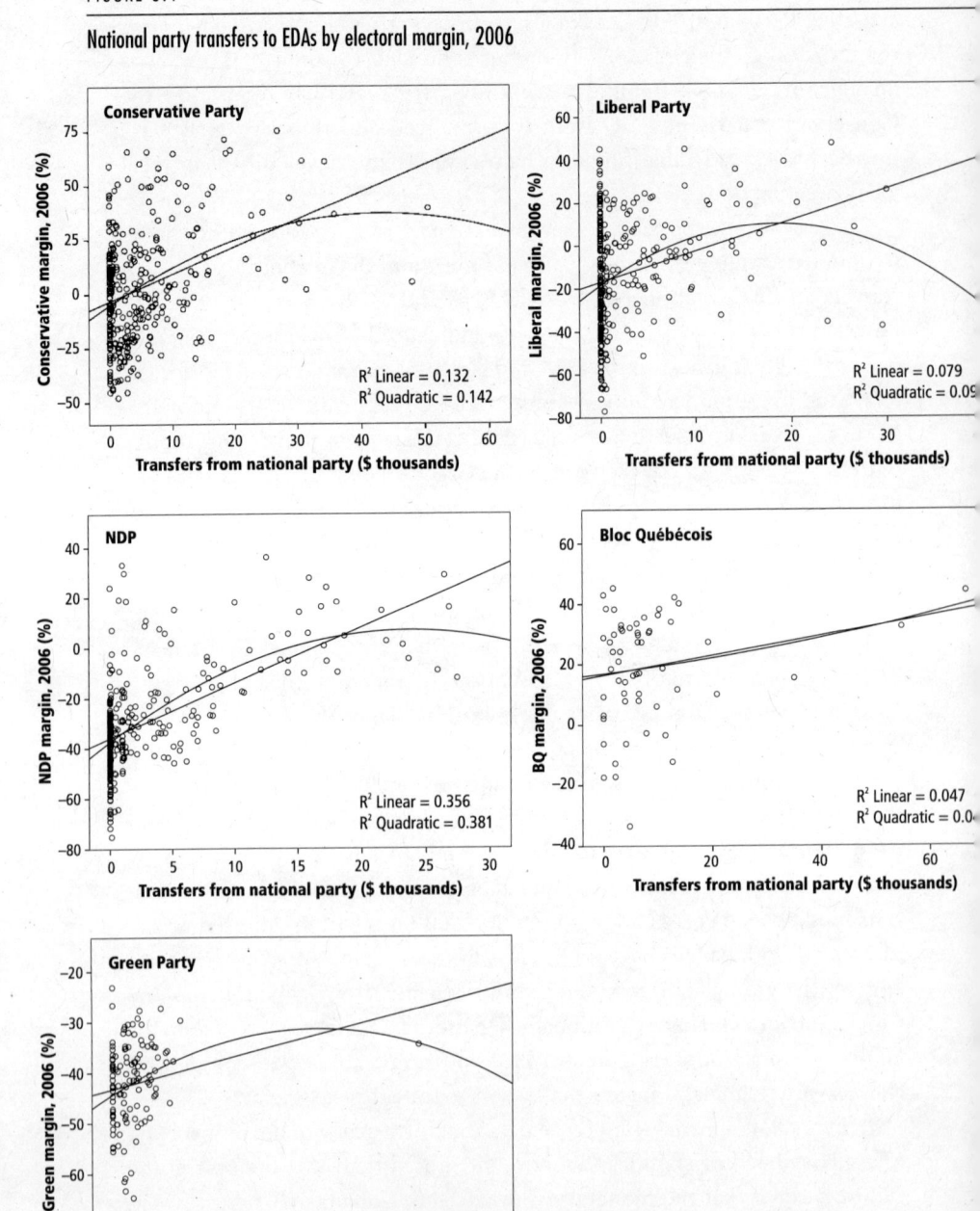

Green Party
R^2 Linear = 0.031
R^2 Quadratic = 0.048

TABLE 6.6

National party transfers to EDAs, 2006 ($)

Party	Total transferred to EDAs	Number of candidates	Average transfer to EDAs with party candidate
Bloc Québécois	469,290	75	6,257
Conservative	1,602,421	308	5,203
NDP	889,947	308	2,889
Liberal	787,026	308	2,554
Green	132,818	308	431

grassroots counterparts. Whether this extends to the party in non-election years is a question that must be asked when more data become available in future years.

Building Local Organizational Capacity: Extra-Campaign EDA Expenditures

Local party associations exist to further a political party's interest in the riding by recruiting candidates and members, raising funds, and communicating the party's message. Some of these activities are basic to the self-maintenance of the local organization, and although volunteer labour is often available, most cost money (even fundraising requires some investment). Carty's analysis (1991, 59) of the situation in the 1980s revealed that local associations of Canada's then-three major parties almost universally took on self-maintaining tasks such as fundraising activities, social events, and membership campaigns. Carty also found that most local associations (65 percent) engaged in policy study and development, and many undertook communications activities such as public meetings (52 percent), publishing a newsletter (46 percent), and getting exposure on local or cable TV (14 percent). Only 9 percent reported doing any local polling. Taken cumulatively, Carty's portrait is one of relatively vigorous local party organizations even outside an election campaign period.

The data contained in the detailed EDA reports for 2004 and 2007 and reported in Tables 6.7 and 6.8 refer only to financial expenditures and therefore are not directly comparable to Carty's results. However, they do confirm that EDAs are active outside the election campaign period. Only the Green Party's EDAs appear to have largely folded up shop outside the campaign period itself. Organizational self-maintenance activities (fundraising,

TABLE 6.7

Extra-campaign EDA activities, 2004 (Mean $ expenditures)

	Conservative		Liberal		NDP		Bloc Québécois		Greens
	Won seat	Lost seat	Won seat	Lost seat	Won seat	Lost seat	Won seat	Lost seat	All EDAs
Radio ads	41	190	337	74	52	7	0	0	1
TV ads	295	58	90	18	0	3	0	0	2
Other ads	5,927	2,377	4,826	3,807	4,164	639	535	355	867
Fundraising activities	1,969	982	5,128	2,471	5,235	591	3,942	17	211
Office expenses	6,281	3,641	6,740	3,095	8,256	1,083	1,839	1,542	332
Polling	552	573	2,495	309	346	140	0	0	0
Professional services	883	422	1,346	653	2,069	649	172	70	55
Research	449	290	100	131	0	1.61	25	0	0
Salaries and benefits	416	114	530	482	2,564	241	0	0	25
Travel and hospitality	805	461	3,117	654	710	218	653	1,339	98
Other (bad debts, conventions)	3,704	730	8,097	2,590	534	340	3,999	499	104
Total*	49,517	23,127	75,514	35,081	60,963	19,591	44,088	25,454	4,083

* Total includes funds transferred from the EDA to other levels of the party organization.

office expenses, professional services, salary and benefits, travel and hospitality, and other spending) figure prominently in the other four parties. These expenditures reflect the cost of doing business as a local party, and although there is some discrepancy between EDAs that won and lost seats and across the parties, these are relatively small. One interesting and somewhat surprising finding is that the NDP EDAs that were successful in the June 2004 election spent considerably more on average on salaries and benefits than did the other parties.

Again confirming earlier research, the NDP also stands out in most expenditure categories for having the largest gap between its electorally successful and unsuccessful grassroots organizations. In other parties (except, of course, for the Greens, where there were no winning EDAs), this gap exists but is more muted. Even in an election year, very little radio or TV ads are run by EDAs. In the case of Conservative, Liberal, and NDP EDAs, a somewhat higher priority attaches to "other advertising," which presumably includes newspaper ads and leafleting. Relatively little is spent on polling or political research, and it is likely that the high levels of policy study and development Carty noted in his survey of local party associations is a voluntary activity undertaken by activists rather than by paid professionals.

We should expect local party activities to significantly decline in non-election years. As Table 6.8 reports, this was not necessarily the case for

TABLE 6.8

Non-election year EDA activities, 2007 (Mean $ expenditures)

	Conservative	Liberal	NDP	Bloc Québécois	Greens
Radio ads	168	46	7	18	11
TV ads	130	1	17	23	0
Other ads	4,606	1,905	419	616	569
Fundraising activities	5,732	4,179	861	3,236	718
Office expenses	5,419	3,083	892	1,546	409
Polling	1,123	560	30	142	47
Professional services	1,373	1,395	545	335	514
Salaries and benefits	1,151	258	176	0	36
Travel and hospitality	2,556	1,641	188	536	90
Other (bad debts, conventions)	3,680	2,347	259	3,192	167
Total*	25,643	14,378	3,536	13,523	1,991

* Total includes funds transferred from the EDA to other levels of the party organization.

EDAs of Canada's political parties. Although average expenditures decreased substantially, many EDAs were spending considerable amounts of money despite the fact that no election occurred in 2007. One of the largest average expenditures for EDAs of all parties was fundraising. In 2007, Conservative, Liberal, and BQ EDAs spent on average between $3,200 and $5,700 on fundraising, with NDP and Green Party EDAs averaging substantially less. Moreover, several EDAs spent money on advertisements, though Conservative EDAs spent by far the most.

Therefore, even though EDAs are far more active when there is a federal election, data indicates that some EDAs are spending money on local party activities such as fundraising, advertising, and travel outside of formal election periods. However, it is difficult to say whether local party activity has been affected by the election finance reforms. We can conclude only that EDAs remain financially solvent and continue to be somewhat active in election and non-election years.

Financial and Electoral Strength – Is There a Relationship?

From the foregoing, it is clear that EDAs in all parties look quite different depending on whether the party's candidate won in 2004. In general, the most affluent and vigorous (in terms of extra-campaign expenditure activities) EDAs are, irrespective of party, ones in which their local candidate took the constituency in the June election. These differences are apparent in the detailed 2004 data, but they also persist in the evidence of the balance sheets for 2005 and 2006. This suggests that there may be some relationship between the strength (proxied here by financial wealth) of an EDA and the electoral performance of its candidate.

As plausible as this relationship sounds, establishing the causal connection between money and votes in statistical research is a challenging undertaking. This is because both measures are indicators of party support within the local community, and there is no easy way of saying which causes which. Although local organizational strength may contribute to a candidate's electoral success, it is also possible that the local organization may itself benefit from a candidate or party's prior local popularity. This subtlety notwithstanding, it is interesting to begin the discussion by looking at the general relationship between a local organization's financial strength and its candidate's electoral strength.

Perhaps the easiest way to appreciate the general nature of these relationships is to inspect scatter plots of local EDA assets and their electoral performance. Figure 6.2 illustrates these simple bi-variate relationships in

FIGURE 6.2

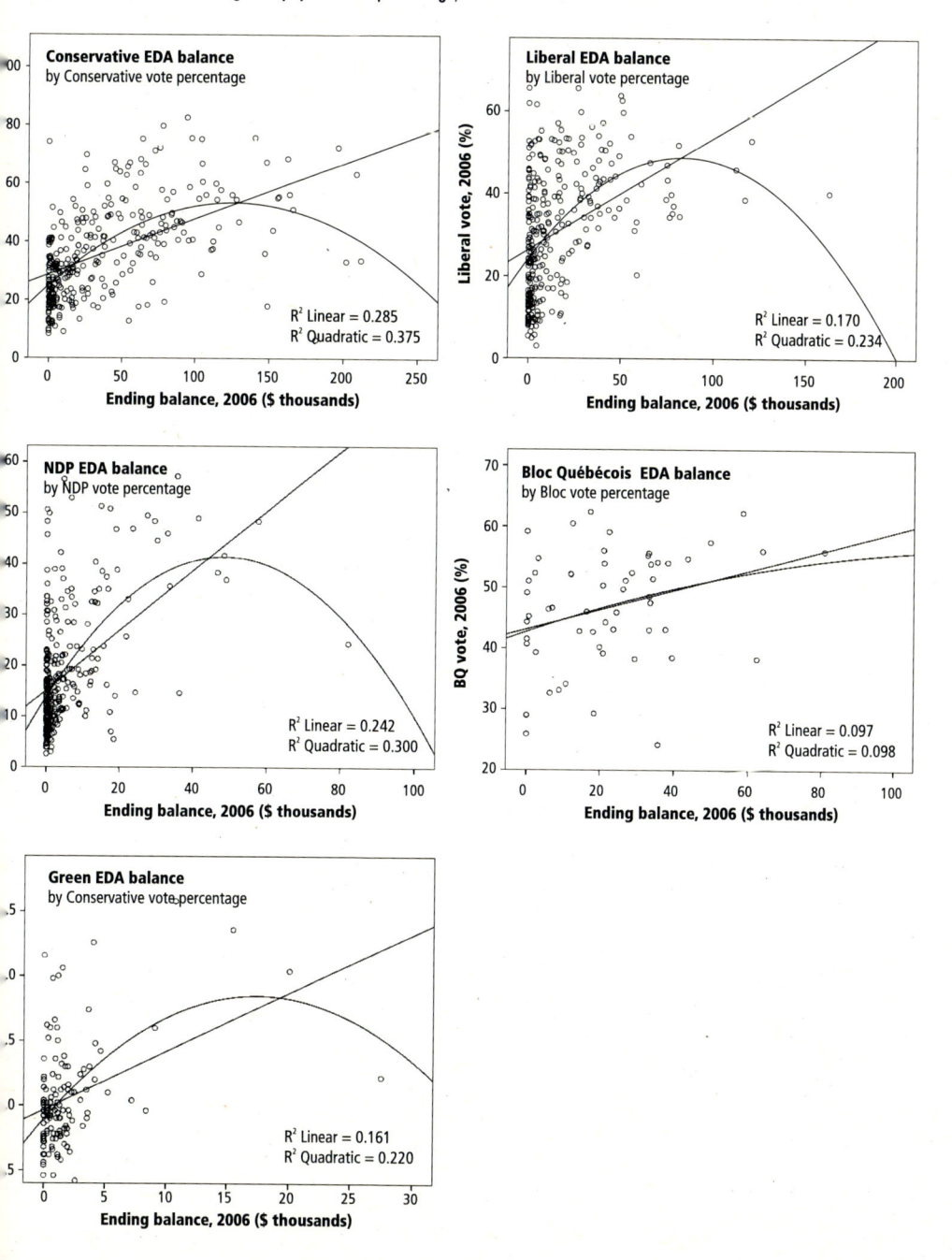

Impact of EDA financial strength on popular vote percentage, 2006

terms of a local party's 2006 net assets and its candidates' share of the total vote in the January 2006 election. These plots show only a modest positive relationship between these measures, implying that electoral and EDA financial support at the local level are somewhat distinct. In all cases, the superimposed linear regression line performs almost as well at summarizing the nature of these relationships as do the quadratic alternatives. The relationship between local organizational assets and popular vote is strongest for the Conservatives, but there is considerable scatter around the lines (and only about 30 percent of the variance in votes across ridings can be statistically attributed to the local asset balance). Among the other parties, the size of the local party organization accounts for 24 percent of the NDP's electoral vote percentage, for 23 percent of the Liberal Party's electoral vote percentage, and for 16 percent of the Green Party's popular vote percentage in each riding. The relationship is weakest among Bloc Québécois ridings, explaining only 10 percent of the variation in the BQ vote percentage. The weakness of these relationships contrasts sharply with the much stronger ties uncovered in previous research between campaign spending by candidates and their vote shares – in 2000, for example, they ranged from 24 percent variance explained for Liberals to 76 percent for the NDP (Carty and Eagles 2005, 48). Clearly, there is no simple correspondence between local EDA organizational strength and the conduct of successful campaigns, and further research will be necessary to more fully appreciate these connections.

Conclusion

What, then, is the general state of the local party following the adoption of recent reforms? Most obviously, there are signs of the continued vitality of grassroots party politics virtually across the partisan board. Local EDAs raise substantial amounts of money, are generally financially solvent, and often serve as sources of revenue for higher levels of party organization. Although Canada's parties remain primarily electoral machines designed to mobilize support in terms of votes, there appear to be significant EDA activities that occur outside the campaign period. The substantial financial transfers involving EDAs and other levels of the party suggest that – if anything – the financial integration of Canada's parties has been increasing over the past several decades.

Our understanding of the impact of reforms to the election finance regime on local party organization is limited by the absence of EDA financial data from the pre-2004 period and by detailed data on the post-reform period being available only for the first year. The situation is complicated further by the fact that 2004 and 2006 are federal election years and therefore do not represent "business as usual" for these electorally oriented organizations. The release of the complete data for 2007 is helpful in this respect, but given the lack of a majority for the government formed in 2004 and the expectation (correct, as it happened) of imminent election calls, it could be that several years will need to pass before we can observe EDAs in circumstances that have in recent decades come to be considered normal. Finally, there is every likelihood that the relations between EDAs and higher levels of party organization will continue to evolve, in part at least as a response to the new transparency in party finances. Political parties are voluntary organizations, and the ties that unite and motivate activists are continually subject to negotiation and renegotiation. Arguably, the terms of the agreements reached across the levels of Canada's party organizations in the future will be more clearly defined, and therefore altered, by the very presence of reliable EDA financial data.

The available data do speak more or less clearly to several hypotheses that might be advanced about local associations in this heavily publicly funded party system. First, there is no sign that the local associations have been rendered anachronistic by the flow of significant public funds to the central party organizations. EDAs in all five parties in most constituencies have been able to maintain some positive asset balances (with no sign yet that these are diminishing) and undertake significant fundraising and party-maintaining activities. In fact, all accounts seem to suggest that EDAs are better off financially today than they were at the beginning of 2004. Whether this is because they are in constant election readiness due to the persistence of minority governments or because the election finance reforms have provided central parties with more consistent funding, local EDAs remain financially viable several years after reform.

Their ability to attract significant amounts of financial contributions suggests that concerns about weakening linkages between grassroots party and civil society are either premature or exaggerated in the Canadian case. However, as evidenced from the Bloc Québécois EDAs' reliance on central party funds and the Conservatives' in-out scheme, the relationship between EDAs, the campaigns they mount, and the central party is still in a state of flux. With the strict restrictions on the sources of funding, and the highly competitive nature of federal politics, EDAs, if they are to be valuable components of a political party's electoral apparatus, may require more intervention from the central party. With the influx of regular, predictable, and sizable allowances from the public treasury going to central parties, it is perhaps surprising to see their continued tendency to tax their grassroots organizations. Whether this situation is tenable over the long term is unclear, now that the books on party finances are completely open for all the participants to see. But for now, at least, the grassroots of Canada's party system seem to be reasonably healthy.

NOTES

Financial support for this research was provided through a Standard Operating Grant from the Social Sciences and Humanities Research Council of Canada.

1 However, the disposition of campaign surpluses is an internal party affair and there is no requirement that these surpluses remain in local coffers. For example, the Liberals in 1988 required candidates to sign over, at the beginning of the election campaign, one-half of all reimbursements to the national party, and some of the NDP's provincial wings have made similar claims on their federal candidates (Carty 1991, 191).

2 Although the legality of this practice following the RCMP raids on the Conservative Party headquarters in April 2008 remains unclear, many, including opposition MPs, argue that it breaks the spirit of the Election Finances Act, since it allows the national party to usurp national spending limits and the local campaigns to be reimbursed for what are essentially expenses of the national campaign. Of course, this controversy is itself evidence of the impact of C-24 reforms, since without them this behaviour would not likely have been discovered. Defenders of the practice argue (variously) that the distinction between national and local expenditures is arbitrary and unclear in practice (Coyne 2008a), or that local campaigns are ineffectual and therefore local parties are behaving rationally in transferring their spending to the national campaign (Frum 2008; Coyne 2008b)

WORKS CITED

Carty, R. Kenneth. 1991. *Canadian Political Parties in the Constituencies.* Vol. 23 of the Research Studies for the Royal Commission on Electoral Reform and Party Financing. Toronto: Dundurn Press.

Carty, R. Kenneth, and Munroe Eagles. 2003. Party Organization and Campaigning at the Grassroots. *Party Politics* 9(5) (Special issue): 539-652.

–. 2005. *Politics Is Local: National Politics at the Grassroots.* Toronto: Oxford University Press.

Coyne, Andrew. 2008a. Let the Parties Work It Out for Themselves. *Maclean's,* 7 May. http://www.macleans.ca/.

–. 2008b. Local Campaigns Are Largely a Fiction Anyway. *Maclean's,* 23 April. http://www.macleans.ca/.

CTV News. 2008. "Harper says Tories followed spending rules." 22 April. http://www.ctv.ca.

Frum, David. 2008. David Frum on Elections Canada: Power-Crazed Bureaucrats or Dangerous Speech-Censors? *National Post,* 18 April. http://network.national post.com.

Geddes, John. 2000. The Black Hole of Election Money. *Maclean's,* 27 March, 34-36.

Johnson, David. 1991. The Ontario Party and Campaign Finance System: Initiative and Challenge. In *Provincial Party and Election Finance in Canada,* vol. 3 of the Research Studies for the Royal Commission on Electoral Reform and Party Financing, ed. F. Leslie Seidle, 39-88. Toronto: Dundurn Press.

Katz, Richard S., and Peter Mair. 1995. Changing Models of Party Organization and Party Democracy: The Emergence of the Cartel Party. *Party Politics* 1(1): 5-28.

Stanbury, W.T. 1991. *Money in Politics: Financing Federal Parties and Candidates in Canada.* Vol. 1 of the Research Studies for the Royal Commission on Electoral Reform and Party Financing. Toronto: Dundurn Press.

van Biezen, Ingrid, and Petr Kopecký. 2007. The State and the Parties: Public Funding, Public Regulation and Rent-Seeking in Contemporary Democracies. *Party Politics* 13: 235-54.

Young, Lisa. 1991. Toward Transparency: An Evaluation of Disclosure Arrangements in Canadian Political Finance. In *Issues in Party and Election Finance in Canada,* vol. 5 of the Research Studies for the Royal Commission on Electoral Reform and Party Financing, ed. F. Leslie Seidle, 3-43. Toronto: Dundurn Press.

7

The Quarterly Allowance and Turnout
Old and New Evidence

PETER JOHN LOEWEN AND ANDRÉ BLAIS

The most recent Canadian elections were contested under substantially different campaign finance rules than those fought in 2000 and earlier. In the past, parties could solicit donations from a large variety of donors – individuals, corporations, and unions. The donations were without limit. Introduced by Prime Minister Chrétien in the run-up to his resignation, Bill C-24 severely limited such corporate and union donations. It also limited the size of individual donations to any single candidate and in total. In short, it changed the rules of the game.

In exchange for limiting donations from private sources, C-24 offers parties generous public subsidies, arguably making parties more dependent on state financing than ever before. The bill also changed the determinant of this funding. Whereas subsidies up to then had been a function of a party's expenditures in the previous election (given the party passed a certain threshold), C-24 calibrated subsidies to absolute vote count.

There are at least three consequences to this legislation that can be explored. First, by making parties more reliant on individual donations, the legislation may advantage parties with broad-based support among the electorate and disadvantage parties whose financial support came from union and corporate donations. This implication is considered throughout this volume. Second, by limiting the size of any one donation, the legislation could reduce the incentives for quid pro quo relationships. In other words, it would reduce corruption, or the possibility of corruption. Third, by tying reimbursements to raw vote totals, the legislation could help in arresting declining turnout. Others have done substantial work on the first of these two implications. We take up the possibility of increased turnout.

The argument for increased turnout is simple on its face: If every vote counts – indeed, each vote is worth about a $1.75 – then (major) parties should seek more voters, regardless of their own position vis-à-vis their competitors. Moreover, individuals face a greater incentive to vote rather than abstain, as a ballot cast for a third-place or worse party would not be wasted but would instead endow that party with future financing.

Our intention is to test whether this occurred. That is, did the introduction of C-24 increase turnout, or at least arrest its decline? This question is much more difficult to answer than it appears on its face. In the next section, we outline this difficulty. We then lay out the tests we use to overcome these difficulties. With our results in hand we demonstrate that there is little reason to believe that C-24 increased turnout by changing the behaviour of individuals and major parties.

We then turn our attention to another possibility. By providing ongoing funds to parties, C-24 may have provided inducements for minor parties to run candidates in as many ridings as possible in a race for public funding. Parties need only win more than 2 percent of the national vote to receive annual funds. This is exactly the strategy that the Green Party took up (see Lambert 2007). Accordingly, we test whether this had the effect of increasing turnout.

Looking for Effects

How can we decisively determine if C-24 had an impact on turnout? We argue that this requires two steps. First, it requires that we clearly state *how* C-24 could have increased turnout. That is, we have to explain a mechanism or mechanisms by which it could do the task. It then requires us thinking up critical tests of these.

In our mind, the mechanism by which C-24 could impact turnout seems fairly straightforward. Political scientists have spent a great deal of time thinking about and measuring what increases and decreases political participation, particularly voting. Two things have proven to be fairly robust predictors of turnout. They do not explain all the differences, but they do consistently explain some variation, so we look to these factors. To wit, the *closeness* of an election consistently predicts whether turnout will be higher or lower than some other jurisdiction that is otherwise the same. So, when the distance between first and second is smaller, more people will head to the polls. And when it is less competitive – that is, when the distance between first and second is larger – voters have less of an incentive to cast a ballot.

Another factor that has clearly been shown to impact turnout is *individuals' preferences*. Imagine an NDP supporter in the constituency of Desnethé-Missinippi-Churchill River in 2006. In that riding, the Conservatives and the Liberals were in a tight race, but the NDP candidate trailed badly. Why would an NDP supporter go to the polls? Well, she may look at the race between the Liberal and Conservative candidates and decide that she really does not want the Conservative to win, so she will hold her nose and vote for the Liberal candidate. She is a *strategic voter*. However, if the distance between first and second *(closeness)* is great, she may decide to stay home anyway. To go to the polls and vote for the NDP would be a wasted vote, and a vote for one of the top two candidates may not make much of a difference, especially if she is indifferent about these two parties.

However, what if a voter had another reason to go to the polls? Say, for example, that by voting she could transfer some money directly to her preferred party. This is exactly what Bill C-24 does. For every vote cast, parties receive $1.75 a year until the next election. If a voter cares deeply about her party's fortunes, this may be enough to induce her to vote. Our hypothetical NDP voter will have an incentive to go to the polls rather than stay home. And if she goes to the polls, she will have an incentive to give her vote to the NDP rather than the other party that she dislikes less. This, then, is one part of the mechanism: C-24 encourages voters to go to the polls, regardless of the competitiveness of the race in their local riding and regardless of their preferences.

The second part of the mechanism has to do with political parties. Canadian political parties have long relied on the state for some of their funding. Some of this comes through the tax credits that the government provides for political contributions. Making it easier for individuals to donate money makes it easier for parties to raise money. In addition to tax credits, the government formerly reimbursed a share of election expenses provided that parties and candidates passed a certain vote threshold. But C-24 changed this. Although maintaining thresholds, it used raw vote totals to determine subsidies. Accordingly, central parties received $1.75 for each vote, regardless of the constituency in which the vote was cast.

This changes the incentives facing parties. If parties want to maximize their return on investment, they will seek to maximize the raw numbers of votes they receive. Accordingly, they will seek out votes in places where each dollar spent will have the greatest impact. We argue that these are likely constituencies where their vote total is relatively low, as each dollar should have a greater marginal impact. This thinking is clearly rooted in the principle of diminishing marginal returns, and it has clear implications for what we should see among parties' spending patterns. Specifically, we should see parties devoting more resources post-C-24 to less competitive constituencies than they did pre-C-24. The second part of the mechanism, then, is clear: Parties will distribute their resources (that is, money) more equally because they want to maximize their raw vote returns.

With these two mechanisms specified, how can we test them? In a previous paper (Loewen and Blais 2006), we specified four simple but critical tests. Indeed, there is not a single test that will demonstrate whether C-24 changed the actions of parties in a way that would affect turnout. Instead, we aimed for an accumulation of several pieces of evidence. To that end, we specified two aggregate-level and two individual-level tests, each of which examines the possibility that C-24 could increase turnout. In this chapter we add data from 2006 to three of the tests. We present these tests, and then turn to an extended discussion of why no positive effects emerge. Following this, we consider another mechanism not considered in our earlier paper, namely, the behaviour of the Green Party of Canada.

Aggregate-Level Tests

We first consider evidence at the constituency or aggregate level. As a first test of the effects of C-24, we consider the relationship of closeness between first- and second-place parties on turnout in constituencies before and after C-24. Following Cox (1997), we know that individuals who prefer a party that is not in the top two in a constituency have little incentive to vote for that party, provided its likely position is clear. Rather, such an individual should defect to her preferred party among the top two. If she is indifferent between the parties, or if the margin between them is wide, then she will abstain. In more competitive ridings where the distance between first and second is smaller, we should observe higher turnout. That is, turnout should be driven up by closeness. Conversely, in ridings where the margin between first and second is larger, turnout should be lower.

How should C-24 change this relationship? If C-24 increases an individual's incentive to vote regardless of the closeness of the race, the effect of closeness on turnout should have decreased. To test if this is the case, we

TABLE 7.1

Closeness and turnout, 2000, 2004, and 2006

	Coefficient	R.S.E.	T score	95% C.I.
Closeness	−.097	0.02	−4.93	−0.14, −0.06
2004	−1.550	0.73	−2.13	−2.98, −0.12
Closeness*2004	0.030	0.03	1.09	−0.02, 0.08
2006	2.767	0.68	4.07	1.43, 4.10
Closeness*2006	0.010	0.03	0.36	−0.04, 0.06
Constant	63.550	0.52	122.58	62.53, 64.57

Adj R^2 = 0.15
N = 917

Note: Dependent variable is constituency turnout (percent). Model is OLS. Robust standard errors, clustered on constituency, are estimated.

specify a simple regression between turnout and closeness with an interaction term for 2004 and closeness and an interaction term for 2006 and closeness.[1] Our results are presented in Table 7.1.[2]

We draw the reader's attention to three things. First, closeness does predict turnout as expected, but the relationship is rather weak. For example, if the margin between first and second increased by 5 percentage points, turnout would decrease only by about half a percentage point. As we stated above, this relationship works at the margin. Second, by looking at the variables for 2004 and 2006, we can see that our models are capturing the differences in overall turnout between these elections. Compared with 2000, turnout was higher in 2006 but lower in 2004. Third, both of the interaction variables – *closeness*2004* and *closeness*2006* – are insignificant. This indicates that closeness had the same impact after C-24 as it did before.

The second part of our proposed mechanism has to do with the efforts of the parties. As C-24 rewards parties for each vote obtained, it makes no distinction between the ridings from which votes are drawn. Parties should thus have an incentive to seek votes in non-competitive constituencies where they have little chance of winning but can likely increase their absolute number of votes. In other words, parties and candidates should be less concerned in 2004 about the competitiveness of a constituency when seeking votes. We can test this through a regression similar to that above.

To conduct this test, we regress a candidate's spending in a riding on the margin of victory in that riding, a dummy for 2004, and an interaction between 2004 and the margin of victory. We exclude 2006 from this analysis

TABLE 7.2

Competitiveness and candidate spending, 2000 and 2004

	Coefficient	R.S.E.	T score	95% C.I.
Closeness	−273.75	24.58	−11.13	−322.0, −225.5
2004	14,099.90	1,340.86	10.52	11,466.6, 29,658.7
Closeness*2004	−120.70	45.80	−2.64	−210.6, −30.8
Constant	37,528.00	727.34	51.60	36,099.5, 38,956.4

Adj R^2 = 0.12
N = 2006

Note: Dependent variable is unaudited and audited campaign expenditures as reported by Elections Canada in 2004 and 2000, respectively. Model is OLS. Candidates who did not report their spending have not been included. Analyses of returns from 2000 suggest little difference between the audited and unaudited summed totals of spending.

on account of ongoing controversy over the accounting of local spending by the Conservative Party, in which the national party transferred funds to the local association, which then paid for a portion of an ad run regionally as a means of circumventing the national spending limit.

Our logic is as follows: the less close the race, the less spending that should occur, on average, as trailing candidates will curtail their efforts, and winning candidates may similarly reduce their efforts. Accordingly, margin should produce a negative coefficient. If C-24 has the expected effect, the interaction term should be significant, and the coefficient should be positive. A positive coefficient indicates that the closeness of a race between first and second has a weaker effect on candidate spending in 2004 than in 2000.[3]

Table 7.2 presents our results. The results are opposite to expectations. Indeed, margin of victory exerts *more* of a negative effect on party expenditures in 2004 than in 2000.[4] In other words, candidates devoted comparatively less to turning out voters in marginal ridings in 2004 than in 2000.[5]

Individual-Level Tests

So far, our detective work has not found much evidence to support the possibility that C-24 could increase turnout. As part of the mechanism we have described involves the actions of individuals, we also have to consider evidence from this level. We have created two tests to uncover possible effects at the individual level. Both use the 2000, 2004, and 2006 Canadian Election Studies. Our first test follows from the logic specified above; the second replicates an earlier test of the determinants of individual-level turnout

(Blais et al. 2001), with a focus on the individual-level factors that C-24 should affect.

For our first test, we apply Cox's logic (1997) (laid out above), and we examine the behaviour of those individuals whose first preference was for a party that finished in third place or worse. We define as preferred the party that receives the highest rating in the pre-election wave of the Canadian Election Study (we exclude ties). These individuals had three options: to abstain, to vote for their preferred third-place party, or to desert and vote for one of the top two parties. We would expect to see more "sincere" votes for the third-place party in 2004 than in 2000, and less abstention or defection to a second-most preferred party (for a longer discussion of sincere voters, see Blais et al. 2001; Blais 2002; Blais, Young, and Turcotte 2005).

For a voter who prefers a third-place or worse party, Bill C-24 should increase her likelihood of voting for that party, as she can endow her preferred party with $1.75 per year, regardless of how far behind it lags. Accordingly, we expect to see less abstention or desertion in 2006 and 2004 than in 2000. We classify as deserters those voters whose preferred party finished in third place and who voted for the first- or second-place party. This party must be their second preferred choice. If C-24 is effective, it should decrease incentives to desert, as voters will be faced with a choice between endowing a continuing benefit to their preferred party and playing a likely very marginal role in choosing between the top two parties.

Finally, we should expect to see more third-party voters. We regard third-party voters as those who prefer and vote for a party that finished third or worse. Put another way, if C-24 was effective in increasing turnout, it should render less effective the individual-level mechanism of Duverger's law (Duverger 1954). Did C-24 achieve these goals?

Table 7.3 presents the distribution of these voters by year. When we consider all of the years together, there is a weakly significant difference in the distributions ($X^2 = 8.65$, $p = .08$). Indeed, it appears that by 2006 there were significantly more third-place party voters and significantly fewer abstainers than in previous elections. When we compare the elections pairwise, we find no significant differences between 2000 and 2004 ($X^2 = 1.3$, $p = .52$) or between 2004 and 2006 ($X^2 = 3.21$, $p = .20$). However, we do find a significant difference between 2000 and 2006 ($X^2 = 8.33$, $p = .02$). In other words, there was less abstention in 2006 than in 2000, and more voters with third-place preferences cast ballots for their preferred parties. We cannot say conclusively whether this is because of a more competitive campaign or because of the incentives of C-24. But it does increase the possibility that

TABLE 7.3

Vote choice of voters with a preference for a third-place party, 2000, 2004, and 2006

	2000	(%)	2004	(%)	2006	(%)
Abstainers	45	(16.8)	42	(13.4)	40	(9.7)
Deserters	70	(26.1)	84	(26.8)	104	(25.2)
Third-place voters	153	(57.1)	187	(59.7)	269	(65.1)
N	268		313		413	
All years	$X^2 = 8.65$, p = .08					
2000, 2004	$X^2 = 1.3$, p = .52					
2000, 2006	$X^2 = 8.33$, p = .02					
2004, 2006	$X^2 = 3.21$, p = .20					

C-24 increased turnout by changing individual behaviour toward voting and away from abstention.

We conducted a final test of the individual-level determinants of the decision to turn out that considers all voters. We largely follow Blais and his colleagues' test (2002). Our model regresses the respondent's reported decision to turn out on age, income, education, political interest, and party identification.

Added to these standard variables are five key variables for testing the effect of C-24. The first is closeness. As above, this measures the distance between the winning and second-place candidates in the respondent's constituency. We should expect a negative coefficient, as the larger the margin, the less incentive the individual has to vote, as her ballot is less likely to be pivotal. We add to this a dummy variable for the 2004 election and another for 2006, and an interaction between 2004 and closeness and 2006 and closeness. If C-24 reduced the importance of strategic considerations in 2004 and increased the incentive for individuals to turn out in 2004, then the interaction term between closeness and 2004 should be positive, lessening the marginal effect of the competitiveness of a race in 2004.

As Table 7.4 demonstrates, the interaction term between closeness and 2004 is not different from zero. Moreover, closeness alone is not significant. Rather than strategic considerations carrying the day, it seems that standard demographic and psychological explanations are driving the turnout decision. To wit, age, university education, high income, political interest, and party identification all predict turnout in the expected direction, and do so significantly.

TABLE 7.4

Individual-level correlates of turnout, 2000, 2004, and 2006

	Coefficient	S.E.	Z score
Closeness	−0.01	0.00	−1.53
2004	0.29	0.14	2.12
2004*Closeness	−0.00	0.00	−0.42
2006	0.48	0.15	3.13
2006*Closeness	−0.00	0.01	−0.03
Age	0.04	0.00	15.10
Income	0.45	0.11	4.16
University degree	0.35	0.10	3.63
Interest	2.19	0.13	16.55
Party ID	0.62	0.07	8.30
Constant	−1.40	0.15	−9.34

Pseudo R^2 = 0.16
N = 7,921

Note: Dependent variable is a dummy variable, indicating whether the respondent voted (1) or abstained (0). Model is a logistic regression.

Weak Incentives and Coordination Failure

We are now left with a question. Why did C-24 not exhibit these possible effects? In our earlier study, we proposed three reasons. First, the provisions of the bill were not well known by voters. Indeed, by 2005, only one in four Canadians was aware of the $1.75 provision (SES Research 2005).

Second, major parties may not have responded to the new incentive structure. They were certainly aware of the legislation, as it was passed into law in June 2003, a year before the next election. Moreover, the parliamentary testimony of both large and small parties prior to the bill's adoption suggests that they understood the logic of the new funding formula (Canada, House of Commons 2003). However, parties and candidates are not perfectly rational actors with the ability to take advantage of every opportunity in an election. The distribution of resources is as likely dominated by past practices, intuition, and instincts as by calculation of future costs and benefits. What is more, few parties would be willing to change past practices for an uncertain payoff in the heat of an election. In the hubbub of an election campaign, parties are interested in winning, not in ensuring they will have more money in the future.

Third, the provisions of the bill created a clear principal-agent problem. The bill provided incentives to the national party, but mobilization generally occurs at the local campaign level. Accordingly, national parties were faced with the difficult task of convincing local candidates to find and spend more resources, especially in marginal ridings. This is at worst impossible and at best difficult to implement. There is just little possibility that a party could coordinate its distribution of resources in a way that would both maximize its chances of winning *and* maximize its expected financial returns after the election.

But What of the Greens?

The evidence seems clear: major parties did not focus on taking advantage of the financial rewards of C-24, choosing instead to focus on winning. But what if a party was not interested in winning, but rather in receiving enough votes to receive the annual subsidy? This was exactly the case with the Green Party. Rather than seek out competitive seats – for example, on Vancouver Island – the party chose to run candidates in every riding in an attempt to pass the national threshold. Moreover, they financed their campaign through loans, with the expectation that they would pass the required threshold. In addition to running candidates in every riding, the Greens also made direct appeals to voters informing them that their vote would be worth $1.75 to the party. These appeals were specifically addressed at those who had previously not voted or who had previously given up on voting. We can derive from this another avenue through which C-24 could increase turnout. By giving small parties incentives to mobilize new voters into the system, C-24 may increase the overall level of turnout. We test this proposition through two tests.

In our first test, we measure the relationship between Green vote and turnout at the constituency level. If the Green Party succeeded by bringing more voters to the polls – rather than just by winning over existing voters – then higher turnout should be associated with higher Green vote totals. As with our models above, we regress turnout on our variable of interest and then interactions between the variable of interest and indicators of 2004 and 2006. If the Green Party did mobilize voters, the relationship between Green votes and turnout should be significant in 2004 and 2006.

Our results, presented in Table 7.5, suggest that there is a relationship between Green vote share and turnout after C-24, but not before. This is consistent with the argument that Green Party efforts may have increased

TABLE 7.5

Turnout on Green Party vote, 2000, 2004, and 2006

	Coefficient	R.S.E.	T score
Green vote %	−0.35	0.23	−1.51
2004	−4.83	0.81	−5.96
Green vote*2004	1.31	0.28	4.76
2006	1.09	0.80	1.36
Green vote*2006	0.80	0.28	2.86
Constant	61.50	0.39	162.44

Adj R^2 = 0.15
N = 917

Note: Dependent variable is constituency turnout (percent). Model is OLS. Robust standard errors with clustering on constituency are reported.

turnout. Indeed, our results suggest that for each percentage point in Green vote in 2004, turnout was 0.96 percentage points higher. In 2006, the effect was about half (0.44 percentage points) but still positive and significant. These results, however, may be the result of unobserved heterogeneity. The Green Party decided to run candidates in every riding in 2004 and 2006, whereas they had run only 111 candidates in 2000. Accordingly, strong Green performances could be correlated with higher turnout simply because new Green candidates performed better in ridings where there is a higher average turnout. To get a better grip on this relationship we need to use a dynamic analysis where we consider the effect of increases in Green vote on increases in turnout. This test is complicated by the fact that ridings in 2004 do not map perfectly onto ridings in 2000. For that reason, we consider provincial averages for 2000 to 2004 (Table 7.6). Constituency-level changes are used for 2004 to 2006 (Table 7.7).

The results are mixed. From 2000 to 2004, there appears to be a clear relationship between increased support for the Green Party and increased turnout. If this can be attributed to the Green Party bringing voters into the system, this supports the contention that C-24 increased voter turnout. However, these results are still at an aggregate level and may be a function of aggregation rather than real changes at the riding level. The results from 2004 to 2006 suggest that this may be the case, as an increase in Green Party vote has no relationship to increases or decreases in turnout. Vote

TABLE 7.6

Changes in provincial turnout and provincial Green vote, 2000 to 2004

	Coefficient	S.E.	T score
Green vote 2004 – Green vote 2000	1.51	0.46	3.26
Constant	–7.86	1.62	–4.87

Adj R^2 = 0.44
N = 13

Note: Dependent variable is provincial constituency turnout (percent). Model is OLS.

TABLE 7.7

Changes in riding turnout and Green vote, 2004 and 2006

	Coefficient	S.E.	T score
Green vote 2006 – Green vote 2004	–0.17	0.11	–1.55
Constant	3.92	0.15	26.69

Adj R^2 = 0.004
N = 308

Note: Dependent variable is constituency turnout in 2006 (percent). Model is OLS.

results do not allow us to disaggregate and redistribute Green Party vote in 2000 constituencies into redrawn 2004 constituency boundaries. Thus, we are left with mixed evidence that Green Party vote is related to increased turnout after the introduction of Bill C-24.

Conclusion

Examining the effect of the per-vote subsidy on voter turnout, we find that there was no change in the relationship between closeness and turnout. This is in addition to no evidence of a change in the spending allocations of parties. We also find that, at the individual level, the decision to turn out was not affected differently by strategic considerations in 2006 and 2004.

Although we had previously argued that Bill C-24 had little effect on turnout, we now find some weak evidence that it did have an effect on the distribution of third-place voters. There is evidence of a difference in the likelihood of abstaining or deserting a preferred third-place party before and after C-24. Moreover, we find that the legislation appears to have created incentives for small parties, namely, the Green Party of Canada. These incentives have likely drawn a small number of new voters into the system, especially when the 2004 election is compared with the 2000 campaign. However, the effect is small, at best.

It remains true that Bill C-24 has just not made substantial strides in arresting turnout decline. As we have argued, this is likely because its mechanism is just not strong enough to change the behaviour of the actors who matter: parties and voters. That said, it is possible that parties will continue to adapt to this new regime and will in time exhibit behaviour more clearly in line with its incentives. Such behaviour could include encouragements to vote that feature explicit mentions of the annual endowment such a vote gives. It could also include parties and other groups urging those already intending to vote to avoid strategic voting on the grounds that they can still reward their favoured party even if its chances of election are dismal. Finally, we could see parties better adapting to the new regime if they systematically increase campaign preparation and expenditures in constituencies where they have little chance of winning but reasonable chances of increasing their vote share. Although we remain skeptical that such actions can produce noticeably large increases in voter turnout, we also recognize that such changes will come slowly, if they come at all.

NOTES

Portions of this chapter are based on material previously published as Peter John Loewen and André Blais, Did Bill C-24 Affect Voter Turnout? Evidence from 2000 and 2004, *Canadian Journal of Political Science* 39(4): 935-43. Reprinted with the permission of Cambridge University Press.

1 This model may seem too simple, as it ignores any number of other possible factors, including riding-level demographics and provincial variations in turnout. We have two responses. First, we have specified models with provincial dummies, and the substantive findings of our model do not change. Second, we take seriously Clarke's argument (2005) that if we do not know the true model of the phenomenon we are specifying, then any addition of variables can increase bias, even if they are a part of the true model. In short, we side here with simplicity.
2 We estimate robust standard errors to account for the possible correlation of error terms as a result of multiple observations being drawn from common geographic units (that is, constituencies).
3 It can be argued that we should employ national party spending, rather than local candidate spending, as it is parties that benefit from the increases in vote count, not local candidates. We agree, but we note two measurement issues that make this impossible. First, it is extremely difficult to track national spending geographically in

Canada. National party spending reports are not itemized geographically. Rather, they are categorized by spending type. Thus, we cannot locate national party spending down to the local level. Second, even when national parties do make transfers to local candidates, the differing accounting practices and financing schemes of the various parties make it very difficult if not impossible to develop comparative measures. Nevertheless, C-24 provides an incentive for parties to transfer money to candidates irrespective of the closeness of the race in the constituency. If this is the case, holding all else equal, total candidate spending should be more weakly related to the closeness of the race in 2004 than in 2000.

4   We performed one additional test, focusing on the spending of NDP candidates in Quebec in 2004. The NDP traditionally runs weak and poorly financed campaigns in this province, and it receives low vote totals as a result. Although the ceiling on their support in the province is low, their vote is likely not maximized. Accordingly, the party should have a greater incentive to spend in weak ridings in 2004, where the returns for spending are greatest. However, regressing NDP candidate spending in Quebec on closeness, a dummy for 2004, and an 2004*closeness interaction shows the same negative sign for the interaction term as above (b = −184.1, s.e. = 113.3).

5   The dummy variable for 2004 is significant and substantively large. Accordingly, candidates spent more on average in 2004 than in 2000. However, the key fact remains that as margins increase candidates reduce their spending faster in 2004 than in 2000. Moreover, there are good reasons why average spending should have increased in 2004: the NDP was richer in 2004 than in 2000, and the folding of the Progressive Conservatives and Canadian Alliance into the Conservative Party eliminated low-spending PC candidates.

WORKS CITED

Blais, André. 2002. Why Is There So Little Strategic Voting in Canadian Plurality Rule Elections? *Political Studies* 50: 445-54.

Blais, André, Elisabeth Gidengil, Richard Nadeau, and Neil Nevitte. 2002. *Anatomy of a Liberal Victory*. Peterborough, ON: Broadview Press.

Blais, André, Richard Nadeau, Elisabeth Gidengil, and Neil Nevitte. 2001. Measuring Strategic Voting in Multiparty Plurality Elections. *Electoral Studies* 20(10): 343-52.

Blais, André, Robert Young, and Martin Turcotte. 2005. Direct or Indirect? Assessing Two Approaches to the Measurement of Strategic Voting. *Electoral Studies* 24(2): 163-76.

Canada. House of Commons. 2003. Standing Committee on Procedure and House Affairs. 30 April. http://www.parl.gc.ca.

Clarke, Kevin. 2005. The Phantom Menace: Omitted Variable Bias in Econometric Research. *Conflict Management and Peace Science* 22(4): 341-52.

Cox, Gary. 1997. *Making Votes Count*. New York: Cambridge University Press.

Duverger, Maurice. 1954. *Political Parties: Their Organization and Activity in the Modern State*. New York: John Wiley and Sons.

Lambert, Lisa A. 2007. The Effects of State Subventions to Political Parties: A Case Study of the Green Party of Canada. MA thesis, University of Lethbridge.

Loewen, Peter John, and André Blais. 2006. Did Bill C-24 Affect Voter Turnout? Evidence from the 2000 and 2004 Elections. *Canadian Journal of Political Science* 39(4): 935-43.

SES Research. 2005. Large Majority of Canadians Unaware of Recent Reforms in Campaign Finance. Press release. http://www.sesresearch.com/library/polls/POLNAT-SU05-T147.pdf.

8

Financing Party Leadership Campaigns

WILLIAM CROSS AND JOHN CRYSLER

As is increasingly the case across Western democracies, political party leaders occupy a central role in Canada's politics and government, dominating both election campaigns and their parties' parliamentary agendas (Cross 2004, 76; Poguntke and Webb 2005). Moreover, following each general election, it is assumed that the leader of the largest parliamentary party shall become prime minister. Given these high stakes, it is perhaps unsurprising that contestants frequently raise and spend millions of dollars in pursuit of a party leadership. Despite the evident importance of these contests to the public interest, traditionally they have been wholly controlled and regulated by the political parties themselves. Canada's new campaign finance regulatory regime, established through legislation taking effect in 2004 and 2007, imposes disclosure requirements and contribution limits on leadership contestants, marking the first time that Parliament has regarded leadership contests not as private matters but as important political events that should be regulated to protect the public interest.

In this chapter we examine the history of the financing of party leadership contests and make a positive case for public regulation on three grounds: the consequential nature of leadership selection; the interests of legitimacy, fairness, and public confidence that apply to general elections apply equally to leadership contests; and the failure of political parties to adequately self-regulate the financing of their contests. We also suggest that although the new regulations are an important step forward, further reforms may be needed. Most notably, the new regime appears too restrictive in terms of opportunities for leadership candidates to raise sufficient funds through contributions and, as a result, money continues to "seep into the political system" (Boatright, this volume) through very large personal loans.

Situating Party Leadership Selection

Consideration of the role of money in leadership contests, and the appropriateness of public regulation of same, is contingent on an assessment of how central these contests are both to the political parties and to the nation's broader politics. In the Canadian case, the answer is clear and unequivocal: leadership selection is one of the central functions of Canada's parties, as well as one of the most consequential activities in political life. There are four factors worth highlighting in this regard: the dominance of the leader over the party's organization, the central role of the leader in setting party policy, the high degree of likelihood that leadership candidates in governing parties will subsequently serve as prime minister or lead a senior ministry, and that leadership selection is one of the very few decisions over which grassroots party members have considerable control.

In terms of party organization, there is no independent party in central office in Canadian parties of the type described by Katz and Mair (1995) and generally found in European parties. The leader of the party largely fills this void, normally exercising almost complete authority over the extraparliamentary party's central operations. In virtually all aspects of party life, including control of the party's purse strings, recruitment of staff, and organization of electoral strategies, the party leader is supreme. And although the party in the constituencies has some independent authority (see Carty and Cross 2006), increasingly the party leader has the ability to encroach upon the local prerogative both in law and in practice (Cross 2006). The leader's organizational dominance demonstrates the importance of leadership contests both to the parties themselves and to the country's broader politics, since the parties' organizational structures, controlled by whomever the party selects as leader, are substantially funded by the public purse.

Party leaders generally are given broad discretion in the setting of policy in Parliament. Very rarely is this policy autonomy questioned within the party. There is no tradition among the major parties of significant independent voting by elected members, or of the extra parliamentary party setting policy positions different from those favoured by the leader. One result of this strong party cohesion is that leadership contests often serve as proxies for ideological disputes within a party (Carty and Cross 2006). Given the leader's dominant role in setting policy direction, party members acknowledge that the best way to influence this is to select a leader who shares their policy perspectives. The results of leadership contests, then, have a significant impact on the menu of policy programs available to voters.

Candidacy in a leadership contest is often a stepping-stone to high public office. Since 1900, twenty men and one woman have been chosen to lead the Liberals and Conservatives (not including interim leaders who were essentially place holders until a formal selection could be organized). Of these twenty-one leaders, fifteen became prime minister – seven Liberals (King, St. Laurent, Pearson, Trudeau, Turner, Chrétien, and Martin) and eight Conservatives (Borden, Meighen, Bennett, Diefenbaker, Clark, Mulroney, Campbell, and Harper).[1] In the case of governing parties, successful leadership contestants automatically assume the premiership without needing to first win a general election (recent cases include Martin in 2003, Campbell in 1993, and Turner in 1984).

Contesting and losing a leadership contest is also often a path to other high public office. In 2010, past leadership contestants held approximately one in five portfolios in the Conservative cabinet, including some of the most senior ministries. This is not exceptional. Chrétien appointed his two main rivals from the 1990 Liberal leadership contest to the positions of minister of finance and deputy prime minister, and Mulroney's senior cabinet ministers included all of his principal leadership rivals. Even in opposition, losing a leadership contest has its benefits. For example, following Stéphane Dion's election as Liberal leader in 2006, he appointed the runner-up as deputy leader and another challenger as the party's candidate in one of the Liberals' safest constituencies. As Carty (1989, 125) has argued, "It seems reasonable to conclude that running for party leadership pays well, even for the losers. Almost all who were defeated have gone on to cabinet positions whenever that was an option, and many have also received public positions after they have left electoral politics."

Leadership selection contests provide grassroots party members with one of the few opportunities to directly influence their parties. Research shows that party members believe that they have too little influence, whereas central party elites have too much (Young and Cross 2002a). With the party leadership often controlling the policy agenda and increasingly interfering in local candidate selection, the one area in which grassroots party members unquestionably hold the balance of power is in the choice of a leader. As described in this chapter, the major parties now offer all of their members a direct say in the selection of leaders. Party elites continue to exert considerable influence, but in no sense can a candidate succeed without winning substantial support from a party's grassroots partisans. The significant role that leadership contests play in engaging grassroots party members is confirmed by evidence that for many party members, participation in a leadership contest is an important motivation in their decision to join a political party (Young and Cross 2002b). In this sense, leadership contests are crucial to the health of political parties, as they allow the parties to engage grassroots members, recruit new ones, and create a general sense of enthusiasm within the party. In addition, these contests provide rare inter-election opportunities for citizens to have some influence on the parties that represent them in Parliament.

In sum, the party leader's dominance over party organization and policy, the fact that participants in leadership contests go on to occupy Canada's highest political offices, and the evidence that leadership contests provide parties with rare opportunities to engage with civil society all demonstrate that party leadership contests are of the utmost importance to political parties and to the Canadian public. Given their central place in our politics, the selection of a party leader cannot be viewed as an internal party affair. The importance of these contests beyond the confines of the political party justifies a critical examination of their financing. To contextualize this analysis, it is necessary to review briefly the means by which party leaders are selected in Canada.

Methods of Party Leadership Selection

The story of changing methods of party leadership selection in Canada is one of a continual shifting of power from the centre to the constituencies, with an increasing number of party members being included in the leadership franchise. It is possible to identify four selectorates charged by the parties, at different times, with the leadership choice: the elected caucus, local and central party elites, party convention delegates, and all members of the party. The changing methods and franchise often have mirrored broader shifts in democratic norms in Canadian society. Thus, we see dramatic changes in the 1920s, 1960s, and 1990s, during periods of increased support for populism and declining confidence in traditional democratic institutions (Carty, Cross, and Young 2000).

For the first half-century after Confederation, the parties' parliamentary caucuses made the leadership choice. At first, the choice was made by a handful of parliamentary elites; this group was gradually expanded until all MPs had a vote. The first significant change to this process occurred in 1919 when the Liberal Party chose Mackenzie King as its leader at a party convention that included not only elected members and central party notables but also representatives of the party's constituency associations from across the country. These early conventions, quickly emulated by the Conservative Party, were relatively small (about a thousand delegates), and party elites (primarily those holding some public or party office) continued to play an important role as ex officio delegates, often comprising as many as half of a contest's voters (for full details of these early processes, see Courtney 1973 and 1995). And, at least in the Liberal Party, these were often essentially stage-managed events in which the outgoing leader selected his replacement and used the convention as a tool to ratify the choice.

The nature of party leadership conventions changed dramatically when the Conservatives and Liberals selected leaders in 1967 and 1968 respectively. These conventions were twice as large as earlier ones, with most of the additional delegates coming from the constituencies. The weakening influence of the party elites was evident in a dramatic increase in the number of candidates and the competitiveness of the contests. No longer was it possible to view these contests as stage-managed ratifications of an elite's choice. The Liberal contest in 1968 drew eight serious contenders and lasted four ballots; the Conservatives attracted nine candidates to their 1967 contest, which was won on the fifth ballot. The increase in the number of delegates chosen at the constituency level soon changed the focus of campaigning. In the 1970s, rather than following the earlier practice of hoping to persuade delegates at the convention, candidates began to focus a significant proportion of their campaign funds and energy at the local level in an effort to ensure that their supporters were elected as convention delegates.

The next significant change came in the 1990s when the parties moved away from delegated conventions to varying methods of party members casting ballots directly for their preferred leadership candidate. Although all these methods allow party members to cast a vote, there are important differences in the ways in which the votes are counted. In some contests, the votes simply are totalled up; the first candidate to receive a majority is elected. In others, each vote is weighted to ensure that all local constituencies, regardless of how many party members vote, have identical influence on the leadership choice; and in others, party members' votes determine, on a proportional basis, the number of delegates each candidate is awarded to a convention at which delegates are required (on the first ballot) to vote according to the local members' preferences (see Cross 2004). All of the major parties currently use some form of direct voting. To meet the challenge of persuading and mobilizing hundreds of thousands of party members, leadership campaign teams have come to resemble those found in general election campaigns, with paid campaign managers, pollsters, media specialists, fundraisers, and other professional staff, all of which has the potential of significantly increasing costs.[2]

Financing of Leadership Campaigns

Questions relating to the costs and financing of leadership campaigns began to be raised during the shift to the large, competitive conventions of the late 1960s. As John Courtney has written: "The cost of mounting a serious campaign for the leadership of either the Liberal or Conservative party has skyrocketed since the advent of modern conventions ... Since 1967 leadership campaigns have become increasingly more highly organized, professionally managed, and technologically sophisticated affairs that carry ever larger price tags" (Courtney 1995, 61). Courtney reports that Robert Stanfield's campaign to win the 1967 Conservative contest cost approximately $150,000 and Trudeau's 1968 Liberal effort about $300,000. Trudeau's spending was a "hundred-fold increase over Lester Pearson's reported spending only ten years earlier" (Courtney 1995, 62).

In the period up to and including these contests, there was no regulation of the financing of leadership campaigns either by the state or the political parties. This approach mirrored the near-complete absence of regulation of party activity in general election campaigns. Prior to 1974, there was no public regulation of the financial activities of parties – no spending limits, no contribution restrictions, and no disclosure requirements. This changed in 1974 with the adoption of the Election Expenses Act. The key provisions of this act included limits on candidate and party spending during election campaigns, partial public funding of election expenses, and a requirement to disclose both contributions and expenses (Stanbury 1986).

Missing from the 1974 legislation was any regulation of party personnel selection contests. Neither leadership campaigns nor local candidate nomination contests were included in the regulatory regime. Both were viewed as the private events of political parties and not as contests worthy of public scrutiny and regulation. None of the contemporary commentary on the legislation noted the absence of regulation for these contests, as it was widely accepted that these were internal party affairs that should be conducted wholly as the parties deemed appropriate.

The parties themselves began to establish some regulation of leadership campaign financing in the wake of the 1974 legislation, suggesting that they believed the principles of transparency, accessibility, and fairness underpinning the new legislation should, at least in part, apply to leadership contests as well. A few general comments can be made about the parties' experiences with self-regulation of leadership campaign financing in the 1974-2004 period. First, there were significant differences between the parties, reflecting their general views toward governmental regulation. At one extreme, the New Democrats imposed highly restrictive spending limits and disclosure requirements; at the other extreme, the Canadian Alliance had virtually no self-regulation for its contests. As Adams (2000, A4) states, the Alliance's laissez-faire approach was "in keeping with the party's libertarian spirit." Second, there was little consistency within the parties over time. For example, although the Conservatives introduced disclosure requirements for their 1976 contest, they did not adopt them in 1983 and did not introduce spending limits until their 1993 contest. In all of the major parties, when spending limits were imposed, they varied from contest to contest, tending to increase over time well beyond the rate of inflation.[3] Third, only in the NDP's contests, and in one Conservative contest, were there any significant restrictions on contribution amounts. Finally, individual candidates frequently ignored or creatively evaded both the letter and spirit of parties' rules, and party officials were largely powerless in disciplining the offenders. To understand better the range of approaches the parties took and to evaluate the success of their efforts, it is worth examining in some detail the financing rules the parties adopted in recent contests. The analysis that follows focuses on 1990-2004. The post-2004 period, when public regulation was in place, is considered separately.

Party Self-Regulation, 1990-2004

Spending Limits

Imposing spending limits is perhaps the most visible act of regulation that parties set for leadership contests. When parties impose a limit, the principal motivation is usually a desire to create a level playing field by preventing candidates with easy access to large amounts of campaign funds from gaining an undue advantage. A secondary rationale is a belief that candidates should not be required to raise excessive amounts of funds, which may make them too beholden to financial contributors. As Table 8.1 illustrates, there is significant variance in limits imposed by the parties, from no limit

TABLE 8.1

Financing of leadership contests, 1990-2004 (prior to public regulation)*

Contest by party** and year (winner)	Method of selection	Disclosure required? Spending	Disclosure required? Contributions	Spending limit	Party levy Entry fee	Party levy Tax	Restrictions on contributions	Total Spending Winner	Total Spending Top Spender
LPC 1990 (Jean Chrétien)	Traditional delegate convention	Yes	Yes (>$100)	$1,700,000	$25,000	20% (expenditures above $250,000)	None	Chrétien $2,446,036	Same
PC 1993 (Kim Campbell)	Traditional delegate convention	Yes	Yes	$900,000	$10,000 (refundable under certain conditions)	N/A	None	Campbell $3,000,000 (est.)	Same
NDP 1995 (Alexa McDonough)	Delegate convention with primaries	Yes	Yes (>$100)	$250,000	$1,000	10% (directed contributions)	$10,000 limit	McDonough N/A	N/A
PC 1998 (Joe Clark)	Direct vote of party members (weighted by constituency) Run-off ballot	Yes	Yes (>$100)	$1,800,000 (extra $500,000 for those on second ballot)	$30,000 (half of it refundable)	15% (expenditures)	N/A	Clark N/A	Hugh Segal $1,200,000 (est.)
CA 2000 (Stockwell Day)	Direct vote of party members	No	No	None	N/A	N/A	None	Day $600,000 (low est.)	Tom Long $3-4 million (est.)

CA 2002 (Stephen Harper)	Direct vote of party members	No	None	$50,000 (half of it refundable)	20% (directed contributions)	None	Harper $1,100,000 (total donations)	Same
NDP 2003 (Jack Layton)	Direct vote of party members and trade union supporters	Yes	Yes (>$100)	$500,000	$7,500 (partially refundable)	20% (directed contributions)	$15,000 limit	Layton $758,436	Same
PC 2003 (Peter MacKay)	Hybrid direct vote/ convention	Yes	Yes (>$200)	$2,000,000	$45,000	N/A	N/A	MacKay >$1,000,000 (est.)	Same
LPC 2003 (Paul Martin)	Hybrid direct vote/ convention	Yes	Yes (>$200)***	$4,000,000	$75,000	20% (expenditures above $400,000)	None	Martin $7,750,000 (est.)	Same
CPC 2004 (Stephen Harper)	Direct vote (weighted by constituency)	Yes	Yes (>$200)	$2,500,000	$100,000 (half of it refundable)	10% (contributions between $25 and $25,000)	No contributions from constituency associations and non-residents of Canada	Harper >$2,000,000 (est.)	Belinda Stronach $5,356,168 (total donations)

N/A = data not available

* The Bloc Québécois' two contests in 1996 and 1997 are not included. Estimates are based on news reports.
** LPC – Liberal Party of Canada, PC – Progressive Conservative Party, NDP – New Democratic Party, PC – Progressive Conservatives, CA – Canadian Alliance, CPC – Conservative Party of Canada
*** The contribution disclosure requirements only applied to cabinet ministers; Paul Martin complied voluntarily.

in the Canadian Alliance contests to a few hundred thousand dollars in the New Democratic Party (NDP) to several million dollars in the Conservative and Liberal contests. For the most part, spending limits have increased over time.

It is also important to note that although party-imposed spending limits may appear to be a significant restraint on candidate spending, in practice this is not necessarily the case, as many categories of expenditures routinely are exempted from the limit. These include expenditures on items such as candidate deposits, auditing and legal expenses, interest on loans, fundraising expenses, child care expenses, salary paid to the candidate, travel and accommodation for the candidate and his or her family, volunteer work done for the campaign, and public opinion polling costs. This list includes some of the most expensive components of leadership campaigning, and their exemption has allowed candidates to spend far in excess of the set limit without violating party rules. The spending limits imposed by the parties also typically apply only to the official period of the race (running from the date the contest is called to the day of the vote). In practice, leadership campaigns often begin months and sometimes years before the official launch of the contest, allowing candidates to raise and spend significant amounts of money outside any regulatory framework.

There is substantial evidence that candidates frequently spent far in excess of any limits (without necessarily violating their party's rules). According to Jean Chrétien's 1990 expenditure reports, his campaign exceeded the party's spending limit by almost $750,000 (Cross 1992, 21). In 1993, Kim Campbell's campaign acknowledged spending more than three times the set limit, claiming that all but $300,000 of the excess spending was on items that were exempt from the spending cap (Courtney 1995, 64). In the 2003 Liberal leadership race, Paul Martin acknowledged spending far in excess of the $4 million spending limit. It appears from disclosure reports that Martin's campaign spent approximately $7.75 million or almost twice the limit.[4] Much of this was presumably spent before the official launch of the leadership campaign, as Martin never completely shut down his campaign efforts after losing the 1990 contest to Chrétien.

Belinda Stronach's overall campaign expenditures in the 2004 Conservative contest also appear to have exceeded the party's spending limit. Stronach's reported expenditures were just shy of the $2.5 million limit, but her campaign reported raising more than $5,356,168 or about $2.8 million in excess of the limit. After subtracting the party's levy on donations and tax on expenditures, the Stronach campaign likely spent at least $1.6 million in excess of the spending limit.[5] It is possible that Stronach's campaign, like that of Martin's, carried a substantial surplus, but the fact that the candidate donated a total of $3.95 million of her own funds, in three separate instalments, suggests that the money raised was spent. As with other leadership races, numerous expenses were exempt from the spending limit, including the registration fee and compliance deposit, up to $100,000 in staff costs for membership data entry, translation costs, and financial and legal costs.

Similarly, Jack Layton's acknowledged expenditures in the 2003 NDP contest far exceeded the $500,000 spending limit. Layton reported spending $758,436, of which his campaign claimed $351,404 was spent on exempt expenses. Most notably, his campaign claimed $269,765 in exempt direct mail, fundraising, and finance costs.

Whether there should be a spending limit and the level at which it is set are often contentious issues within a party. Prospective candidates and their supporters take different positions, often dependent upon what they perceive to be their strategic interest. There is evidence that high spending limits, and the ease with which leading candidates can spend in excess of the limits, have discouraged some candidates otherwise thought to be competitive from entering leadership races. For example, Jim Prentice, Chuck Strahl, and then-Progressive Conservative leader Peter MacKay decided not to become candidates in the 2004 Conservative leadership race at least in part because of difficulties in raising the amount of money necessary to compete with other top contenders (*Cheadle* 2004).[6] The high spending limit in the Liberal race of 2003, combined with Paul Martin's dominance in organization and fundraising, resulted in candidates departing from the race and prevented would-be candidates from entering. As an analysis of Allan Rock's departure from the race concludes, "Fund raising and organization had increasingly become worrisome for the Rock campaign, as it had for all others considering a challenge to Martin" (Brown 2003, A4).

The fundraising pressures on campaigns increase when candidates are required to pay substantial sums of money to the party, a practice often justified as necessary to offset various costs associated with holding the leadership contest. Payments to the party tend to take the form of one or several of the following: a registration fee, a levy on contributions, or a tax on expenditures (see Table 8.1). The registration fee helps prevent "frivolous" candidates from entering and often part or all of it is refunded to candidates who abide by the contest's rules. The party may also take a percentage of contributions raised, usually ranging from 10 to 20 percent. Often such a levy is imposed only on directed contributions (donations to individual candidates that flow through the parties so that the donor may obtain a party-generated tax receipt). Finally, the party may impose a tax on expenditures. Once again, this tax typically ranges between 10 and 20 percent.

Obviously, these rules can work against underfunded candidates and, as with spending limits, are often the subject of intense debate among those charged with setting a leadership contest's rules (Flanagan 2007, 115-20). For example, there was disagreement over the drafting of financial regulations leading up to the Liberal Party's 2003 race. Draft regulations of the leadership expenses committee would have required a $100,000 upfront deposit and a 20 percent levy on all expenditures. Together these measures would have resulted in candidates giving the party $200,000 of the first $700,000 they spent. Several candidates successfully lobbied the committee to adopt rules that made the contest more accessible: a $75,000 deposit and a 20 percent levy on all expenditures above $400,000. Together, these measures meant that a candidate would give the party only about $114,000 of the first $700,000 spent.

Contribution Limits
As seen in Table 8.1, there are few instances in which parties placed any restrictions on contributions to leadership campaigns. This approach mirrors the 1974 legislation that relied on disclosure and spending limits, but not contribution limits, to reduce the influence of money on politicians. The only significant exceptions are the NDP's cap on contributions in the 2003 and 1995 contests ($15,000 and $10,000 respectively) and the Conservatives' ban on contributions from non-residents of Canada and constituency associations in 2004. The latter restriction is presumably to prevent MPs from raising more money than they need for general election campaigns, husbanding the surplus in their constituency associations, and then funnelling that money either to their own leadership campaign or to one of their allies.[7]

Disclosure Requirements
Similar to spending and contribution limits, and as illustrated in Table 8.1, the parties have taken markedly different approaches to requiring disclosure of leadership financing. Again, the approaches taken by the NDP and the Canadian Alliance are the most distinct, with the Canadian Alliance requiring no disclosure and the NDP requiring full disclosure – including partial pre-vote reporting. There are two main reasons for a party to require their candidates to disclose their contributions and these largely parallel the

rationale for general election disclosure. First, there is a well-established tradition that candidates for public office should not be the secret beneficiaries of donors' largesse but rather that these relationships should be made transparent and subject to public scrutiny. Second, disclosure is necessary to enforce any other financial regulations (such as spending limits, contribution restrictions, or the party's levy on campaign revenues and expenditures). Thus, parties that do not set any restrictions on the raising and spending of leadership campaign funds have less incentive to require candidates to disclose their financial activity.

In terms of party leadership selection, there are three main dimensions of disclosure: (1) whether the information is reported solely to the party; (2) the relative comprehensiveness of the reported information; and (3) whether the disclosure is made before the conclusion of the contest. First, although most of the parties requiring disclosure make the information public, this is not always the case. Sometimes a party's rationale for requiring disclosure is not transparency but to ensure that other rules are followed. In such instances, the party may see no need to make that information public. In other cases where disclosure rules apply, only partial summary information from candidates' disclosure reports is made public.

Second, in terms of the comprehensiveness of the information disclosed, parties have set various thresholds for the size of contributions that must be disclosed, with most falling in the $100 to $200 range. Many of the disclosure reports made public by parties and candidates do not provide sufficient information to allow readers to clearly identify the contributors. Occasionally, only names (or in the case of corporate contributions, registration numbers) are provided without addresses or cities. The NDP's 2003 contest was an exception in that the reports did include the city and province of the contributors.

Finally, the timing of the disclosure requirements is often at issue. Some parties require candidates to make partial disclosure during the course of the campaign. This allows for public scrutiny of these returns prior to the leadership vote, which raises the possibility of the media or a competing candidate criticizing the sources of another candidate's funds. More common, however, is for parties to require the disclosure reports well after the end of the leadership campaign. Until the Liberals' 2003 race, which compelled candidates to disclose contributions every sixty days during the campaign (and every week during the final month of the campaign), only the NDP required interim reports identifying contributors.[8]

It is impossible to know for certain if candidates were complying fully with disclosure requirements, since official auditing of candidates' accounts and statements typically did not take place. The Liberals' 1990 race demonstrates the problem. Candidates were required to report donations of $100 or more. Contributions disclosed by leading candidates Martin and Chrétien amounted to only about one-third of their total reported expenditures. There is no way of knowing what the sources of these other funds were. Nonetheless, it may be unlikely that the candidates raised this large a share of their funds in contributions of $100 or less (Cross 1992, 21).

There are two main impediments to the parties' effective enforcement of their own financing rules in leadership campaigns. First, there is a substantial disincentive for parties to discipline a leadership contestant because the opprobrium that would fall upon the sanctioned candidate would likely spill onto the party as well, especially if the candidate in question wins the leadership contest. Second, leadership candidates have little to lose in breaking party rules, which do not have the force of law, and any breaches usually are not revealed until after the contest (if at all), when it is too late to have an impact on the outcome. The parties' unwillingness and general inability to effectively police the financing of their own leadership contests strengthened calls for public regulation.

Public Regulation of Leadership Financing

The Royal Commission on Electoral Reform and Party Financing

The first significant proposal to include party leadership contests within the campaign financing regulatory framework was made by the Royal Commission on Electoral Reform and Party Financing in 1991. The commission recommended that candidates be required to disclose their expenditures and contributions in excess of $250 and that campaigns be limited to spending an amount equal to 15 percent of the election expenses permitted for their party in the most recent general election (about $1.9 million, at the time, for major parties) (Canada, RCERPF 1991, 285).

The commission balanced what it saw as the interests of legitimacy, fairness, and public confidence against the parties' claims that there was no significant public interest in the operation of these contests. The commission rejected arguments that "parties are essentially private, self-regulating organizations made up of volunteers" (Canada, RCERPF 1991, 282). Instead, it found that leadership selection contests were highly consequential events in which genuine public interests were at stake, and that the public had a right to ensure these campaigns were conducted in a fair and transparent fashion. As evidenced in the following passage, the commission found that the parties had largely failed in their efforts to self-regulate these contests adequately:

> These efforts at self-regulation have not assuaged concerns that the role of money in the selection of national leaders has the potential to undermine the integrity and fairness of the process. At the same time, it remains difficult for party officials to enforce the rules that do exist. (281)

The commission's recommendations were not acted upon by Parliament and, until the 2004 changes came into effect thirteen years later, leadership contests continued to operate independent of the campaign finance regulatory framework.

Regulatory Approaches in Other Jurisdictions

Three Canadian provinces currently impose some form of regulation on leadership contests (British Columbia since 1995, Manitoba since 2002, and Ontario since 2005). All three provincial regimes include disclosure requirements, though none imposes spending limits and only one includes contribution limits. With respect to disclosure, the threshold for the public identification of donors ranges between $100 and $250. Ontario has the most aggressive approach to the timing of disclosure, requiring reporting within ten business days after a contribution is deposited. Neither British Columbia nor Manitoba requires disclosure reports before the conclusion of the contest. British Columbia and Manitoba require candidates to disclose information on expenditures, and only Manitoba places a limit on contributions, where the maximum an individual can contribute to any combination of leadership contestants is $3,000 and organizations such as corporations and unions are prohibited from contributing.

The experience of leadership selection in Britain is an interesting comparative case because of the shared parliamentary system, as well as the move to some form of membership vote in all three of the major parties. In the past, when the parliamentary party selected the leader, financial regulations were not needed. However, with the expansion of the selectorate, the cost of campaigning has increased dramatically, leading to recent attempts to regulate leadership campaign spending. For example, in its 2005 leadership contest, the Conservative Party set a spending limit of £100,000, in 2007 the Liberal Democrats set a spending limit of £50,000, and Labour imposed no spending cap in its contest to replace Tony Blair. Since the enactment of the Political Parties, Elections and Referendums Act in 2000, leadership contests became subject to partial public regulation. The act requires public disclosure of all donations above £1,000. This rule applies to any party member receiving donations in support of a quest to attain any position, including leader, within the party. Data on each donation must be submitted to the Electoral Commission within thirty days of the date of donation; this information is then posted on the commission's website.

Public Regulation of Federal Leadership Contests
Bill C-24, which brought about the first comprehensive changes to Canada's electoral finance regime since the adoption of the 1974 law, came into effect on 1 January 2004. The bill's provisions included, for the first time, state regulation of the financing of both party candidate nomination and leadership contests. With the passing of this legislation, Parliament definitively expressed its view on the debate over the appropriateness of state intervention into these areas of party decision making. In terms of leadership selection, the federal government now requires disclosure of contributions. In addition, it requires information on contributors to be published prior to the conclusion of the contest, imposes a limit on contributions from individuals, and prohibits union and corporate donations. This regime does not include a spending limit.

In 2007, the new Conservative government adopted Bill C-2 (the Accountability Act). The new act essentially adheres to the principles of the 2004 changes but establishes a more restrictive regime. The limit on contributions by individuals to all political entities, including leadership campaigns, was reduced from $5,000 (as set in 2004) to $1,000 (subject to indexation). Similarly, the amount that nomination and leadership contestants and general election candidates can contribute to their own campaign in excess of the contribution limit was reduced from $5,000 to $1,000. The specific provisions of the current regulatory regime applying to leadership contests may be summarized as follows:

- Anyone who accepts a contribution for a leadership bid – before or during the contest period – must register with Elections Canada as a leadership contestant once the party officially calls the contest.
- Once a person registers as a leadership contestant, that person is deemed to have been a candidate from the time he or she first accepted a contribution or incurred a leadership campaign expense.

- Candidates must file periodic pre-vote reports disclosing the name and address of all who contribute in excess of $200.
- Candidates may accept contributions only from Canadian citizens and permanent residents of Canada – corporations, trade unions, and associations are prohibited from contributing.
- Individuals may not contribute more than $1,000 in total (subject to annual indexing) to any combination of leadership contestants in a single leadership contest.
- Candidates may contribute no more than $1,000 of their own money, beyond the contribution limit, to their campaign.

The new regime treats leadership campaigns both more strictly and more leniently than it does parties and candidates in general election campaigns. The strict pre-vote disclosure requirements do not apply to general elections, and by not imposing a spending limit on leadership contests, the campaign finance regime has continued to treat leadership campaigns more leniently than election campaigns.

Impact of the New Regulatory Regime on Leadership Contests

The first leadership contest by a major party to be held under the new regime was the Liberal contest in 2006.[9] Although it is too early to assess fully the impact of the new financing regime, the Liberal case does allow us to make tentative observations.

On election night in January 2006, Prime Minister Paul Martin announced that he would resign as Liberal Party leader as a result of his government's electoral defeat. The Liberal caucus selected an interim leader, and the contest to replace Martin was opened officially on 7 April 2006. A series of delegate election meetings, in which all party members who had joined by 1 July were eligible to vote, were scheduled in the party's constituencies and clubs for the weekend of 29 September to 1 October. Delegates were allocated to the leadership candidates on the basis of the proportion of the vote they received in each constituency. The elected delegates were required to vote for the candidate to whom they were pledged on the first ballot of the 3 December convention but were free to vote as they wished on subsequent ballots. In addition to those elected in the constituencies, approximately one-fifth of the convention delegates had ex officio status (such as MPs, former candidates, party officials, and constituency executives) and were subject to no first-ballot restrictions. Eleven people registered as candidates, and by the time of the convention eight remained in the race.

According to Liberal Party president Mike Eizenga, the party did four things to make the 2006 contest more accessible than the 2003 race. It (1) reduced the spending limit from $4 million to $3.4 million; (2) reduced the entry fee from $75,000 to $50,000; (3) stipulated that there would be no exempt expenditures – all expenditures, including previously exempt ones such as polling and tour expenses, would be included in the spending limit; and (4) raised the threshold after which the 20 percent tax on expenditures would apply from the first $400,000 spent to $500,000.[10] Together, these changes reduced the amount of funds candidates needed to raise to be competitive. As it turned out, even these changes overestimated the ability of the party's candidates to raise funds in the new regulatory environment.

There is considerable evidence to suggest that all of the candidates, including the front-runners, had difficulty raising sufficient funds to compete effectively in the eight-month-long contest. However, since this difficulty in raising funds affected all candidates to some degree, the more restrictive fundraising environment may have helped produce a more competitive contest. As Table 8.2 illustrates, we confine our analysis here to the top four finishers (Dion, Ignatieff, Rae, and Kennedy), who also bested the other candidates in terms of funds both raised and spent.

In contrast to past contests, there is no evidence that any candidate spent more than the party's nominal limit of $3.4 million. According to disclosure reports, the top spender was Bob Rae at $2.99 million, and no other candidate, including the winner Stéphane Dion, came within $1 million of the limit. It appears that this fiscal restraint was driven more by necessity than by design. All four of the major candidates had trouble raising sufficient funds from individual contributors and took out hundreds of thousands of dollars in loans, mostly from themselves and their family, friends, and close supporters. For example, Rae's brother lent his campaign $720,000 and Rae himself lent $125,000. In addition, three of the top four candidates incurred hundreds of thousands of dollars in unpaid claims from suppliers. According to the candidates' final reports, submitted to Elections Canada months after the conclusion of the contest, all of them owed substantial sums in loans and unpaid claims (the average debt owing was $603,516.75). This amount would have been substantially higher had the party not decided to return the 20 percent levy on expenditures above $500,000 after the convention. The levy had been imposed to help defray the costs of the convention, but when the convention turned a profit and it was apparent that all of the campaigns were running significant deficits, the party decided to return the levy. The party also returned the candidates' $50,000 entry fees, which

TABLE 8.2

Liberal leadership contest 2006: Expenditures, contributions, and debts of the top four candidates ($)

	Stéphane Dion	Michael Ignatieff	Bob Rae	Gerard Kennedy
Expenditures	1,882,367.92	2,316,027.85	2,987,556.95	1,425,086.09
Contributions	953,396.12	1,500,469.08	2,149,868.57	689,338.19
Loans incurred	705,000.00	570,000.00	845,000.00	451,170.00
Unpaid claims	293,707.03	247,239.74	0.00	311,682.10
Repaid loans	150,000.00	40,503.78	623,478.08	195,750.00
Debt owing* (May-June 2007)	848,707.03	776,735.96	221,521.92	567,102.10
Debt owing** (June 2008)	600,000.00	100,000.00	0.00	300,000.00

* Debt owing is that portion of loans that have not been repaid (excluding interest) plus any remaining unpaid claims.
** Estimates from media reports.
Source: Candidate final reports filed with Elections Canada in May-June 2007 except where otherwise noted.

assisted efforts to retire campaign debts. Despite the party's generosity, six leadership contestants (including the winner Stéphane Dion) missed the final deadline to repay their loans three years after the completion of the contest (McGregor 2010).

There are several reasons why the Liberal leadership candidates had such difficulty raising funds for the 2006 contest. First, the Liberals had been humiliated very recently by a serious fundraising scandal (resulting in the conviction of several party operatives) and had suffered an electoral defeat after a long run in office. These factors made fundraising pitches a tough sell. Second, with eleven candidates in the race, there was great demand on the available funds. This was exacerbated by the fact that eight of these candidates were from the Toronto area and were "seeking money from the same pool of donors" (Taber 2006, A5). Third, the ban on union and especially corporate donations eliminated a rich source of funds tapped by candidates to raise millions of dollars in past contests. For example, in 2003, Martin received donations of $100,000 from each of nine separate corporate donors and millions of dollars in smaller corporate donations. Fourth, the $5,400 limit on individual contributions made fundraising more challenging given that many individuals donated larger amounts in past contests. Again, to use Martin's 2003 campaign as an example, he attracted over $1.5 million in individual contributions of $10,000 or more. Moreover, as of 1 January 2007, the limit on individual contributions was lowered to $1,100, meaning that candidates then had to solicit much smaller contributions in order to clear their campaign debts.

Although the restrictive fundraising environment made life for the candidates more difficult, forcing some campaigns to scale back their operations and to ask paid staffers to work as volunteers, there is some evidence these fundraising restrictions had a positive impact on the competitiveness of the race. We may speculate that in a relatively unregulated fundraising environment one or two of the better-known candidates would have been well positioned to raise and spend enough funds to marginalize other potential rivals, as was the case in each of the past three contests. Under the new rules, however, four serious candidates emerged, both in terms of delegate support and funds raised. And for the first time in the history of the Liberal Party, a candidate who did not top the first ballot won the convention (see Table 8.3). Although it is difficult to isolate the precise impact of the new regulations on the competitiveness of the contest, there can be little doubt that these rules contributed to a levelling of the playing field on which the race was run.

The practice of making public the names of individual contributors and the amounts they donate before the selection date had a major impact on at least one of the candidates. When reports were made public in May 2006, the media discovered that Joe Volpe's campaign had accepted $108,000 in donations from twenty current and former executives of the generic drug company Apotex Inc., their spouses, and their children. All of these contributions reached the legal limit of $5,400, including $27,000 in donations from five donors under the age of eighteen (Bryden and Panetta 2006). Some alleged that the $108,000 might constitute a concealed corporate donation, which is illegal under the Canada Elections Act – a claim Volpe and his contributors flatly denied. Although it is not illegal for those younger than 18 to donate, Volpe returned the $27,000 contributed by minors to demonstrate that his campaign would abide by "the spirit" of the law (ibid.). The other $81,000 was not returned. Even without an official sanction by the state, the impact of the disclosure on the Volpe campaign was high. Volpe was forced to return tens of thousands in contributions, and the controversy dogged him throughout the campaign.

Overall, the new regulatory regime appears to have worked fairly well. All of the candidates complied with the various disclosure requirements,

TABLE 8.3

Liberal leadership convention results, 2006

Candidate	1st ballot	2nd ballot	3rd ballot	4th ballot
Michael Ignatieff	1,412 (29.3)	1,481 (31.6)	1,660 (34.5)	2,084 (45.3)
Bob Rae	977 (20.3)	1,132 (24.1)	1,375 (28.5)	–
Stéphane Dion	856 (17.8)	974 (20.8)	1,782 (37.0)	2,521 (54.7)
Gerard Kennedy	854 (17.7)	884 (18.8)	–	–
Ken Dryden	238 (4.9)	219 (4.7)	–	–
Scott Brison	192 (4.0)	–	–	–
Joe Volpe	156 (3.2)	–	–	–
Martha Hall Findlay	130 (2.7)	–	–	–
Total	4,815 (100)	4,690 (100)	4,817 (100)	4,605 (100)

Notes: Hall Findlay was eliminated after the first ballot, and Brison and Volpe withdrew voluntarily. Dryden was eliminated after the second ballot and Kennedy withdrew voluntarily. Rae was eliminated after the third ballot.

making it the most open and transparent contest ever held by a major federal political party. In addition, the restrictions on contributions were effective in making the contest more accessible to candidates who would have been unable to attract the millions of dollars from large corporations and wealthy individuals necessary to be competitive in past contests. However, this first test of the rules by a major political party also reveals several areas of concern.

As noted above, all of the major candidates took out loans worth hundreds of thousands of dollars to help finance their campaigns. There are no limits on the amount that can be loaned to leadership candidates. Furthermore, corporations and unions, which are prohibited from making contributions, are permitted to make loans. The absence of restrictions on loans has been criticized for giving those candidates who are wealthy – or who have wealthy friends, family, or close supporters – an advantage in building up campaign funds quickly over their less wealthy and less connected competitors. Under the law, any loan that is not repaid within eighteen months of the leadership selection date is treated as a contribution.[11] Any remaining loan amount over the contribution limit of $1,100 constitutes an illegal contribution, although it is possible for Elections Canada to allow candidates to write off loans (Bryden 2009). In the context of a leadership campaign, however, there is little practical difference between funding that comes from a large contribution and a large loan to be repaid after the contest. Moreover, extensions to repay the loan may be granted indefinitely by Elections Canada or the courts, and a candidate may default on a loan that is deemed truly uncollectible.

In his recommendations to the House of Commons Standing Committee on Procedure and House Affairs in January 2007, the chief electoral officer summarized the current situation with respect to political loans as follows:

> The loans granted by lenders – who are not in the business of lending, who lend money at non-commercial rates, with terms that are not available to others, or in cases where there is little prospect of reimbursement – may be perceived as a means to influence the political entity to which the funds are provided. (Chief Electoral Officer 2007, 35)

As such, the chief electoral officer made a series of recommendations to impose "additional controls and [make] these transactions more transparent and the rules governing disclosure more consistent from one political entity to the other" (ibid., 37). In 2007, the Conservative government introduced legislation that largely follows the chief electoral officer's recommendations and proposes these changes to the Canada Elections Act: (1) a prohibition on union and corporate loans to federal political entities; (2) counting loans and loan guarantees toward an individual's contribution limits; (3) restricting loans greater than the contribution limit to financial institutions lending at commercial rates of interest; and (4) requiring more detailed information on the loan, lender, guarantor, and repayment schedule in disclosure reports.

The governing Conservatives have introduced legislation to implement these recommendations and to create tighter rules for the treatment of unpaid loans.[12] Although the new loan regime would apply to all political entities, the minister responsible, Steven Fletcher, claimed that the rationale for the bill was "to remove the loopholes that were discovered during the [2006] Liberal leadership contest" (Bryden 2009). These proposals, however, have not escaped criticism. The National Citizens Coalition has argued that such stringent limitations infringe on free speech, the National Women's Liberal Commission expressed concern that bank loans would be more difficult for women to obtain than men, and some senior officials from financial institutions expressed concern at becoming the sole source of large political loans

(Bédard 2007). Former leadership contestant Gerard Kennedy, who had taken out large personal loans from family members and supporters, predicted that under this regime banks would lend only to candidates with significant personal assets (Bryden 2009).

The practice of using large loans to fund leadership campaigns, besides revealing a loophole in the legislation, revealed that the new restrictions on contributions resulted in candidates having a difficult time raising adequate funds to participate in a vigorous national contest. This is worrisome, as leadership contests provide the parties with rare opportunities to engage their supporters from every corner of the country in a consequential political decision. The 2006 leadership contest, which took place under more favourable fundraising conditions than those currently in place, raises the spectre of threadbare and scaled-back campaigns in future contests. This points to a contradiction in the 2004 legislation: although contribution limits and a ban on corporate and union donations were also imposed on political parties, this was offset by a new annual public subsidy to the parties worth millions of dollars. For leadership contestants, by contrast, there was no public funding introduced to offset the more restrictive contribution limits. During the 2006 Liberal leadership race, Eddie Goldenberg – Jean Chrétien's long-time chief policy adviser and key architect of the 2004 changes – admitted that by not introducing public funding for leadership campaigns, "a mistake was probably made" (Bryden 2006).

For a long time, leadership candidates have received indirect public financing through the practice of directed contributions, whereby contributions to leadership candidates flow through the parties, earning the contributors substantial tax credits. The experience of the federal Liberals suggests that direct public funding may also be needed. As Goldenberg suggested to the Canadian Press, a possible option would be to introduce a system whereby individual contributions raised by leadership candidates are matched by contributions from the state. This reform would help ensure that candidates are able to raise enough funds for a vibrant campaign that connects with voters across the country, and it would reward those candidates successful at attracting large numbers of small donations from their supporters.

Finally, control over leadership campaign expenditures is another area in which reforms might be considered. It has long been acknowledged that spending limits are necessary to level the playing field for elections of all types. Spending caps help ensure that elections are not won by one side vastly outspending the other. The 1974 legislation imposed spending limits on political parties and candidates in election campaigns, and the 2004 legislation applied spending limits to candidate nomination contests. However, the state has yet to establish limits for leadership contests. The parties themselves have acknowledged the need for spending limits by imposing them for most contests in recent decades. The parties' lack of success in enforcing these limits suggests that state intervention is appropriate. The government appears to have given some consideration to including spending limits for leadership campaigns in the 2004 legislation. However, in the end, it was persuaded by the argument that parties should be left to their own approaches on this issue. The government's house leader, Don Boudria (2003) argued that there is such diversity among the parties in terms of size and resources that "it is impossible to have the same size [that is, spending limit in leadership contests] for everyone and think that the structure will fit everyone well." The chief electoral officer, in his recommendations to the House of Commons Standing Committee on Procedure and House Affairs in 2007, also alluded to the difficulty in setting an appropriate spending limit for leadership contests when he observed that "there is insufficient data available to Elections Canada to make a recommendation to assist Parliament in the setting of such limits" because so few contests have occurred under the new rules (2007, 33-34).

Spending limits, however, need not be one-size-fits-all. The practice in candidate nomination contests is instructive in this regard. The legislation sets a relatively high limit that is restrictive only in the most competitive contests. Parties that believe this limit is too high are free to impose a lower one on their candidates, and some do (as did the New Democrats in the 2006 election). A similar approach might be taken with respect to leadership contests.

Conclusion

For years, the debate over whether Canada's campaign finance regulatory regime should be expanded to include party leadership selection centred on an argument over whether parties are essentially private or public organizations. This argument has been won by those who see parties as public instruments in the practice of Canadian democracy. To steal a phrase from van Biezen (2004) and Epstein (1986), Canadians view political parties as the "public utilities" of their democracy. This view is supported by public opinion data consistently finding strong support for the proposition that "without parties, there can't be true democracy" (Howe and Northrup 2000;

Blais and Gidengil 1991). Canadians adhere to this conviction even while they are increasingly critical of the performance of their parties.

Importantly, Canadians not only think that parties are essential to their democracy but they put their money where their mouth is. Taxpayers have subsidized the work of parties since 1974, and they increased this support dramatically in 2004 with the introduction of annual allowances to the parties. Leadership campaigns themselves do not receive direct public financing, but they benefit from public dollars through tax credits that are made available to contributors.

Given the central, and privileged, place of parties in Canadian democracy and the investment that taxpayers make in their operations, citizens have every right to demand that the key functions of parties, including leadership contests, be conducted in a way that reflects their democratic values. Beginning in the 1970s, the parties attempted to self-regulate these contests, but these efforts largely failed. Not only did the parties take very divergent approaches, with some rejecting regulation altogether, but they also displayed an inability to enforce their own rules and penalize those who violated them.

The regulatory framework established through the legislation enacted in 2004 and 2007 takes some very important steps toward ensuring transparency, fairness, and accessibility in Canadian leadership contests. Although further reforms are still needed, the significance and effectiveness of the new regulatory regime should not be discounted. The experience of the Liberal leadership contest in 2006 suggests that the era in which big money dominates party leadership contests is over.

NOTES

We would like to thank Tom Flanagan for providing data and for helpful comments on an earlier version of this chapter.

1 Conservative leaders Stanfield, Drew, Bracken, and Manion failed to become prime minister during this period. We have excluded Conservative leaders selected between 1994 and 2003, when the party was essentially split into two and was not electorally competitive. Stéphane Dion is the only former Liberal leader not to become prime minister, and current leader Michael Ignatieff has not yet served as prime minister.
2 For a compelling insider's view of a modern leadership campaign, see Flanagan 2007, 96-136.
3 The NDP's spending limit was $15,000 in 1975, $150,000 in 1989, $250,000 in 1995, and $500,000 in 2003. The Liberals' spending limit was $1.65 million in 1984, $1.7 million in 1990, and $4 million in 2003. The Conservatives' spending limit was $900,000 in 1993, $1.8 million in 1998, $2 million in 2003, and $2.5 million in 2004.

4 The Martin campaign transferred $3.8 million in surplus funds to the Liberal Party after the convention (*Kitchener-Waterloo Record* 2004), leaving approximately $8.5 million from the $12.3 million raised. When the party's 20 percent tax on expenditures greater than $400,000 (up to $4 million) is applied, a further $720,000 can be subtracted. This leaves approximately $7.75 million in apparent campaign expenditures.
5 According to the Stronach campaign's list of contributors over $200, $4.23 million was raised in contributions above $25,000. The party's 20 percent share works out to $846,000. In addition, $1,126,168 was raised in contributions between $200 and $25,000. The party's 10 percent share works out to $112,616.80. When the levies are added to the tax on expenditures of 10 percent on $2,496,482 (or $249,648.20), the party would have taken in at least $1.2 million. However, the Conservatives later claimed that Stronach did not in fact pay the full amount and owed the party as much as $380,000 (a figure that the Stronach camp disputed) (Campion-Smith 2005).
6 The Progressive Conservative Party and the Canadian Alliance merged to form the Conservative Party of Canada in December 2003. The party held its inaugural leadership vote in March 2004. The contest was exempt from changes that were made to the Canada Elections Act that came into effect 1 January 2004.
7 An example of this practice occurred in the 2003 Liberal leadership contest, during which John Manley's abortive campaign received a $96,000 contribution from his own constituency association.
8 Although the Liberals' pre-vote disclosure requirements in 2003 applied only to cabinet ministers, Paul Martin (who was not in cabinet at the time) complied voluntarily.
9 The provisions of Bill C-24 applied up until 1 January 2007, almost a month after the completion of the contest, at which point Bill C-2 came into effect. After this date, Bill C-2's lower contribution limit applied to contributions solicited by candidates who were attempting to clear their campaign debts.
10 From an appearance on the CTV program *Canada AM* on 20 March 2006.
11 After the 2006 Liberal leadership contest, nine candidates were granted eighteen-month extensions to repay their campaign loans after the initial eighteen-month period expired in June 2009 (Bryden 2009).
12 At the time of writing, the most recent version of this legislation was Bill S-6, which died when Parliament was prorogued in December 2009.

WORKS CITED

Adams, Paul. 2000. Klees Withdrawal Offers Insight into Campaign Financing. *Globe and Mail*, 6 April, A4.

Bédard, Michel. 2007. *Legislative Summary: Bill C-54, an Act to Amend the Canada Elections Act (Accountability with Respect to Loans)*. Library of Parliament. http://www.parl.gc.ca/.

Blais, André, and Elizabeth Gidengil. 1991. *Making Representative Democracy Work: The Views of Canadians*. Toronto: Dundurn Press.

Boudria, Don. 2003. Testimony to the Standing Committee on Procedure and House Affairs, House of Commons, Ottawa, 3 April. http://www.parl.gc.ca/.

Brown, Jim. 2003. Rock Won't Seek Leadership. *Vancouver Sun*, 15 January, A4.
Bryden Joan. 2006. Donation Limits on Leadership Candidates Went too Far, Law Architect Admits. *Canadian Press*, 13 September.
–. 2009. Tories to Turn Off Taps on Political Loans. *Canadian Press*, 11 March.
Bryden, Joan, and Alexandra Panetta. 2006. Volpe Returns Controversial Donations but Corruption Cloud Lingers. *Canadian Press*, 1 June.
Campion-Smith, Bruce. 2005. Stronach Biggest Spender in Bid for Party Leadership. *Toronto Star*, 20 August, A12.
Canada. RCERPF (Royal Commission on Electoral Reform and Party Financing). 1991. *Reforming Electoral Democracy*. Ottawa: Ministry of Supply and Services.
Carty, R. Kenneth. 1989. Is There Political Life after Losing the Race? *Journal of Canadian Studies* 24(2): 116-34.
Carty, R. Kenneth, and William Cross. 2006. Can Stratarchically Organized Parties Be Democratic? Evidence from the Canadian Experience. *Journal of Elections, Public Opinion and Parties* 16(2): 93-114.
Carty, R. Kenneth, William Cross, and Lisa Young. 2000. *Rebuilding Canadian Party Politics*. Vancouver: UBC Press.
Chief Electoral Officer. 2007. *Recommendations of the Chief Electoral Officer of Canada to the House of Commons Standing Committee on Procedure and House Affairs Respecting Specific Issues of Political Financing*. http://www.elections.ca/gen/rep/oth/jan2007/jan2007_e.pdf.
Cheadle, Bruce. 2004. 2.5-M Spending Cap Placed on Conservative Campaigns. *Winnipeg Free Press*, 18 January, A6.
Courtney, John. 1973. *The Selection of National Party Leaders in Canada*. Toronto: Macmillan.
–. 1995. *Do Conventions Matter?* Montreal and Kingston: McGill-Queen's University Press.
Cross, William. 1992. Financing Leadership Campaigns in Canada. *Canadian Parliamentary Review* 15(2): 16-23.
–. 2004. *Political Parties*. Vancouver: UBC Press.
–. 2006. Candidate Nomination in Canadian Political Parties. In *The Canadian General Election of 2006*, ed. Jon Pammett and Christopher Dornan, 171-95. Toronto: Dundurn Press.
Epstein, Leon. 1986. *Political Parties in the American Mold*. Madison: University of Wisconsin Press.
Flanagan, Tom. 2007. *Harper's Team: Behind the Scenes in the Conservative Rise to Power*. Montreal & Kingston: McGill-Queen's University Press.
Hamilton Spectator. 2006. Honey of a Donation. 27 May, A14.
Howe, Paul, and David Northrup. 2000. Strengthening Canadian Democracy: The Views of Canadians. *Policy Matters* 1: 5.
Katz, Richard, and Peter Mair. 1995. Changing Models of Party Organization and Party Democracy: The Emergence of the Cartel Party. *Party Politics* 1(1): 5-28.
Kitchener-Waterloo Record. 2004. Martin Surplus Wipes Out Liberal Debt. 19 January, A3.
McGregor, Glen. 2010. Leadership Aspirants Miss Debt Deadlines. *Montreal Gazette*, 5 January, A8.

Poguntke, Thomas, and Paul Webb. 2005. *The Presidentialization of Politics: A Comparative Study of Modern Democracies*. Oxford: Oxford University Press.

Stanbury, William. 1986. The Mother's Milk of Politics: Political Contributions to Federal Parties in Canada, 1974-1984. *Canadian Journal of Political Science* 19(3): 795-821.

Taber, Jane. 2006. A Summer of Backyard Party Politics. *Globe and Mail*, 27 June, A5.

van Biezen, Ingrid. 2004. Political Parties as Public Utilities. *Party Politics* 10: 701-22.

Young, Lisa, and William Cross. 2002a. The Rise of Plebiscitary Democracy in Canadian Political Parties. *Party Politics* 8(6): 673-99.

–. 2002b. Incentives to Membership in Canadian Political Parties. *Political Research Quarterly* 55(3): 547-69.

9

Lessons from the American Campaign Finance Reform Experience

ROBERT G. BOATRIGHT

Many scholars have noted that the United States and Canada have undertaken overhauls of their campaign finance laws at similar times, in response to similar crises. Yet, American politics for the past three decades has been characterized by attempts by politicians and political organizations to circumvent existing laws, whereas there is less evidence of such deliberate attempts in Canada. This has been characterized by some as evidence of differences between the two nations' political cultures (see Lipset 1991; Wilcox 2005). Similarly, former prime minister Joe Clark (2004, 400) has observed, in reference to the most recent Canadian campaign finance legislation, that "Canada has a new policy because the United States has an old problem." In Clark's view, Canada has few of the campaign finance troubles of the United States, but changes in American law provided the Chrétien government a convenient means of signalling that it cared about reform despite that American-style legislative changes provided an imperfect fit to the regime's problems.

Whatever the impulses behind the two nations' campaign finance reform movements, it does seem evident that Canadian campaign finance problems have not reached the scale of American problems, in large part simply because the sums of money spent in American elections in the 2000s dwarf the sums spent in Canadian elections. Whether this is cultural, institutional, or a consequence of the two nations' prior campaign finance regimes, the rapid pace of adaptation in the United States to the Bipartisan Campaign

Reform Act (BCRA) of 2002 provides one with an opportunity to ask two questions. First, are politicians, parties, and organized interests responding to Canada's new campaign finance laws in the way that they have in the United States? And second, do such responses accord with the motives of reformers, or do they amount to a circumvention of the law?

In the first post-BCRA elections, ongoing American groups reduced their contributions to the parties and their advertising expenditures, and shifted their resources toward "ground war" tactics. Changes in campaign finance law certainly have something to do with this change, but there is ample evidence that the enactment of BCRA merely pushed groups in a direction they were already headed. The polarization of the electorate during the Bush presidency and groups' analysis of what was effective precipitated a shift in group tactics from persuasion to mobilization. This shift coincided with the enactment of BCRA. Any analysis of the American case is complicated by unique features of the elections of the past decade, just as one might expect an analysis of Canadian elections to be complicated by the resurgence of the Conservative Party. Thus, a major task in any comparison of the two nations' experience with campaign finance reform is to separate immediate political events, legal changes, and ongoing developments in political strategy from each other.

To separate these factors, I first consider the past three decades' worth of campaign finance practices and law in the United States, and the fit between American and Canadian theories of the role of money in politics. I then turn to consideration of the consequences of BCRA, with particular attention, given the content of the 2003 reforms to Canadian law, to adaptations by business groups and labour unions to the limitations on soft money contributions and issue advocacy. I close with some comments on ways in which the culture and institutions of the two nations have led to different responses to reform. I focus here primarily on adaptations by organized interests and less on the adaptations of parties, in part because the adaptations of parties are easier to identify – one can measure their adaptations to a large extent simply by measuring their overall funding before and after BCRA – and in part because the verdict on Canadian campaign finance seems to be that, like the American parties, Canadian parties have not suffered major financial reversals (Cross 2004, 151-54). In addition, the public funding provisions of the Canadian bill are likely to further insulate parties from financial reversals, should they remain in place. Interest group adaptations are less predictable than those of the parties. Although American interest groups tend to be better financed and more involved in elections than their Canadian counterparts, there is potential for their strategies to be adopted in Canada.

A Brief History of American Campaign Finance Reform

Before the early 1970s, the United States had a patchwork of campaign finance regulations, as befit a system that was largely dominated by political parties and political patronage. At various times in the first half of the twentieth century, laws were passed requiring candidates to report receipts and expenditures, and prohibiting banks, corporations, and labour unions from donating directly to candidates, but there was no individual law establishing a set of campaign finance rules (Corrado 1997, 30-31). During the late 1940s, the American Federation of Labor responded to these restrictions by forming the first political action committee (PAC); several peak business organizations followed suit in the 1960s. A PAC can solicit voluntary contributions from individual employees of a corporation or members of a union and then contribute from these funds to candidates for office.

The 1974 Federal Election Campaign Act (FECA) amendments established limits on the amount of money individuals can contribute to politicians ($1,000 per election cycle), political parties ($20,000 per cycle), PACs ($5,000), and in sum ($25,000), and they established limits on the amount of money a PAC can contribute to a candidate ($5,000) or a party ($15,000), although there is no aggregate limit on what PACs can contribute.[1] The original version of FECA (passed in 1971) also established limits on candidate spending and on contributions by a candidate to his or her own campaign. These candidate spending limits were subsequently overruled by the Supreme Court in the *Buckley v. Valeo* decision (424 US 1 (1976)), which established candidate spending as a freedom of speech issue. Another bill of that era, the Revenue Act of 1971, created a system of voluntary public funding and spending caps for presidential candidates.

FECA also established an enforcement body, the Federal Election Commission (FEC) to monitor campaign finance practices. The FEC is a bipartisan organization appointed by Congress, with three Democratic members and three Republican members; the FEC budget is set by Congress. In its first major decision, the SUN-PAC decision (FEC 1975-23), the FEC ruled that connected PACs – that is, PACs run by a corporation or a labour union – could have their overhead expenses paid for by their parent organization (Sorauf 1997, 130-33). FECA and the SUN PAC decision thus gave the imprimatur to PACs, and by 1980 the number of PACs had grown to 2,551, up from 608 in 1974 (Ornstein, Mann, and Malbin 2002, 106). The number of

PACs continued to grow, albeit at a slower pace, until it reached over 4,000 by the early 1990s.

According to most analyses, the reforms associated with FECA did contain political spending during the late 1970s and early 1980s (Sorauf 1994, 230-35). Although the pace of candidate and party spending may have been held in check, however, FECA was widely criticized for the proliferation of PACs and was often held responsible for the increasing security of incumbent members of Congress. Despite the fact that no individual business organization could plausibly claim credit for ensuring the election or re-election of a member of Congress on the basis of its direct contributions, many critics argued that office-holders were now beholden to business PACs in general (see, for example, Sorauf 1997, 125). Despite the perception that business groups would, on average, favour Republican candidates, Democratic House members reaped the majority of corporate PAC contributions in all but one election cycle between 1978 and 1994 (inclusive; Ornstein, Mann, and Malbin 2002, 107-9). The chairman of the Democratic Congressional Campaign Committee (DCCC) during the 1980s, Tony Coelho, is often credited with having convinced business PACs that the Democrats would be the majority party for the foreseeable future and that PAC contributions would ensure continued access to congressional leaders (Jackson 1988, 82-87).

During the 1990s, however, three noteworthy practices began to undermine the FECA regime. First, beginning in 1996, both parties began to solicit soft money – unlimited contributions from individuals, corporations, or unions to the parties. Soft money could not be used to directly advocate for the election of a candidate, but it could be used to air advertisements that discussed issues of concern to the parties and could be used for get-out-the-vote drives and other expenses that stopped short of direct advocacy (Malbin 2003b, 5-6).[2] In 1996, the six party campaign committees raised and spent $262 million in soft money, and this amount nearly doubled again in 2000, with the parties raising and spending a total of $495 million in soft money (ibid.). Second, organized interests also began to undertake extensive issue advocacy campaigns. The American Federation of Labor and Congress of Industrial Organizations (AFL-CIO) spent an estimated $35 million in treasury funds on issue advocacy during the 1996 election, airing as much as $1 million worth of television advertisements in the districts of some individual Republican House members (Dark 1999, 184-86). These advertisements did not explicitly direct viewers to vote for or against a candidate, but they often described the representative's voting record in harsh terms and closed with an exhortation to listeners to telephone the representative and tell him how they felt about his voting record. Other organizations, including groups closely tied to the insurance and pharmaceutical industries, ran their own multi-million-dollar issue advocacy campaigns during the 1998, 2000, and 2002 election cycles (Baker and Magleby 2002; Magleby and Tanner 2004). In short, the distinction between issue advocacy and express advocacy for a candidate's election had collapsed. And third, beginning in 1996, presidential candidates began to seriously consider rejecting public funding and the corresponding spending limits; Republican candidate Steve Forbes rejected public funds in 1996 and 2000, Republican nominee George W. Bush rejected them in 2000 and 2004, and Democratic candidate Howard Dean and eventual Democratic nominee John F. Kerry rejected them in 2004. By 2008, it was apparent that no serious primary campaign could be run using matching funds, and Barack Obama declined public funds in the general election as well. These decisions removed the upper limits on candidate spending during the primary and increased the importance of early fundraising in presidential campaigns.

The set of campaign reforms championed by senators John McCain and Russell Feingold, which eventually became BCRA, addressed the first two of these problems. BCRA prohibited soft money contributions entirely at the federal level. It also prohibited groups that accept corporate or labour funds (a category that includes most advocacy groups as well) from airing radio or television advertisements that name a candidate during the thirty days preceding a primary election or the sixty days preceding a general election. In addition to these two major components, BCRA doubled the amount of money individuals can give to candidates or parties, as well as the aggregate amount individuals can give, and indexed that amount to inflation. It left the limits on PAC contributions unchanged. Despite rhetoric to the contrary, there is little evidence to suggest that the authors of BCRA believed that the bill would limit overall spending, would decrease the electoral advantage of incumbents, or would eliminate large donors from politics. Given concern over the threat of quid pro quo corruption, real or implied, in soft money contributions, one aim of BCRA was simply to remove the potential for large, unregulated contributions to the parties; another was to eliminate the possibility that individual organized interests could sway election results through thinly veiled advocacy campaigns. BCRA, then, was largely intended to put campaigns back on the footing they had been on during the 1970s and 1980s. The law has since been weakened substantially by the Supreme Court; although the court upheld the core of the decision in its *McConnell v. FEC [Federal Election Commission]* ruling, it overturned the act's provisions concerning self-financed candidates in the 2008 *Davis v. FEC* decision, it weakened the act's electioneering restrictions in the 2006 *FEC v. Wisconsin Right to Life, Inc.*, and it struck down the electioneering restrictions entirely, along with previously established prohibitions on express advocacy by corporations, in its 2010 *Citizens United v. FEC* decision.[3]

Canada and the United States: Theoretical Paradigms

Perhaps the best-known paradigm used to assess American campaign finance is the hydraulic theory. In this theory, money, like water, will continue to seep into the political system. Reforms can change the direction that the money takes, but money will eventually seep back into the system as political actors identify and exploit loopholes in the law. Arguments in favour of this theory range from those of John McCain himself – who has argued that campaign finance reforms are likely to be necessary every decade or two but that they are still worthwhile – to those of libertarian critics of BCRA, who have argued that the best means of addressing money in politics is to provide clear channels for it to take, and then to try to maximize transparency and provide voters with the tools to accurately observe the flow of money into the system (see, for example, Smith 2001, 220-25). It is worth noting that this goal of transparency can easily be separated from arguments for or against any particular type of regulation, and that reform proponents have also often sought to strengthen disclosure requirements. Transparency has, however, been a key part of the arguments made by BCRA opponents.

A second paradigm is what one might call the push-pull distinction (see Boatright et al. 2003; Boatright et al. 2006). In contrast to the hydraulic theory, this paradigm distinguishes between money that is "pushed" into the system by partisan or ideologically charged individuals or groups and money that is "pulled" into the system by rent-seeking politicians. This distinction roughly parallels the distinction often made between influence-seeking and access-seeking groups in politics. This perspective also seems to grant greater strength to the McCain-Feingold reforms; if a percentage of the soft money raised by the parties was money that politicians coaxed out of unwilling donors, one could have expected BCRA to reduce the amount of money spent on politics, even while it permitted donors fired up by the high stakes of the election to find alternate channels for their money. Pushed money, in this argument, will find a way into the system, but politicians will find it more difficult to pull money into the system.

A third paradigm worthy of consideration is the "single-minded seeker of re-election" paradigm, generally associated with the work of David Mayhew (1975). Given that members of Congress are ultimately the authors of campaign finance laws, it is arguable that Congress is unlikely to take actions that will decrease the security of its own members. For instance, many have described BCRA as an "incumbent protection act" because of its restrictions on issue advocacy and its (since overturned) provisions penalizing self-financing candidates, the vast majority of whom are non-incumbents (see Campbell 2003; Steen 2003). Some analysts have gone so far as to describe BCRA exclusively in terms of partisan self-interest (see Samples 2006).

These different paradigms are worth noting in this context for two reasons. First, given that a major intention of both the American and Canadian campaign finance reforms has been to limit the role of corporations and labour unions in funding campaigns, it is worth asking about these groups' motives – do they seek to push their money into political campaigns, or is their money pulled into campaigns by politicians? If, as I argue below, their money is largely pulled in both systems, restricting their contributions may reduce the overall amount of money in the system without harming the effectiveness of these groups in politics. And second, given that the adaptations of both group types are largely what one might call extra-legal – by which I mean not against the law but largely outside the scope of past or present campaign finance law – it becomes difficult to argue that these groups' adaptations were necessarily unforeseen consequences of the law. Rather, they were part of an ongoing development by such groups in how they engage in political discourse with their members and the public.

Noticeably absent from the paradigms of American campaign finance outlined above, though, is any sort of notion of group restraint. That is, it is assumed that groups, candidates, and parties will aggressively test the limits of the law. When comparing the United States and Canada, this assumption provides a test of the chicken-or-the-egg question that dominates so many comparative studies of the two nations: If Canadian political actors do not respond as Americans have, is this a consequence of institutional differences between the two systems or of cultural differences between the two nations? And moreover, are cultural differences a consequence of institutional differences, or a cause? Some Canadian groups, most notably the National Citizens' Coalition, have pushed the limits of Canadian campaign finance law, but the absence of any broadly based group challenge to new Canadian party financing laws (of the type that unified the *McConnell* plaintiffs) provides some evidence that Canadian groups have been more quiescent about reform than have Americans.

Institutional Differences
The most evident institutional difference relevant to campaign finance reform is that of the political system itself: Canada's is party based, whereas the US's is far more candidate-centred. It is true that the larger American interest groups have increasingly sought to aid their favoured parties, but to the extent that most groups have wielded clout over legislators, it has been because the parties could not take their support for granted. Even in the highly partisan elections of the past decade, trade associations have actively sought out Democrats to support, liberal advocacy groups such as the Sierra Club and Planned Parenthood have supported Republicans in general elections and primaries, and conservative advocacy groups such as the National Rifle Association have similarly supported Democrats in numerous instances. The ability of groups to work to cultivate cross-partisan support for their issues has been an integral feature of their appeals to voters and candidates. In the Canadian system, the inability of candidates to break with their party leadership while still remaining party members in good standing certainly limits the influence of organized interests in many ridings, particularly those where there are contested nomination campaigns.

A second important institutional difference is that Canadian elections have historically been called by the governing party, whereas American elections occur on a regular schedule (though Canada's Conservative government passed legislation in 2007 establishing fixed election dates). Cross (2004, 123-24) contends that this is one reason why there is a permanent class of campaign professionals in the United States yet there is none in Canada. Similarly, American interest groups maintain permanent electoral wings and consistently plan election strategies and solicit political contributions. Absent the ability to plan for an election, Canadian interest groups would seem less able to engage in election-oriented mobilization or issue advocacy efforts. The distinction made in BCRA between electioneering and pure issue advocacy is based on calendar dates that all involved understand – groups know well in advance when the sixty-day window before the general election will kick in, and they are able to develop strategies that move from television and radio advertising to other types of communications well in advance of elections. The inability of Canadian groups to exercise such foresight would appear to have three major consequences:

(1) groups cannot develop long-range electoral strategies; (2) groups may be in the awkward position of having to rapidly shift their strategies should they be surprised by a writ of election; and (3) groups with close connections to the majority party may garner inside information about an impending election and have an advantage over other groups.

Cultural Differences
The basic cultural distinctions between Canadian and American politics, as described by commentators such as Lipset (1991) need little elaboration. These may well manifest themselves in a willingness on the part of Canadian groups to follow the spirit (and not just the letter) of the law, to pursue their political goals through the bureaucracy and the cabinet rather than through elections (Presthus 1973). These cultural differences may also manifest themselves in agreement by all parties on the merit of the ideas behind the law, and in efforts to call attention to loopholes before they become integral features of campaign financing. As the description below shows, American parties and groups have done none of these things.

A second important difference, which bridges the gap between cultural and institutional characteristics of the Canadian system, is the breakdown of contributions from corporations and labour unions. The relationship between the Canadian Labour Congress and the NDP is much more of a patron-client relationship than has been the case for the AFL-CIO, or any of its member unions, and the Democrats in the United States. Corporations, in addition, are much less partisan in their giving in Canada than in the United States. This appears to be true not just with contributions to the parties but also with independent expenditures (see Young and Everitt 2004, 106-8). These breakdowns indicate that although the evolution in interest-group strategies in the United States has been driven largely by the competition between organized labour and peak business associations, the fact that this adversarial relationship is not reinforced by the parties in Canada may mean that political strategies in Canada should not develop in the same manner as those of the United States.

A related issue is the lack of correspondence between American and Canadian interest groups. Of the major contributors to the Canadian parties listed by Cross (2004, 149), only one (the United Steelworkers) exists under the same name in the United States. Of the thirty-three interest groups listed by Young and Everitt (2004, 108) that were active in the 2000 election, *none* is a formal affiliate of American organized interests. There are, to be certain, many organizations in each country that can be closely matched to those of the other, but one should not expect sharing of explicit technological or strategic details of any political activity. In many cases, this is because Canadian parties fulfill the functions that American groups might fulfill. To cite one example, Cross notes that the increasing importance of computer-generated lists in contacting and mobilizing voters may well centralize the activities of the parties in Canada; in the United States, such lists have facilitated the centralization and coordination of interest group activities as well.

Hence, even if Canadian groups wished to adopt American-style activities, it is not clear that they can do so for organizational or financial reasons. Of the groups Young and Everitt discuss, very few seem to be organized in such a way that they have either the ability or the will to engage in a national campaign, or are able to direct their resources toward competitive ridings in the manner that the parties do. Although American interest groups have made credible claims that their issue advocacy efforts influenced election results, there is little evidence of similar successes in Canada. It is, for instance, possible that advocacy groups could seek to develop comprehensive voter lists, but the parties already have such lists and cannot share them. As I note below, two group types that may resemble Americans in their adaptations are organized labour and (potentially) conservative advocacy groups.

These exceptions aside, however, the American situation presents a case study of the sort of guidance Canadian groups might seek in attempting to maximize their electoral clout, but it is equally likely to provide a cautionary tale to Canadians of the sort of outcomes that have been averted through the more extensive contribution limits and electioneering restrictions put in place through the new Canadian finance regime.

Adaptations to BCRA in 2004 and Beyond

Going into the 2004 election, Democratic elites fully expected President Bush to forego matching funds during the Republican primary season, and they expected that the increased limits for individual donors would help Bush substantially. Democrats did not expect that their nominee would be able to forgo matching funds as well, and they therefore expected that their candidates would spend all their money against each other. They thus anticipated two immediate consequences from BCRA. First, they expected that Bush, with no primary opponent, would have the luxury of spending tens of millions of dollars on unanswered advertisements attacking the Democrats' de facto nominee.[4] Meanwhile, the absence of soft money would prevent the

Democratic Party from mounting an effective response to Bush during this bridge period between the end of primary competition and the convention (after their conventions, both presidential nominees receive an equivalent grant for campaign expenses). Second, they expected that the liberal groups that had spent significant sums of money on issue advocacy during the 1996 and 2000 elections would similarly be incapable of providing help during election season. Democrats, then, expected Bush to be among the greatest beneficiaries of the new law. Their expectations shaped the political strategies of parties and interest groups long before the 2004 campaign actually began.

Political Parties
Fundraising figures from the past four American elections make it difficult to argue that either party was harmed by BCRA. Figure 9.1 shows fundraising by all six party campaign committees over the period from 2000 to 2008. At the presidential level, hard money fundraising by both parties surpassed their hard and soft money fundraising levels of 2000 (Corrado 2006). At the congressional level, fundraising by each of the four party committees was down slightly from 2002, but the Democratic committees more than doubled their hard money fundraising from previous cycles, and the spending ratio between the parties in the House and Senate was not dramatically different from what it had been in 2000 or 2002.

The surprising fundraising numbers at the presidential level no doubt bear some relation to the close, and highly contentious, 2004 election, but they also show the resilience of the parties, and they bear testament in particular to the increased emphasis on grassroots fundraising by the Democratic National Committee (DNC). Fundraising at the congressional level also may be influenced by context; because it was evident throughout the year that the presidential election would be close and costly, the presidential campaign committees may have absorbed money that might otherwise have gone to the congressional committees. In addition, few political elites believed that it was likely that the Democratic Party could gain a majority in either the House or the Senate, so there may have been less of an incentive for donors to give to the parties than there had been in 2000 or 2002. In 2006, with Republican majorities looking more tenuous in both chambers, Democratic committee receipts increased almost 50 percent, while Republican receipts remained constant. Congressional party receipts in 2008 continue this trend. The DNC's fundraising fell off substantially in 2008, but this was clearly a consequence of Barack Obama's decision to raise his own

FIGURE 9.1

Party campaign committee fundraising, 2000-08

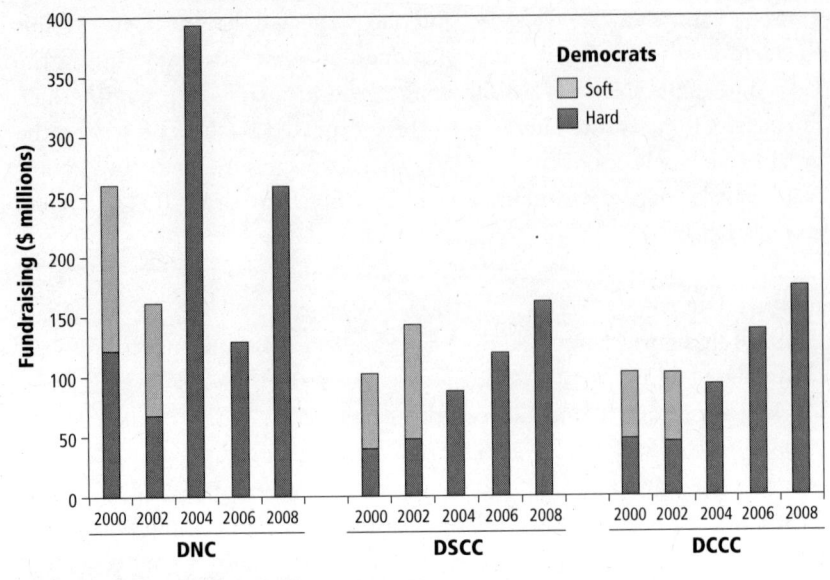

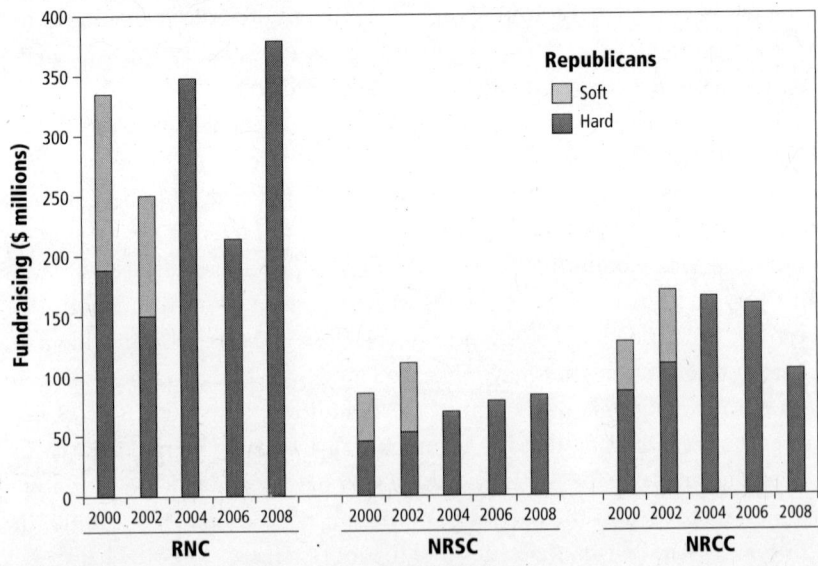

DNC – Democratic National Committee, DSCC – Democratic Senatorial Campaign Committee, DCCC – Democratic Congressional Campaign Committee, RNC – Republican National Committee, NRSC – National Republican Senatorial Committee, NRCC – National Republican Congressional Committee
Source: Federal Election Commission.

money in the general election – declining the flat public funding grant accepted by John McCain and by all previous major party nominees since the passage of FECA. Those who wished to support Obama could give either to Obama or to the DNC, whereas those who wished to support McCain could give only to the Republican National Committee.

Early in the 2004 election season, several prominent Democratic elites began to explore the development of new "527" organizations – so named because of the section of the US tax code under which they were organized. These organizations would seek to offset the Bush advantage during the summer of 2004. Although PACs and political parties are technically 527 organizations, a 527 organization that is not a PAC and is thus not subject to contribution limits can legally be formed. Many ongoing interest groups had 527 accounts prior to 2004, but in 2004, several new 527 organizations were formed that had no connection to established groups. The largest of these organizations tended to be identified not by their issues of concern (as would be the case for a traditional advocacy group) but by their political function. Two large organizations, America Coming Together (ACT) and the Media Fund, were established by prominent Democratic activists, and an umbrella fundraising group, the Joint Victory Campaign, was established to channel contributions to these two groups. ACT and the Media Fund raised and spent a combined $139 million in 2004. The Media Fund was primarily a vehicle for advertising, whereas ACT engaged in voter registration and get-out-the-vote work, following the strategy employed by the AFL-CIO in the past several elections. These groups benefited from several large individual contributions – most notably, those of financier George Soros and insurance company owner Peter Lewis. Yet, they also received much of their start-up money from labour unions. Labour contributed a total of $92.0 million to 527 groups, as compared with $54.8 million in 2002 (Boatright et al. 2006). Corporations gave $69.1 million to 527 groups, as compared with $16.3 million in 2002. As large as these numbers may appear, they did not replace the soft money that labour and corporations had previously given, and much of it stayed close to the donors; for instance, $63.1 million of the money contributed went to the 527 funds of the two largest labour unions, the Service Employees International Union and American Federation of State, County and Municipal Employees, not to the new quasi-party 527 organizations.

To those who argue that BCRA has not worked, 527 organizations clearly constitute compelling evidence. However, they were not *prima facie* evidence that BCRA merely directed political money in a new, and potentially less transparent, direction. These groups focused primarily on the presidential election, and FEC decisions after the election made it clear that many of their activities were illegal. Their activities were premised in part on the accurate assessment that the FEC would not act quickly enough to shut down these groups. Although the FEC did decide after the 2004 election to penalize many 527 organizations, they remained active in 2006 and 2008, albeit to a lesser degree than in 2004. This declining role may have been a partial consequence of the 2008 Democratic nominee not needing 527 support as badly as groups believed Kerry would in 2004.

Furthermore, there was a marked change in the types of corporations that donated money – large, publicly traded companies had comprised the bulk of soft money donors, whereas the major corporate 527 donors tended to be smaller, privately held companies (see Boatright et al. 2006). If one assumes that privately held corporations have more freedom to give for ideological purposes than do publicly traded ones, it becomes evident that for corporations, pushed money remained in the system whereas pulled money largely disappeared, to be redirected into other, possibly non-political, activities.

It seems doubtful that anything like 527 groups could develop as a response to the 2003 reforms to Canadian law. It is therefore worth investigating other types of adaptations unions and business groups made following BCRA. For the most part, these adaptations represent an extension of strategies both types of groups had pioneered in 1996, 1998, and 2000. For both labour unions and business groups, member communication had been growing in importance over the past several election cycles, and it had become obvious by 2004 that these activities made sense even apart from the fact that they were advantageous under BCRA.

Organized Labour
From 1996 through 2002, organized labour had been both a major soft money contributor to the Democratic Party and a major purchaser of issue advocacy advertisements. Yet, during this period, views within the AFL-CIO about these two practices had evolved significantly. First, within the organization, there was a growing sense that union support for the Democratic Party had not prevented the party from enacting legislation harmful to unions. Second, internal polls indicated that the AFL-CIO had little success in mobilizing non-union members to vote for pro-labour candidates in 1996 or 1998, but the organization's member contacting program did appear to have swayed union members to vote for Democrats.[5] Accordingly, the AFL-CIO began to invest in repeated member contacts, using paid and

volunteer organizers to discuss politics with members. The union began to build up an extensive database on members, including members' issues of concern and voting histories. The AFL-CIO could then concentrate on those less likely to vote, and it could approach these individuals with political information relevant to their lives and concerns. By 2000, 26 percent of voters were from union households, up from 19 percent in 1992 (Rosenthal 2002, 552).

In 2002, the AFL-CIO had ceased all of its political advertising by early September (when the sixty-day window would have taken effect had BCRA been law). In 2004, it aired only one-third the number of ads it had run in 2000, and it sought instead to emphasize member communication. In addition, the political strategy of America Coming Together, which received ample union funding, was basically the AFL-CIO strategy applied to non-union members. Although ACT suspended operations in early 2005, the individual unions have continued to follow the same basic strategy since then, albeit through their own 527s rather than through outside groups. Union 527s were among the biggest advertisers, as well, in 2008, although they focused their attention more on congressional races than on the presidential race.

These developments were likely encouraged by BCRA but were not clearly caused by it. Another development that can be read as a response to BCRA is the creation of Working America, a type of non-union union within the AFL-CIO, which anyone can join free of charge. Membership in Working America does not confer voting rights within the union or any other benefits, but it does provide the AFL-CIO with a larger number of individuals whom it can contact while still having these contacts serve as membership communications. And, perhaps of particular importance, the AFL-CIO can solicit contributions to its PAC from these individuals, who will have no competing union allegiances for their money. This is no substitute for organizing new dues-paying union members, but Working America does show the priority unions have placed on member communication in the post-BCRA environment.

Business Groups

Leaders of peak business organizations tend to frame most business spending in elections in reactive terms. For instance, several major business groups formed The Coalition: Americans Working for Real Change to run advertisements responding to the AFL-CIO's electioneering activities in 1996. Industry-supported organizations with vague names such as Citizens for Better Medicare, the United Seniors Association, and Americans for Job Security also engaged in late issue advocacy activity, choosing districts where liberal groups had been active (Baker and Magleby 2002; Magleby and Tanner 2004).

Soft money spending by business groups was not necessarily a reaction to other groups' activities, but it was often pulled money. As of early 2001, many major companies had adopted policies against giving soft money (Mullins and Mitchell 2001); others had announced their support for a soft money ban but continued to make soft money donations. In 2004, many of the same corporations declined to donate to 527s (Cummings 2004). To a degree, PACs came to replace some of the soft money corporations had given to the parties, but the increase in total PAC spending did not dramatically outstrip the secular increase in PAC fundraising that had been going on for decades, nor does the increase seem surprising given the heightened public interest in the 2004 elections.

The major shift since 2004 in business group strategy was business's increased focus on communication with employees. In 1998 and 2000, according to many in the business community, labour successfully outmobilized business, and in those elections, business groups' strategies of issue advocacy and soft money contributions were not an adequate counterweight to labour's efforts. As a result, the larger trade groups, such as the Business-Industry PAC, the Chamber of Commerce, and the National Federation of Independent Business, sought to expand their own grassroots efforts. These groups, as well as several other industry-specific groups, have sought to use the Internet to provide customized candidate information to businesses, and they have trained business owners in how they can encourage workers to vote and provide information to workers without expressly advocating for any candidate.

There were some adverse consequences for business groups from BCRA, to be certain. The diminished role of industry-sponsored front groups following the passage of BCRA no doubt hurt some major industries. For the most part, however, business groups' strategies likely would have been little different (albeit more costly to individual companies) had BCRA not been in place in 2004. Spending by business groups on congressional races in 2008 also has shown that corporate groups can still raise enough money to communicate with the public, particularly when they are in the role of defending against attacks by labour. As was the case for organized labour, BCRA at most pushed business groups in a direction that they either would have or should have (in the view of trade association leaders) taken anyway. It is difficult, then, to expect a radical change in business advocacy now that the Supreme Court has lifted the electioneering restrictions; the restrictions were doing little to restrain the "pushed" spending of groups.

Summary

Many recent analyses of BCRA have claimed that it has had little influence on campaign fundraising, and the large sums spent in the 2008 presidential and congressional races provide some evidence of this. BCRA has, however, changed the priorities of many groups. In regards to parties, business organizations, and labour groups, then, BCRA had three major consequences.

First, the soft money prohibitions do not appear to have harmed the ability of either party to raise money, but they have arguably forced the parties to be more aggressive in their fundraising, particularly in their efforts to procure small contributions. Because the Republican Party has traditionally raised more hard money than the Democratic Party and because of the demonstrated skill of President Bush at raising hard money, it had been expected that the Democratic Party might be at a disadvantage. This has not been the case so far, but it may be so in future elections. The Democrats have outperformed expectations since 2004 in part because of antipathy toward President Bush among their supporters and in part because of the small donor databases they had built in 2002. The increase has occurred primarily in contributions from individuals – particularly small donations – not in PAC contributions. However, anticipation on the part of party elites that the Democratic Party would have fundraising difficulties led to the formation of several quasi-party organizations. It remains to be seen whether these groups will persist in future elections, but at the moment it appears that their fundraising successes in 2004 will be hard to match in the future. These groups did, however, provide an opportunity for groups and individuals who had pushed their money into the system in the past in the form of issue advocacy expenditures or soft money contributions to maintain or increase their political spending.

Second, there has been no overall decline in issue advocacy, despite the restrictions (Boatright et al. 2006; Franz, Rivlin, and Goldstein 2006). There has been a change, however, in the types of groups that aired advertisements; traditional and familiar issue-based groups advertised less, with new 527 groups, which often had names unfamiliar to the public, taking their place. It is difficult to know whether this would have been the case in elections less heated than that of 2004, although several ephemeral groups formed to air advertisements in the 2008 presidential primary and general election campaigns. Even had the Supreme Court not struck down the restrictions, they would have gradually been rendered obsolete. They applied only to television and radio advertising; Internet-based communications will likely be harder to regulate. BCRA's restrictions were narrowly tailored to apply to advertisements that "refer to a clearly identified candidate" and were targeted at that candidate's constituency or potential constituency. These limitations were designed to protect "pure" issue advocacy, but it is possible for groups to run advertisements discussing issues that are of importance in an election that do not mention candidates or parties. In 2004 and 2006, some groups simply responded by running advertisements earlier. In elections where the contestants are well defined early or where particular themes (such as "change") are strongly associated with one party or candidate, such ads can still be effective. This may all be a moot point following the *Citizens United* decision, but the discussion above of electioneering shows that groups can adjust their advocacy work to new regulations without also increasing their spending; the same will be true now that electioneering has been deregulated.

Third, there has been a marked increase since 2004 in the use of "ground war" tactics – voter registration drives, get-out-the-vote efforts, and various forms of personal contacting. Interest groups, parties, and candidates have all adopted this micro-targeting approach. For business groups, this has often taken the form of Internet-based workplace communication. For labour unions and liberal advocacy groups, this has taken the form of door-to-door campaigning and extensive volunteer work in swing states. Some of this likely would have happened without BCRA, but BCRA did encourage this development. In 2004, there was little persuasion that could be done, and thus unions chose to focus their efforts on working-class voters in swing state cities while conservative groups sought to mobilize voters in more conservative areas of these same states. This type of strategy may be useful in future elections, as well, but a less polarized United States could severely diminish the value of such tactics. Even by 2008, parties and groups were casting their nets somewhat more broadly in their mobilization efforts, and they will likely continue to expand their focus as technological tools for this sort of targeting develop.

What Canada Can Learn from the American Response to BCRA

The Canadian prohibition on corporate and labour contributions may yet yield similar consequences to those in the United States, but any such changes will be tempered by the smaller role organized interests play in

Canadian campaigns, the more fragmented (and less polarized) politics of Canada, and the institutional differences between the two nations. Let us first consider the broader lessons of BCRA, and then look at their applicability to particular types of groups.

Canadian parties have effectively insulated themselves from adverse consequences by increasing their level of public funding. Regardless of its short-term effects, many American observers have argued that it was good discipline for the parties to be forced to seek new donors – and that the Democrats, in particular, were forced to abandon their reliance on large soft money donors and cultivate new hard money donors. Although some have decried the rise of 527 groups, in the United States it can be argued that it is more ethical for the parties to refrain from directly soliciting corporate or labour contributions, even if corporations and unions continue to push money into the system through other means. In the Canadian case, it seems that the ability of parties to solicit these donations is now effectively curtailed, but the ability of companies to push money into the system is now more effectively limited than in the United States as well.

Second, organized interests, particularly business groups, tend to be happier when they are not "shaken down" by politicians for contributions. The Canadian ban on corporate and labour contributions may prevent the type of influence peddling that it was aimed at, but it would seem that if businesses or unions want to continue to spend money to influence elections, they ought to be able to redirect money that had been given to the parties toward developing methods of communicating with their own members about political issues. If these groups follow the American example, businesses and unions will be able to achieve their electoral goals more effectively while spending a fraction of the money they had spent before.

Third, get-out-the-vote efforts generally seem preferable to contributions or advertising for groups concerned about public benefits. As noted above, the number of persuadable voters can determine the merits of these strategies, yet it seems that in the Canadian case the organizations that have been barred from contributing to the parties are precisely those that, by virtue of their membership, have the best ability to communicate with their members (or employees) and to narrowly target communications, in terms of geography or the issues of importance to these voters.

And fourth, the issue advocacy restrictions in Canada, following the *Harper v. Canada (Attorney General)* decision, were less porous than in the United States even before the *Citizens United* decision. Although American interest groups found numerous ways to circumvent these laws, the broader nature of the Canadian statute (and corresponding lack of free speech absolutism) would appear to effectively eliminate large-scale interest group advertising from campaigns. Because Canadian elections do not occur on a regular schedule, groups also cannot deliberately advertise immediately before the restrictions take effect. Groups can still advertise before an election has been called, but there is less rationale for doing this in Canada than in the United States.

It would be complicated to look for a shift in group finances in the elections following the passage of the 2003 reforms in part because of the lack of a Canadian equivalent to PACs, in part because of the public financing provisions for parties, and in part because many Canadian groups were less active than American groups to begin with. If one is looking for adaptations that resemble those of American groups, there are two possibilities.

First, there is a resemblance between the approaches of organized labour in the two countries, although in Canada, as in the United States, changing tactics may not be entirely caused by reform laws. According to Jansen and Young (2009), during the early 2000s, the Canadian Labour Congress (CLC) had been growing somewhat frustrated with its inability to translate financial support for the NDP into political gains for labour, and this relationship had become one between party and labour elites, with little relevance to the CLC rank and file. Following the enactment of the 2003 reforms (though not necessarily because of it), the CLC began to provide issue information to members that encouraged them to "vote their interest" but did not explicitly endorse any candidate or party. This opens up the possibility that parties other than the NDP may pick up on CLC issues, and it may expose deficiencies in the NDP response to labour's efforts in a way that the two entities' financial relationship does not. For an American parallel, it is important to note Jacobson's contention (1999) that in the 1996 election year, although the AFL-CIO was spending money to help Democratic candidates, it was actually the failure of the Democratic Party to field strong candidates, not the labour effort, that held back Democratic gains in Congress.

The CLC, then, has shown an ability to adapt to, and perhaps even to benefit from, the new regulations. It appears from Jansen and Young's (2009) analysis that the CLC effort may mirror the AFL-CIO's in its features, but it is not necessarily directed toward non-members. The CLC also is hampered by the fact that its main client is a party without a realistic chance of gaining a majority in Parliament. This factor alone may reduce the urgency of the CLC's activities; whereas organized labour in the United

States had a realistic chance of helping to propel the Democrats to the presidency or to a House or Senate majority, the CLC can likely expect little more than to help the NDP gain a large enough number of seats to support a Liberal minority government.

A second potential American-style response, in the wake of the 2006 Conservative victory, might come from the National Citizens' Coalition (NCC) and the constellation of related groups that abetted the rise of the Reform Party in the 1990s. Given Stephen Harper's experience as president of the NCC and the NCC's role in challenging prior campaign finance statutes, one might expect the current Canadian leadership to have some ideological distaste for a finance regime like that set up by the 2003 reforms (despite that both parties agreed on the contours of the law when it was passed and that it arguably benefits the governing party). Harper's December 2008 effort to eliminate public subsidies for parties supports this view. Apart from this, however, Harper's election poses the potential for a greater integration of organized interests into the policy debates of government than has previously been the case. Cross (2004, 9, 156-57) contends that the Canadian Alliance had developed close working relationships with several fiscally conservative groups, including the NCC and the Canadian Taxpayers Federation, and that the Alliance and the NDP sought (separately) to create networks of party-based and interest group-based experts who could help the parties develop long-term goals and strategies. Furthermore, Cross notes that the development and formalization of such networks (in the form of policy foundations) could be beneficial to Canadian democracy. Such developments are arguably taking place in the United States; the development of niche-based 527 groups by the Democrats was in part due to a desire to replicate the organizational structure that Republican Party leaders, think tanks, and conservative interest groups had developed during the 1970s and 1980s. In the wake of a campaign finance bill that would appear to distance the parties from the electorate in Canada, the accident of a former interest group leader's elevation to a party leadership position may accomplish similar goals in Canada.

Conclusions

Despite similarities between the American and Canadian reforms, the reforms had different goals and arose as a response to different political problems. Young (2004) evaluates Canadian campaign finance with regard to four goals: accountability, transparency, integrity, and equity. Presumably these goals also figure into defences of the 2003 reforms. The first three have been introduced into American campaign finance debates as well, but few proponents of BCRA seriously felt the act would equalize campaign funding disparities between candidates or between parties. If one seeks equity, one is bound to advocate public funding or mandatory spending caps and to make efforts to limit interest group advocacy.

Canadian political scientists worry, however, that when the pursuit of equity leads to public financing, it can limit the responsiveness of politicians to the electorate. And when one considers the role of the electorate in campaigns, it is difficult not to also include organized interests, including labour unions and corporations. The governments of both the United States and Canada sought to restrict the political activities of corporations and unions while still preserving the rights of such groups to talk to their members and to allow people who belong to, or are influenced by, these groups to voice their political views. As the above discussion shows, corporations and unions still have the ability to engage in the political process, as they should. The major questions are whether their new activities are more beneficial to democratic politics than were their prior ones (that is, whether member communication is normatively superior to televised appeals or campaign contributions), and whether these new activities are as transparent and measurable as were their prior activities.

There are normative considerations, as well, in the question of whether Canadian interest groups will follow the American model in switching to more sophisticated member communications. Again, the evidence suggests that they can, but it does not suggest that they will. One of the most persuasive arguments American groups made against BCRA was that the parties should not have a monopoly in defining what an election is about. When its major provisions were all in place, BCRA slightly reduced the ability of groups to dictate the content of election campaigns, and in Canada the 2003 reforms and the third-party advertising restrictions clearly do the same. The history of recent Canadian elections demonstrates that Canadian parties already have more power than their American counterparts to decide what an election will be about. In both countries, it is worth more carefully considering the issue of who "owns" elections and who should dictate election content. Many Canadian politicians have warned of the dangers of interest groups usurping the parties' role in defining election issues (see, for example, summaries of campaign finance politics in Jensen 1992; Carty, Cross, and Young 2000, 95; and Young 2004). There is a danger as well, however, in giving groups too little of a role. American reformers may find much to applaud in Canada's campaign finance efforts, but in both the United States and Canada, it remains too easy to demonize organized interests. In both nations, now may be an important time to more fully articulate the role organized interests should have in elections.

NOTES

This chapter is a condensed version of the chapter on US interest groups in my forthcoming book *Interest Groups and Campaign Finance Reform in the United States and Canada* (University of Michigan Press). Thank you to the University of Michigan Press for granting permission for this chapter to appear here; to Lisa Young and William Cross for fielding questions about Canadian campaign finance; and to Michael Malbin, Mark Rozell, and Clyde Wilcox, my coauthors on related work.

1 For a summary of FECA, see Potter (1997); for comparisons of FECA and BCRA, see Currinder (2005) and Malbin (2006a).
2 Soft money as a category had existed since 1980, as detailed by Corrado (1997, 171-73), but the aggregated amount of soft money raised and spent never exceeded $100 million before 1996.
3 The overruled express advocacy prohibitions were initially upheld by the court in its 1990 *Austin v. Michigan Chamber of Commerce* decision.
4 According to many accounts, Bill Clinton was able to do this to Robert Dole in 1996. During that election, however, Clinton did accept matching funds and both parties were able to spend soft money.
5 These comments, as well as information below on union and corporate strategy, are drawn from interviews conducted for the 2003 Boatright, Malbin, Rozell, and Wilcox project (Boatright at al. 2003, 2006).

WORKS CITED

Baker, Anna Nibley, and David B. Magleby. 2002. Interest Groups in the 2000 Congressional Elections. In *The Other Campaign: Soft Money and Issue Advocacy in the 2000 Elections*, ed. David B. Magleby, 51-78. Lanham, MD: Rowman and Littlefield.

Boatright, Robert G., Michael J. Malbin, Mark J. Rozell, Richard Skinner, and Clyde Wilcox. 2003. BCRA's Impact on Interest Groups and Advocacy Organizations. In Malbin 2003a, 43-60.

Boatright, Robert G., Michael J. Malbin, Mark J. Rozell, and Clyde Wilcox. 2006. Interest Groups and Advocacy Organizations after BCRA. In Malbin 2006b, 112-40.

Campbell, James. 2003. The Stagnation of Congressional Elections. In Malbin 2003a, 141-57.

Carty, R. Kenneth, William P. Cross, and Lisa Young. 2000. *Rebuilding Canadian Party Politics*. Vancouver: UBC Press.

Clark, Joe. 2004. What's Right and Wrong with Democracy in Canada. *Election Law Journal* 3: 400-1.

Corrado, Anthony. 1997. Money and Politics: A History of Federal Campaign Finance Law. In Corrado et al. 1997, 25-60.

–. 2006. Party Finance in the Wake of BCRA: An Overview. In Malbin 2006b, 19-37.
Corrado, Anthony, Thomas E. Mann, Daniel R. Ortiz, Trevor Potter, and Frank J. Sorauf. 1997. *Campaign Finance Reform: A Sourcebook*. Washington, DC: Brookings Institution.
Cross, William P. 2004. *Political Parties*. Vancouver: UBC Press.
Cummings, Jeanne. 2004. Companies Pare Political Donations. *Wall Street Journal*, 7 June, A3.
Currinder, Marian. 2005. Campaign Finance: Funding the Presidential and Congressional Elections. In *The Elections of 2004*, ed. Michael Nelson, 108-32. Washington, DC: Congressional Quarterly.
Dark, Taylor E. 1999. *The Unions and the Democrats: An Enduring Alliance*. Ithaca, NY: Cornell University Press.
Franz, Michael M., Joel Rivlin, and Kenneth Goldstein. 2006. Much More of the Same: Television Advertising Pre- and Post-BCRA. In Malbin 2006b, 141-60.
Jackson, Brooks. 1988. *Honest Graft: Big Money and the American Political Process*. New York: Knopf.
Jacobson, Gary C. 1999. The Effect of the AFL-CIO's "Voter Education" Campaign in the 1996 House Elections. *Journal of Politics* 61(1): 185-94.
Jansen, Harold, and Lisa Young. 2009. Solidarity Forever? The NDP, Organized Labour, and the Changing Face of Party Finance in Canada. *Canadian Journal of Political Science* 42: 657-78.
Jensen, Jane. 1992. Innovation and Equity: The Impact of Public Funding. In *Comparative Issues in Party and Election Finance*, ed. F. Leslie Seidle, 110-77. Toronto: Dundurn Press.
Lipset, Seymour Martin. 1991. *Continental Divide: The Values and Institutions of the United States and Canada*. New York: Routledge.
Magleby, David B., and Jonathan W. Tanner. 2004. Interest Group Electioneering in the 2002 Congressional Elections. In *The Last Hurrah? Soft Money and Issue Advocacy in the 2002 Congressional Elections*, ed. David B. Magleby and J. Quin Monson, 63-89. Washington, DC: Brookings Institution.
Malbin, Michael J., ed. 2003a. *Life after Reform: When the Bipartisan Campaign Reform Act Meets Politics*. Lanham, MD: Rowman and Littlefield.
–. 2003b. Thinking about Reform. In Malbin 2003a, 3-20.
–. 2006a. Assessing the Bipartisan Campaign Reform Act. In Malbin 2006b, 1-18.
–, ed. 2006b. *The Election after Reform: Money, Politics, and the Bipartisan Campaign Reform Act*. Lanham, MD: Rowman and Littlefield.
Mayhew, David. 1975. *Congress: The Electoral Connection*. New Haven, CT: Yale University Press.
Mullins, Brody, and Charlie Mitchell. Saying "No" to Soft Money. *National Journal*, 24 March, 870-75.
Ornstein, Norman J., Thomas E. Mann, and Michael J. Malbin. 2002. *Vital Statistics on Congress*. Washington, DC: American Enterprise Institute.
Potter, Trevor. 1997. Where Are We Now? The Current State of Campaign Finance Law. In Corrado et al. 1997, 5-24.

Presthus, Robert. 1973. *Elite Accommodation in Canadian Politics.* Toronto: Cambridge University Press.
Rosenthal, Steven. 2002. Response to Malbin et al. *Election Law Journal* 1: 546-47.
Samples, John. 2006. *The Fallacy of Campaign Finance Reform.* Chicago: University of Chicago Press.
Smith, Bradley A. 2001. *Unfree Speech: The Folly of Campaign Finance Reform.* Princeton, NJ: Princeton University Press.
Sorauf, Frank J. 1994. *Inside Campaign Finance: Myths and Realities.* New Haven, CT: Yale University Press.
–. 1997. Political Action Committees. In Corrado et al. 1997, 121-64.
Steen, Jennifer. 2003. The "Millionaire's Amendment." In Malbin 2003a, 159-74.
Wilcox, Clyde. 2005. Campaign Finance Law Enforcement in Canada and the United States. In *The Delicate Balance between Political Equity and Freedom of Expression: Political Party and Campaign Financing in Canada and the United States,* ed. Steven Griner and Daniel Zovatto, 33-42. Washington, DC: International Idea/Organization of American States.
Young, Lisa. 2004. Regulating Campaign Finance in Canada: Strengths and Weaknesses. *Election Law Journal* 3: 444-62.
Young, Lisa, and Joanna Everitt. 2004. *Advocacy Groups.* Vancouver: UBC Press.

10 Conclusion

HAROLD J. JANSEN AND LISA YOUNG

Although they have been in effect for over six years, we still do not know the full impact of the 2004 reforms to party and election finance in Canada. Under any circumstances, such a significant set of reforms would take some time to alter the behaviour of candidates, parties, and other political actors. These reforms, however, occurred in a period of considerable upheaval in Canada's partisan landscape. The Progressive Conservatives and Canadian Alliance merged to form the new Conservative Party of Canada. This merged party successfully challenged and ended the Liberal Party's domination of party politics. The Liberals struggled to regain their credibility after the sponsorship scandal and are on their third leader since the 2004 party finance regime came into effect. Shortly before the new laws, the New Democrats elected Jack Layton as leader and he helped to reinvigorate a party that had struggled since 1993. Finally, the Green Party's popularity has grown markedly. The net result of this increasingly complicated and newly competitive partisan landscape has been a series of minority governments, starting in 2004. Because of this upheaval, it has been difficult to differentiate between the effect of the reforms and the consequences of an unusually competitive period in Canadian politics.

Nevertheless, the new party finance laws have both shaped and been shaped by these developments. Part of the reason for the Conservatives' success has been their ability to raise money from individual supporters, which has allowed them to thrive in the permanent campaign environment of the last six years. Besides being able to outspend their opponents at election time, the Conservatives have been able to advertise extensively between elections and maintain constant election readiness. The Liberals have been unable to catch up to the Conservatives' advantage in fundraising, and this has had tangible consequences for the party's ability to contest elections. As the only major party to conduct leadership contests under the new rules, the Liberals have been further limited by the restrictive rules governing party leadership fundraising. All of this has had real electoral consequences for the party: the 2008 election campaign marked the first time the Liberals were unable to spend close to the maximum allowed by law (see Figure 5.3). The Green Party's rise to prominence was at least partly motivated by the prospect of the financial rewards under the new system. The continued success of the Bloc Québécois in Quebec is at least partly fuelled by its enriched financial position as a result of the new laws. This has made a majority government remarkably difficult to attain. It is clear that party finance rules have become an important part of the backdrop for this period of Canada's electoral politics.

The Politicization of Party Finance

One of the consequences of this hyper-competitive electoral environment has been that the laws governing party finance have themselves become a battleground for parties trying to maximize their own electoral success and render their competitors less able to compete electorally. This is a break from past practice, when changes to party finance laws typically had agreement from all of the parties in Parliament. The opposition of the Canadian Alliance and Progressive Conservatives to the passage of Bill C-24 in 2003 broke with that practice and arguably opened the door to future unilateral changes to election finance rules. This can be seen with the passage of the Accountability Act in 2006, which lowered the limit on individual donations to $1,000 (adjusted for inflation) from $5,000. The donation provisions of the act had the support of the Conservatives, Bloc, and NDP. Vulnerable on ethics issues in the wake of the sponsorship scandal, the Liberals refused to take a position one way or another. Given the Liberal Party's reliance up to that point on larger donations raised at intimate dinners with the party leader, it was clear that the purpose of the legislation was to financially hamper the former governing party.

The Harper government's attempt to abolish the quarterly allowance to parties in November 2008 took the politicization of party finance to an entirely new level. The government initiated the change without consulting or gaining the support of any of the opposition parties, all of whom would have been significantly affected by the move. The minority government clearly overreached in these attempted changes and misread the opposition's determination to stand them down. The near formation of a coalition government by the opposition parties forced the government to retreat quickly.

The government's retreat on this proposal does not necessarily spell the end of unilateral changes to party finance laws. The idea of eliminating the quarterly allowance remains alive in the media (for example, Flanagan 2009; Milke 2009). Should the Conservatives win a majority, we might well expect to see the quarterly allowance abolished or at least altered in some way. Members of the Conservative government have indicated a desire to revisit the issue of the quarterly allowance under more favourable political conditions (Flanagan and Coletto 2010, 1). The 2004 reforms have made party finance a contentious issue; it appears it will remain so into the near future.

The Ban on Corporate and Union Donations

Even if elements of Canada's party finance regime remain contentious, there appears to be wide acceptance of the idea that corporations and unions should be removed from the political arena as donors. With the Accountability Act, the Conservatives (with the support of the Bloc Québécois and NDP) extended the ban on corporate and union donations to the local level, thus eliminating the last vestige of corporate and union finance in Canada's federal party system. Even in their aborted attempt to alter party finance laws in late 2008, the Conservatives did not try to reinstate them. Given the Liberals' history of scandal, the Conservatives' success with raising money from individual donors, and the NDP's continuing support for the ban on corporate and union donations, it is difficult to envision circumstances where those donations would be allowed.

It is noteworthy that corporations and unions appear to have accepted these restrictions as well. Unions have been content to shift their efforts to third-party advertising outside the writ period and to communicating with their members during campaigns (Jansen and Young 2009). As Boatright notes in Chapter 9, Canada thus far has not experienced the kinds of efforts to circumvent the ban as one finds in the American experience.

In all probability, the Quebec model of *financement populaire* has become the norm in Canadian politics at the federal level for the foreseeable future. It would be impossible to tie the absence of corporate and union contributions to any shifts in policy outcomes, but it is clear that the ban is consistent with prevailing notions of ethics and, if anything, has a modest positive effect on public confidence in the integrity of the electoral system. In the 2008 Canadian Election Study, over three-quarters of the respondents thought the ban on corporate and union donations was a good thing, and only 7 percent of respondents thought that the ban was bad, indicating that this provision enjoys wide public support.[1]

Individual Donations

Given that the ban on corporate and union donations looks to be a relatively permanent feature of the regulatory regime for party finance in Canada, individual donations will remain the only source of private money for political parties for the foreseeable future. The major limitation on individual donations is the $1,100 cap on individual donations to parties. Although this is consistent with the long-standing intention of Canadian election finance law to encourage political parties to seek small donations from large numbers of donors and to prevent parties from being beholden financially to relatively few donors, it is certainly arguable that this limit is unduly restrictive. The low limit can make it difficult for parties to raise the necessary funds to conduct their operations. This is particularly the case for small and newer parties, which typically rely on some larger donations to get started. An overly restrictive limit thus might make the party system less dynamic and responsive.

Although the ban on corporate and union donations might be argued to increase voter confidence in the integrity of the electoral process, it is not clear that a modest increase to the individual donation limit would create the impression that Canadian political parties are beholden to the wealthy. Indeed, were a future government to decide to eliminate or curtail the public financing of parties, such an increase might be necessary to ensure that political parties have the necessary funds to carry out their roles in the political system (Flanagan and Coletto 2010).

The Necessity of State Funding

If the primacy of individual donations is now a well-established component of Canada's election finance regime, the same cannot be said of public financing, particularly the quarterly allowance instituted in 2004. Although accepting the arguments Justin Fisher and Richard Katz offer in Chapters 2 and 4, respectively, of the potentially corrosive impact of state subsidies on political parties as agents of democracy, we argue that a wholesale elimination of the quarterly allowance would be detrimental to electoral democracy in Canada. Electoral competition in Canada requires vibrant political parties to structure debates, recruit political elites, and offer competing policy directions. A majority government that is not held accountable by similarly vibrant opposition parties is an undesirable outcome for Canadians. In the absence of contributions from unions or corporations, Canadian parties are limited in their ability to raise adequate funds to staff their extra-parliamentary organizations, conduct leadership contests, and communicate their ideas to voters. This is particularly true in the short to medium term when Canada's major parties seem unable to earn a majority of the seats in the House of Commons. In a period of perpetual minorities, more frequent elections have become the norm, and this has placed a strain on party coffers. Impoverished parties will yield impoverished political debate; this is not a desirable outcome either for the parties or for democracy in Canada more generally.

But to say that state subsidies are an important support for Canadian parties that should be protected does not imply that these subsidies must remain in their current form. As noted by several of the contributors to this collection, some parties have been clear winners under the current formula. The Bloc Québécois, in particular, is so well funded relative to its electoral needs that it has little incentive to raise money from individual donors. Parties largely dependent on the state for their financial support offend notions of parties as predominantly private organizations, able to persuade at least a small proportion of their supporters to make modest contributions. When Canadian parties once again reconsider the rules governing party and election finance, they might consider capping the extent to which a party can rely on state subsidies – for instance, by requiring that no more than 60 percent of a party's income (excluding election expenses reimbursements) come from public funds, and capping the quarterly allowance when this requirement is not met. This creates a clear incentive for parties to continue to engage with individual donors while still guaranteeing a minimum income for parties tied to their electoral support. Alternatively, parties might consider tying the quarterly allowance to some sort of voluntary demonstration of support from individual Canadians, such as a box on individual income tax returns, allowing Canadians to direct their share of the allowance to a particular party, although the experience of the United States suggests that it is not clear that such a system would generate sufficient income to replace revenue lost from the elimination of the current quarterly allowance system (Flanagan and Coletto 2010, 6-8). Whatever the means chosen, the quarterly allowance should be delivered in a way that encourages parties to remain connected with and responsive to the citizens they are supposed to represent.

Unfinished Business in Party Finance

Encouraging parties to remain connected with and responsive to civil society should be a central public policy goal in regulating party finance. The chapters in this book have pointed to numerous areas where the current regulatory regime could be strengthened to serve this public policy goal more clearly.

One of these areas is leadership selection. This is an important part of party life, as it provides an opportunity for party members to take an active role. The typical swelling of membership rolls around leadership selections suggest that Canadians are more likely to engage with their parties at these times. In some ways, the new party finance rules strengthen this connection. As Cross and Crysler note in Chapter 8, candidates for the leadership of a registered political party must now raise money only from individuals. However, the limitations on individual donations appear to make running such campaigns difficult. Only one major party's leadership has been contested under these rules, and candidates seemingly had trouble raising enough money to run national campaigns. The debts incurred have hampered the ability of the candidates' party to raise money for a number of years, and if left unpaid threaten the coherence of the ban on corporate or union contributions as unpaid loans become de facto contributions. Understanding that engaging a wide range of party supporters in the selection of a leader is one of the critically important functions Canadian parties perform, some consideration should be given to the issue of whether the current arrangements allow parties to fulfil this function. When (or if) Canada returns to a four-year election cycle and parties are not as focused on election readiness, they might give some consideration to finding a means to provide candidates for their leadership with either start-up funds from party coffers or some kind of matching funds to enhance their fundraising capacity. This would be an entirely appropriate use of state funds, as it allows parties to engage Canadians in the selection of a party leader.

Another critical aspect of party organization in Canada is the balance between national parties and local party organizations, as discussed by Coletto and Eagles in Chapter 6. Because party members engage largely at the local level, and focus much of their effort on the selection and support of local candidates, the vibrancy of this level of party organization remains important for parties as democratic organizations. The 2004 reforms concentrate state funds at the national level, and because contemporary fundraising techniques such as direct mail or Internet-based donations enjoy economies of scale at the national level, the potential remains for local party organizations to become financially subordinate to the national party. Although there is some evidence that party revenue has become more centralized since 2004 (Coletto, Jansen, and Young 2009), Coletto and Eagles provide evidence that local party organization remains vibrant and important. The potential for this to change, however, remains, and this balance continues to be an important consideration in future efforts to amend the rules.

Finally, it is reasonable to argue, as F. Leslie Seidle does in Chapter 3, that state-funded parties should be held to higher standards than were their privately funded predecessors. To the extent that we conceive of parties as public utilities, they are subject to public regulation and can be required to meet specific public policy requirements. Currently, parties do little in the way of engaging their members in policy development (Cross and Young 2006), a tendency that has been only exacerbated in the current context of frequent elections and permanent campaigning. Seidle suggests using public funding to encourage parties to engage in greater research and policy development. The relative failure of parties to engage an increasingly diverse Canadian electorate also suggests a weakness in the way parties connect with Canadian society. Seidle points to the possibility of using public financing to encourage parties to increase their societal inclusiveness. Both of these are good examples of the kinds of demands Canadians can now reasonably make of their public utility parties.

Conclusion

Canada's political parties face numerous challenges as they enter the second decade of the twenty-first century. They face declining memberships, an aging volunteer base, and the task of engaging an increasingly diverse and complex electorate. At the same time, they do so in one of the most competitive and difficult electoral environments in the last several decades. Minority governments have become the rule, and political parties must be in a constant state of electoral readiness. The combined weight of these challenges has placed considerable stress on the capacity of political parties to connect citizens with their governments.

These stresses are also taxing the financial resources of Canada's parties. The declining volunteer and membership base means that political parties have to rely on professionals to perform tasks that were once done by volunteers. The more complex electorate requires parties to craft increasingly complex campaigns that recognize that a one-message-fits-all electoral campaign will no longer suffice. New media provide new opportunities for parties but also compete with traditional media for limited campaign resources. Finally, spending money to build up party organization or policy capacity has had to take a backseat to being able to respond to an imminent election call.

It is in this context that the party finance reforms of 2004 were introduced. These changes have been the biggest change to the legislative framework governing Canada's parties since they first became subject to regulation in 1974. Parties have simultaneously been adjusting to the demands of the new legislation and the new social and political realities. As the chapters in this volume have demonstrated, the impact of these changes is already being felt and will continue to shape party organization and political competition in Canada for years to come.

NOTE

1. The fieldwork of the 2008 Canadian Election Surveys was conducted by the Institute for Social Research (ISR) at York University and the study was financed by Elections Canada. The principal co-investigators were Elisabeth Gidengil (McGill University), Joanna Everitt (University of New Brunswick-Saint John), Patrick Fournier (University of Montreal), and Neil Nevitte (University of Toronto). Neither the Institute for Social Research and Elections Canada nor the Canadian Election Survey Team are responsible for the analyses and interpretations presented here.

WORKS CITED

Coletto, David, Harold Jansen, and Lisa Young. 2009. Election Finance Law and Party Centralization in Canada. Paper presented at the annual meeting of the Canadian Political Science Association, Ottawa.

Cross, William, and Lisa Young. 2006. Are Canadian Political Parties Empty Vessels? Membership Engagement and Policy Capacity. *Choices* 12(4): 14-28.

Flanagan, Tom. 2009. Cut the Subsidy, Then Make It Easier for Parties to Raise Their Own Money. *Globe and Mail*, 17 August, A11.

Flanagan, Tom, and David Coletto. 2010. Replacing Allowances for Canada's Political Parties? *University of Calgary School of Public Policy Briefing Papers* 3(1): 1-14.

Jansen, Harold J. and Lisa Young. 2009. Solidarity Forever? The NDP, Organized Labour and the Changing Face of Party Finance in Canada. *Canadian Journal of Political Science* 42(3): 657-78.

Milke, Mark. 2009. Subsidizing Canada's Breakup. *Calgary Herald*, 15 November, A12.

Contributors

André Blais is Professor of Political Science and Canada Research Chair in Electoral Studies at the Université de Montréal.

Robert G. Boatright is Associate Professor of Political Science at Clark University in Worcester, Massachusetts.

David Coletto is Chief Executive Officer of Abacus Data Inc. in Ottawa.

William Cross is the Hon. Dick and Ruth Bell Chair for the Study of Canadian Parliamentary Democracy at Carleton University in Ottawa.

John Crysler is a doctoral candidate in Political Science at Carleton University in Ottawa.

Munroe Eagles is Professor of Political Science and Director of Canadian Studies at the University at Buffalo.

Justin Fisher is Professor of Political Science and Director of the Magna Carta Institute at Brunel University in London, United Kingdom.

Harold J. Jansen is Associate Professor of Political Science at the University of Lethbridge.

Richard S. Katz is Professor of Political Science at The Johns Hopkins University in Baltimore, Maryland.

Peter John Loewen is Assistant Professor of Political Science at the University of Toronto Mississauga.

F. Leslie Seidle is Research Director (Diversity, Immigration and Integration) at the Institute for Research on Public Policy in Montreal.

Lisa Young is Professor of Political Science at the University of Calgary.

Index

2004 reforms. *See* Bill C-24
2006 reforms. *See* Accountability Act (Bill C-2)

Abbott, Jim, 69, 70
Aboriginal people, public funding and, 50
accessibility: and diversity of House of Commons, 54; to electoral competition, 54; Lortie Commission and, 49; public funding and, 54; pushed vs. pulled money and, 178. *See also* participation in public life
Accountability Act (Bill C-2), 45; Bill C-24 and, 170n9; content of, 5; and EDAs, 110; introduction of, 4; and leadership contests, 160-61; and Liberal Party, 98; limit on individual donations, 199
Adams, Paul, 151
advertising: AFL-CIO and, 187; BCRA and, 187, 189-90; BQ and, 93; CPC and, 98, 199; get-out-the-vote efforts vs., 191; by interest groups, 192; Liberal Party and, 98; saturation, 70; in US, 176, 177
advocacy. *See* issue advocacy
America Coming Together (ACT), 185, 187
American Federation of Labor and Congress of Industrial Organizations (AFL-CIO): advertising by, 187; The Coalition and, 187; and Democratic Party, 181, 186, 192; issue advocacy campaigns by, 176-77; member contacting program, 186-87; and PACs, 175; voter mobilization, 185, 187
American Federation of State, County and Municipal Employees, 185
Apotex Inc., 164
Australia, registration of political parties in, 3

Barbeau Committee (House of Commons Committee on Election Expenses), 41

Index

BCRA. *See* Bipartisan Campaign Reform Act (BCRA)
Bill C-2. *See* Accountability Act (Bill C-2)
Bill C-3, 43
Bill C-24, 4, 44, 92-94; and Bill C-2, 170n9; and BQ, 68-69; and cartel party model, 68, 69, 75, 83; as "closed shop situation," 69; closeness of election and, 137-38; consequences of, 130-31; and corporate/union donations, 49, 130; CPC and, 72, 99-101; donor influence and, 44; and EDAs, 71, 104-5, 108, 110; and election expenses reimbursements, 85; and electoral democracy, 14-16; and Green Party, 68, 69, 95-96, 142; impact of, 205; and individual contributions, 75; and leadership contests, 160; and Liberal Party, 46, 48, 68, 72-73, 97-99; and NDP, 70-72, 96-97; and new parties, 69, 70, 95; objectives of, 44; party responses to, 85-101, 138; PC/Alliance opposition to, 199; per-vote subsidy under, 44-45, 85; and policy development, 52, 54; political developments since, 102; previous regulatory regime and, 4-5; and principal-agent problem, 139; public awareness of, 138; public funding in, 44-45; quarterly allowance under, 86; and Quebec, 69; RCERPF and, 5, 7; reasons for, 7-10; and small parties, 131, 142; and spending limits, 85; and state money for political parties, 85; tax credits under, 85, 86; and third-party/place voters, 136-37, 141; and voter turnout, 131-39, 141-42
Bipartisan Campaign Reform Act (BCRA): adaptation to, 173-74; and advertising, 187, 189-90; Bush and, 183; and business groups, 188-89; and campaign funding equality, 194; and campaign fund-raising, 189; and corporate donations, 186; Democratic Party and, 182-83; electioneering vs. pure issue advocacy in, 180; and 527 organizations, 185-86; and "ground war" tactics, 190; as incumbent protection act, 179; and issue advocacy, 189-90; and parties vs. interest groups in determining content of campaigns, 194-95; and partisan self-interest, 179; provisions of, 177-78; and soft money, 177; Supreme Court and, 177-78
Birch, Sarah, 22
Blair, Tony, 160
Blais, André, 12, 137
Bloc Québécois (BQ): ban on corporate and union contributions, 7; as beneficiary of funding regime, 11; Bill C-24 and, 8, 68-69, 92-94; campaign expenses, 70; and cartel model, 69, 83, 92; and coalition, 94; and corporate donations, 200; and CPC, 69, 94; dominance in Quebec, 94; election expenses of, 93; election spending by, 93f; electoral success of, 16; financial standing of, 16; formation of, 43; individual donations and, 91f, 91t, 92, 92t, 94; intra-party transfers of money within, 118t; and Liberal-New Democratic coalition, 1; and Liberal Party, 83; and minority government, 4; 1993 election and, 3; non-public donations to, 46, 47t; and Parti Québécois, 93; quarterly allowance and, 87-89t, 90f; sources of revenue, 87-89t; and spending limits, 93; state funding and, 92, 199, 202; state

funding vs. non-public donations to, 45-46, 47t; state subsidies and, 94; success of, 43-44; and syndicate, 11, 82-83; and union donations, 200

Bloc Québécois EDAs: activities of, 122t, 123t; Bill C-24 and, 110; building of, 119; contributions to, 114, 115t; corporate contributions to, 116; expenditures of, 123t; financial balance by vote percentage, 125f, 126; financial resources, 109t, 110, 111, 112t, 113t, 118, 127; fundraising by, 124; intra-party transfers to, 119, 120f, 121t

Boatright, Robert, 16, 200

Boudria, Don, 44-45, 168

British Columbia, regulation of leadership contests in, 159

Buckley v. Valeo, 175

Bush, George W.: BCRA and, 182-83; Democratic Party and, 182-83, 189; hard-money fundraising by, 189; and polarization of electorate, 173-74; and public funds, 177

business donations. *See* corporate donations

business groups (US). *See* corporations (US)

campaign expenses/spending: and electoral impact, 70, 71f; exemptions from limits, 154; increases in, 31; party taxes on, 156; and size of party, 70; spending limits on, 158

campaign finances: disclosure of, 105; equity in, 194; illegal, 10; inequities in, 15; in US compared to Canada, 173

campaign finances (US): BCRA and fundraising, 189; "ground war" tactics in, 174; hydraulic theory, 178; push-pull distinction, 178; regulation of, 175-78; single-minded seeker of re-election paradigm, 179; testing of limits of law in, 179

campaigns: candidate-centred, 106-7; cartel parties and, 25; complexity of, 205; of CPC, 98; and financial accounting, 107; funding of, 3; interest groups and, 194-95; of Liberal Party, 98; local, 106-7; near-permanence of, 21; permanent environment of, 198-99; professionals in US, 180; rising costs of, 21; shift to local level, 149; spending limits for, 15

Campbell, Kim, 152t, 154

Canada Elections Act: about, 3; fifty-candidate rule, 54, 67; House of Commons Standing Committee on Procedure and House Affairs and, 55; 1996 amendments to, 50; review of political financing provisions, 55; 2007 changes to, 166. *See also* Accountability Act (Bill C-2); Bill C-24

Canadian Action Party (CAP), 70

Canadian Action Party et al. v. Attorney General of Canada, 70

Canadian Alliance: Bill C-24 and, 8, 83, 199; corporate donations and, 72; and corporate/union donations, 99; election spending by, 93f; formation of, 3; and individual donations, 99; and leadership contest financing, 152t, 153t, 154, 156; merger with PC Party, 3-4, 44; relationship with fiscally conservative groups, 193; revenue from individual fundraising, 91t, 92t; self-regulation by, 151; and state funding, 8; state funding vs. non-public donations to, 46, 47t

Canadian Auto Workers (CAW), 76

Canadian Charter of Rights and Freedoms, 50, 56n9

Canadian Election Studies (CES), 55n1, 135, 201

Index

Canadian Labour Congress (CLC), 181, 192-93
Canadian Taxpayers Federation, 193
candidates: appointment of, 14; as centre of campaigns, 106-7; deposits, 42-43; electoral performance, and EDAs, 124; Green Party, 131; national parties and, 128n1, 139; party leadership and, 180; party self-regulation and, 151; political parties and selection of, 3; polling by, 77; recruitment of, 107; reimbursement of, 42, 128n1; spending thresholds for, 49; state support for, 4; and voter turnouts, 135. *See also* leadership candidates
candidates (US): contributions to own campaign, 175; issue advocacy campaigns and, 176-77; self-financing of, 179; spending as freedom of speech issue, 175; spending limits, 175
cartel parties: and activists within parties, 65; BQ and, 69, 92; campaigns run by, 25; characteristics of, 25-26; competition and, 102; defection from, 65; first-past-the-post system and, 77; freedom from popular constraints, 77; Green Party and, 69, 96; media and, 67; negative outcomes of, 32; new parties and, 65; Scarrow on, 26-27; state funding and, 23, 25-26
cartel party model, 7, 60-67; and anti-party-system parties, 66; Bill C-24 and, 68, 69, 75, 83; BQ and, 83; coalition government and, 84; and collusion, 31, 62, 68, 82; and competition, 62; contributions and, 84; and democracy, 66-67, 68, 78-79; and expansion of resources for non-government parties, 74-75; and freedom from reliance on contributions, 75; governing parties and, 61-62; and Green Party, 75, 83; as ideal type, 66; and independence of central parties, 77; and inter-party dynamics, 61; and intra-party transfers of individual donations, 77; and Liberal Party, 73; and loyalty, 34; majority governments and, 78, 84; and mass party, 61; minority governments and, 77-78; and NDP, 71; opposition parties and, 82, 84; and party finance regime, 73-74; and prisoner's dilemma, 79n4; and restriction of policy competition, 64; and smaller parties, 75; and state finance and party collusion, 8; and state/party relationship, 66; state subsidies and, 11, 61, 75, 78, 84; and tragedy of commons, 79n4; in US, 62; and voter turnout, 78
Carty, R. Kenneth, 106-7, 108-9, 117, 121, 123, 147
catch-all parties, 62-63, 64, 66
central parties. *See* national parties
Chrétien, Jean: appointment of political rivals, 147; and Bill C-24, 4, 9, 44, 130; and BQ, 94; and changes in American law, 173; leadership campaign expenditures, 158; on parties and democracy, 80n7; and Quebec sovereignty movement, 94; spending on leadership campaign, 152t, 154
Citizens United v. FEC, 178, 190, 191
civil society: individual donations and, 76-77; parties and, 83, 84, 203; political parties and, 23, 61, 75; state and, 84, 85
Clark, Joe, 152t, 173
class, political parties and, 63
Clift, Ben, 28-30, 29-30, 31, 33, 34
Clinton, Bill, 195n4
The Coalition: Americans Working for Real Change, 187

coalitions: BQ and, 94; and cartel party model, 84; and electoral competition, 84, 102; elimination of public subsidies and, 12, 48, 200; of Liberal and ND parties, 1
Coelho, Tony, 176
Coletto, David, 12, 15, 203-4
collusion: cartel party model and, 25, 26-27, 31, 62, 68, 82; of opposition parties, 82; of political parties, 8
competition: cartel parties and, 25, 62, 102; equal/equitable, 4, 11, 21-22; fundraising, 23; protection of parties from, 23; state subsidies and, 84; and syndicate, 84-85. *See also* electoral competition
Conservative Party (UK): corporate donations to, 22; and spending limits, 159
Conservative Party of Canada (CPC): advertising by, 98, 199; Bill C-24 and, 72, 99-101; BQ and, 69, 94; as cadre party, 106; and cartel model, 62; contribution limits for leadership campaigns, 156; corporate donations and, 72; cost of leadership contests, 150; election campaigns, 98; and election expenses reimbursement, 101; election spending by, 93f; and elimination of party subsidy, 1-2, 100-102, 199-200; financing of leadership contests, 153t, 154; formation of, 3-4, 44; and fundraising, 11-12, 15, 74, 83, 97, 99-101; income sources, 11-12, 15; and individual donations, 72, 91f, 91t, 92t, 97-98, 100, 198-99; intra-party transfers of money within, 114, 118t, 127, 135; leaders as prime ministers, 147; leadership selection contests, 149, 170n6; Liberal Party compared to, 100-101; as minority government, 1-2, 44; and quarterly allowance, 87-89t, 90f, 100, 101; RCMP raids and, 128n2; sources of revenue, 87-89t; and state subsidies, 82, 94; state subsidies vs. non-public donations to, 47t; vote of non-confidence against, 1
Conservative Party of Canada EDAs: activities of, 122t, 123t; building of, 119; contributions to, 114, 115t; expenditures of, 123t; financial balance by vote percentage, 125f, 126; financial resources, 15, 109t, 110, 111, 112t, 113t; fundraising, 124; intra-party transfers to, 118, 119, 120f, 121t, 135; taxing of, 118
constituency associations. *See* electoral district associations (EDAs)
contributions. *See* donations
corporate donations: banning of, 7, 10, 16, 45, 49, 159, 163, 190-91, 200-201; BCRA and, 177; BQ and, 200; and Canadian Alliance, 72, 99; to CPC, 72; direct solicitation of, 191; to EDAs, 104, 107-8; and fundraising, 202; and government contracts, 94; and influence peddling, 191; and Liberal Party, 72, 73, 75, 76, 98; limitations on, 130; maximum under 2004 reforms, 5; and NDP, 70, 96, 200; partisanship of, 181; PC Party and, 99; public reaction to ban on, 201; as pushed vs. pulled, 179; and Reform Party, 72; in US compared to Canada, 181
corporate donations (US): bank donations, 175; BCRA and change in types of corporations, 186; and organized labour, 187; as pushed vs. pulled, 186
corporations: and Conservative Party (UK), 22; contributions to EDAs, 115t, 116; and Democratic vs. Republican Party, 176; influence over policy making, 9; and Liberal

Party, 76; limiting role of, 179; and pushing vs. pulling of money, 191
corporations (US), 187-89; BCRA and, 188-89; communication with employees/members, 188, 191; and 527 groups, 185, 188; organized labour compared to, 188; and soft money, 188
corruption: and Barbeau Committee, 41; and finance reform, 31; interest group financing and, 63; limitation on donation size and, 130; and regulation, 3, 13; soft money and, 177; state funding and, 22, 32, 34; voluntarist tradition and, 29
Courtney, John, 150
Cox, Gary, 133, 136
Cross, William P.: on campaign professionals in US, 180; on computer-generated lists of voters, 182; on individual donations to leadership campaigns, 203; on networks of party-based and interest-group based experts, 193; and party leadership contests, 14; and policy foundations, 52
Crysler, John, 14, 203

Davis v. FEC, 178
Day, Stockwell, 152t
Dean, Howard, 177
democracy: cartel party model and, 66-67, 68, 78-79; electoral, 14-16; individual donations and, 76; leadership contests and, 169; parties and, 80n7; policy foundations and, 193; political parties and, 2, 12, 21, 45, 49, 80n7, 168-69, 201; politics and, 78-79; reforms and, 14-16
Democratic National Committee (DNC), 183, 185
Democratic Party: AFL-CIO and, 181, 186; and BCRA, 182-83; and Bush, 182-83, 189; business PACs and, 176; fundraising, 189, 191; individual donations and, 189; and soft vs. hard money, 191; unions and, 181, 186
Denver, David, 21
Dion, Stéphane: appointment of other leadership contestants, 147; CP television advertising and, 15; leadership campaign spending, 162, 163t, 169n1; Liberal fundraising under, 98; quarterly allowance maintaining Liberals under, 99; repayment of leadership campaign loan, 163
disclosure: of campaign financing, 105; EDAs and, 105; of election expenditure, 150; in leadership contests, 145, 156-58, 160, 164-65; leadership selection and, 157; as necessary for regulation, 157; provincial regulation of, 159; rationale for, 157; RCERPF and, 158-59; timing of, 157, 159
Dole, Robert, 195n4
donations: Bill C-2 and, 160; cartel party model and, 26, 84; and corruption, 22, 29; as dominant source of income, 4; get-out-the-vote efforts vs., 191; hard vs. soft money, 79n6; from individuals, 7; and influence, 9, 11, 38; to leadership contests, 155-56, 157, 167; limits on size of, 7, 97, 157; matched by state, 167; new sources of, 191; PACs and, 175; provincial regulation of limits on, 159; reliance upon, 67; and survival vs. decline of parties, 24; tax credits for, 4, 54, 132; in UK, 26, 29; unrepaid loans as, 165-66. *See also* corporate donations; fundraising; individual donations; union donations
Dubé, Antoine, 69
Duverger, Maurice, 106, 136

Eagles, Munroe, 12, 15, 203-4
EDAs. *See* electoral district associations (EDAs)
Eizenga, Mike, 162
election campaigns. *See* campaigns
Election Expenses Act, 41-42, 54, 150
election expenses/spending: BQ compared to other parties, 93; closeness of race and, 135; competitiveness and, 135; disclosure of, 150; by Green Party, 95; by Liberal Party, 97; margin of victory and, 135; by NDP, 96-97; as percentage of spending limits, 92, 93f; polling by candidates and, 77; public funding of, 150; rebate of, 4; regulation of, 6t; reimbursement of, 85, 101; in US, 173
Election Finances Act, 128n2
elections: closeness of, and voter turnout, 131-32, 133-34, 135; cost of, 54; and EDA activity, 121, 123-24; fixed dates for, 180; interest groups and, 180; margins of victory in, 119, 120f; minority governments and frequency of, 202; ownership of, 194; parties' roles between, 45; party labels on ballots in, 41; presidential (*see* presidential elections); readiness for, 85, 98, 199, 203, 204, 205; regulation of, 4; rising cost of, 41; short-term success in, 26; timing of, 85, 202, 203, 205; uniqueness of law regarding, 7; in US vs. Canada, 180. *See also* leadership campaigns/contests
electoral competition: accessibility to, 54; Bill C-24 and, 137-38; coalitions and, 84, 102; cost of, 63; fairness in, 41; fundraising restrictions and, 164; individual donations and, 94; Liberal Party and, 98; media and cost of, 63; minority governments and, 15-16; NDP and, 97; and party spending, 135; political parties and, 3; and provision of public services, 63; state funding and, 201-2; and voter turnout, 132, 133-34, 141; Westminster tradition and, 84
electoral district associations (EDAs): activities of, 121-24, 126; autonomy of politics of, 108; Bill C-24 and, 71, 104-5, 108, 139; building of, 119; campaign financial accounting and, 107; candidate success and, 124; contributions to, 117; corporate donations to, 104, 107-8; disclosure requirements for, 105; electoral performance and, 124-26; expenditures of, 121, 123-24; financial autonomy of, 117; financial reports to Elections Canada, 104; financial resources, 15, 108-13, 127; fundraising by, 124; impact of reforms on, 106, 126-27; incumbency status, 106, 111, 113t; individual donations to, 77; intraparty transfers and, 77, 107, 116-21, 126, 127; limits on funding sources, 104; and local campaigning, 106-7; minority governments and, 127; national parties and, 12, 17, 108, 117-18, 139, 203-4; and policy, 121; public funding and, 108; purpose of, 121; reforms and, 12; registration of, 104; relations with other party levels, 127; revenue sources, 113-21; as source of revenue, 107; studies of, 105; taxing by central parties, 117-18, 128; taxing of, 12; transparency of finances, 104-5; union donations to, 104, 107-8; and vote raising, 106
electoral economy model, 26-28
Epstein, Leon, 40, 54, 168
equality/equity: in campaign financing, 15, 194; of competition, 4, 11,

21-22; financial, 22; public funding and, 39; spending limits and, 194
Europe: and civil society–political party ties, 61; independent parties in, 146; Phillips inquiry and, 23; political parties in, 3, 7, 12, 20, 49
Everitt, Joanna, 181

FEC v. Wisconsin Right to Life, Inc., 178
Federal Election Campaign Act (FECA), 175, 185
Federal Election Commission (FEC), 175, 186
Feingold, Russell, 177, 178
Figueroa v. Canada (Attorney General), 17n1, 43, 67
Fisher, Justin: on cartelization, 7; and cartels and party collusion, 31; and changes in district-level campaigns, 21; on comparative approach, 33, 34; and new institutionalism, 28-30, 33; and normative institutionalism, 31; on parties and democracy, 45, 201; on public funding debate, 11; on subsidization as corrosive to parties, 201
527 organizations, 185-86, 188, 189, 191, 193
Flaherty, Jim, 48
Fletcher, Steven, 166
Forbes, Steve, 177
France, state vs. voluntarist funding in, 29
fundraising: in absence of corporate/union donations, 202; BQ and, 94; competition in, 23; at congressional level, 183, 184f; costs of, 100; CPC and, 11-12, 15, 48, 74, 83, 97, 99-101, 118; by DNC, 183, 185; by EDAs, 124; and electoral competition, 164; leadership contests and, 155-56, 162, 163-64, 167, 199, 203; Liberal Party and, 97-98, 100, 163, 199; NDP and, 100; from numerous small contributions, 75, 76; by political parties, 38; popular vote and, 90; in presidential campaigns, 177; at presidential level, 183, 184f; short-term electoral success vs. revenue maximization in, 26; by US political parties, 183, 184f; and vote share, 94. *See also* donations

Gauja, A., 2
Germany: appearance of corruption and political parties in, 22; electoral economy model in, 28; electoral law and party finance in, 31; party foundations in, 51; public funding of foundations, 57n14; scope of funding to political parties in, 67
Gingrich, Newt, 62
Goldenberg, Eddie, 167
Gomery Commission, 10, 45, 73
Green Party: as beneficiary of funding regime, 11; Bill C-24 and, 68, 69, 95-96, 142; BQ compared to, 95; and cartel model, 69, 75, 83, 96; election spending by, 93f, 95; elimination of annual financial subsidy and, 2; individual fundraising, 95-96; international name recognition, 70; intra-party transfers of money within, 118t; and Liberal-New Democratic coalition, 2; numbers of candidates, 95, 139, 140; as part of syndicate, 82-83, 96; and per-vote subsidy, 12, 139; public funding vs. non-public donations to, 46, 47t; quarterly allowance and, 87-89t, 90f, 95; revenue from individual fundraising, 91f, 91t, 92t; rise of, 50, 198, 199; running of candidates, 131; share of vote, 69, 95; sources of revenue, 87-89t; spending by, 69; subsidies and reimbursements,

69; and syndicate, 11; and voter turnout, 12, 139-41
Green Party EDAs: Accountability Act and, 110; activities of, 121, 122t, 123t; Bill C-24 and, 110; contributions to, 114, 115t, 116; expenditures of, 123t; financial balance by vote percentage, 125f, 126; financial resources, 109t, 110, 111; fundraising by, 124; intra-party transfers to, 119, 120f, 121t

hard money: and Democratic Party, 191; party fundraising and, 183, 184f; Republican Party and, 189; soft vs., 79n6
Hargrove, Buzz, 76
Harper, Stephen: and 2004 reform legislation, 9; and abolition of quarterly allowance, 199-200; BQ and Mulroney's Quebec coalition, 94; campaign spending by, 153t; elimination of public subsidies for parties, 193; and NCC, 193; proroguing of Parliament, 1, 48; and state financing of parties, 8
Harper v. Canada (Attorney General), 191
Hopkin, Jonathan, 20, 23, 34
House of Commons: Committee on Election Expenses (Barbeau Committee), 41; diversity of, 54; Standing Committee on Procedure and House Affairs, 44-45, 55, 166, 168; women in, 50-51

ICM Research, 27
Ignatieff, Michael, 98, 163t, 169n1
individual donations: Accountability Act and, 199; BCRA and, 177; Bill C-24 and, 75; BQ and, 92, 94, 202; and broad-based party support, 130; and Bush, 182; Canadian Alliance and, 99; and central parties, 77; and civil society, 76-77; CPC and, 72, 97-98, 100, 198-99; Democratic Party and, 189; to EDAs, 77, 115t, 116; and electoral competition, 94; *financement populaire* and, 7; Green Party and, 95-96; increase in, 201; and leadership campaigns, 203; Liberal Party and, 97-98, 162, 163-64, 199; limits on, 7, 161, 175, 201; NDP and, 96; as only source of private financing, 86; quarterly allowance tied to, 202; revenue from, 91f; and share of vote, 96; small and numerous, 75, 76; tax credits for, 54, 67
influence: corporate/union donations and, 191; donors and, 44; pushed vs. pulled money and, 178
institutions/institutionalism: actor-centred, 30-31; historical, 30; new, 29-30, 33; normative, 28-29, 30, 31; and party finance reform, 28-30; path dependency in, 30
interest groups: ban on contributions from, 16; in Canada compared to US, 174-75, 179-80, 181-82, 191-92, 194-95; and candidate-party links, 180; and corruption, 63; and cross-partisan support, 180; and elections, 180, 194-95; 527 accounts, 185; and issues vs. political function, 185; and member communications, 194; separation of parties from, 64; in US, 174-75
International Institute for Democracy and Electoral Assistance (IDEA), 38
issue advocacy: BCRA and, 189-90; campaigns, 176-77; in Canada vs. US, 191-92; groups, 180

Jacobson, Gary C., 192
Jansen, Harold J., 11-12, 15, 30, 84, 192
Jenson, Jane, 49
Joint Victory Campaign, 185

Jouvenel, Bertrand de, 64

Katz, Richard: on British electoral system, 77; and Canadian syndicate, 82; and cartel parties, 25-26; cartel thesis and state funding, 11, 33, 40, 83; and cartelization thesis, 7; collusion and cartel model, 82; on independent parties, 146; and mass party, 19; and negative outcomes of cartel parties, 32; on parties as agents of democracy, 201; and parties' reliance on public funds, 11; and quarterly allowance, 84; and state finance and party collusion, 8
Kennedy, Gerard, 163t, 167
Kerry, John F., 177, 186
King, Mackenzie, 149
Kirchheimer, Otto, 62
Kitschelt, Herbert, 65
Kopecký, Petr, 32-33
Koss, Michael, 30-31, 33, 34

Labour Party (UK), 22, 159-60
labour unions. *See* unions
Lambert, Lisa, 90
Layton, Jack, 153t, 155, 198
leaders of parties: appointment of, 14; and candidates, 180; central role of, 145; choice of successors, 149; direct voting for, 149-50; and local prerogatives, 146; organizational dominance of, 146; and policy, 146-47; as prime ministers, 145, 147. *See also names of individual leaders*
leadership campaigns/contests: big money and, 169; Bill C-2 and, 160-61; Bill C-24 and, 160; contribution limits for, 145, 156; cost of, 145, 150; and democracy, 169; disclosure and, 145, 156-58, 164-65; entry fees, 162-63; financing of, 150-51, 158-61; fundraising for, 167, 203; and ideological disputes, 147; importance of, 146, 148, 158-59; and individual donations, 203; Liberal Party, 97, 161-65, 170n11, 199; limits on size of contributions to, 157; loans and, 167; and party discipline, 158; party self-regulation of, 151; public funding and, 146, 167; and public interests, 158-59; public regulation of, 160-61; as public vs. private matters, 145; RCERPF on, 158-59; regulation of, 5, 145-46, 150-51, 158-61, 169; restrictions on fundraising for, 199; self-regulation of, 14, 151-56, 159, 169; spending limits, 151-56, 167-68; state funding for, 203; and tax credits, 169; wealth and, 14
leadership candidates: appointment to high public office, 147; breaches of party rules, 158; campaign spending by, 154-55; compliance with disclosure requirements, 158; directed contributions to, 167; disclosure and, 164-65; discouragement from running due to expenses, 155; donation of own money, 161; fundraising by, 162, 163-64; loans, 162, 165-66; nomination contests, 168; payment to parties, 155-56; registration of, 155, 160; regulation of, 160-61; spending by, 162
leadership selection: by caucuses, 148-49; and democracy, 148; disclosure and, 157; elites and, 149; importance of, 146; membership involvement in, 146, 147-48, 149, 203; methods of, 148-50, 159-60; by outgoing leader, 149; and parties as private vs. public organizations, 168; and policy, 147
Lewis, David, 41
Lewis, Peter, 185

Liberal Democrats (UK), 159
Liberal Party: 1993 election and, 3; Accountability Act and, 98; advertising by, 98; Alliance-PC merger and, 3-4, 97, 198; Bill C-24 and, 9-10, 44, 46, 48, 68, 72-73, 97-99; BQ and, 83; as cadre party, 106; and candidates' reimbursements, 128n1; cartel party model and, 73; compared to CPC, 100-101; contributions to, 48; corporate donations and, 72, 73, 75, 76, 98; cost of leadership contests, 150; decline of, 3-4, 16, 73; disclosure of contributions to leadership contests, 157; dominance of party politics, 198; election spending by, 93f, 97; and electoral competition, 98; ethics package, 9-10; financing of leadership contests, 152t, 153t, 154; fundraising, 97-98, 100, 163, 199; individual donations to, 91f, 91t, 92t, 97-98, 199; influence of donors to, 44; intra-party transfers of money within, 118t; leaders as prime ministers, 147; leaders of, 198; leadership contests, 3, 97, 154-55, 161-65, 169; leadership selection, 149; liabilities of, 9; membership list, 46, 48; minority government by, 4; NDP and, 1, 97; non-public donations to, 46, 47t; public funding vs. non-public donations to, 46, 47t; quarterly allowance and, 87-89t, 90f; in Quebec, 10, 16, 73; scandals and, 3, 9-10; sources of revenue, 87-89t; sponsorship scandal and, 4, 10, 198, 199; state funding and, 98-99; and syndicate, 11, 82-83, 97, 99
Liberal Party EDAs: activities of, 122t, 123t; contributions to, 114, 115t; corporate contributions to, 116; expenditures of, 123t; financial balance by vote percentage, 125f, 126; financial resources, 15, 109-10, 111, 112t, 113t, 118; fundraising by, 124; intra-party transfers to, 119, 120f, 121t; taxation of, 118
Lijphart, Arend, 78
Lipset, Seymour Martin, 181
loans: for leadership campaigns, 165-67; repayment of, 170n11; unions co-signing, 71; unpaid, as de facto contributions, 203
local associations. *See* electoral district associations (EDAs)
Loewen, Peter John, 12
Longley v. Canada (Attorney General), 103n2
Lortie Commission. *See* Royal Commission on Electoral Reform and Party Financing (RCERPF)
Lösche, Peter, 22

MacIvor, Heather, 56n9
MacKay, Peter, 153t, 155
Mair, Peter: on British electoral system, 77; and Canadian syndicate, 82; and cartel parties, 25-26; cartel thesis and state funding, 33, 40, 83; collusion and cartel model, 82; on independent parties, 146; and mass party, 19; and negative outcomes of cartel parties, 32; and parties' reliance on public funds, 11; and quarterly allowance, 84; and state finance and party collusion, 8
majority governments: accountability to opposition parties, 202; BQ and, 94, 199; and cartel party model, 78, 84
Manitoba, regulation of leadership contests in, 159
Manley, John, 170n7
Martin, Paul: Alliance-Progressive Conservative merger and, 3-4; campaign spending, 153t, 154, 155; corporate donations to, 163; and

disclosure requirements, 170n8; individual contributions to, 164; leadership campaign expenditures, 158; resignation of, 161
Marzolini, Michael, 77
mass parties, 19-20, 61, 66, 106
Matlow, J., 50
May, Elizabeth, 95, 96
Mayhew, David, 179
McCain, John, 177, 178, 185
McClelland, Ian, 42
McConnell v. FEC, 177-78, 180
McDonough, Alexa, 152t
media: cartel parties and, 67; and cost of electoral competition, 63; knowledge of public funding, 27; new vs. traditional, 205
Media Fund, 185
Meech Lake constitutional accord, 43
members: of business groups, 191; of interest groups, 194; of labour organizations, 191, 192
members of political parties: cartel, 25; in cartel parties, 25, 26; decline in, 21, 63, 204-5; elites vs., 147; "instant," 107; and leadership selection, 146, 147-48, 149, 203; Liberal, 46, 48; and policy development, 204; supporters vs., 26
Michels, Robert, 65
Milliken, Peter, 111
minority governments: BQ success and, 199; and cartel party model, 77-78; and EDAs, 127; and election costs, 202; and electoral competition, 15-16; and electoral readiness, 204, 205; series of, 4; survival in Westminster model, 101
MORI, 27
Mulroney, Brian, 94, 147

National Citizens Coalition (NCC), 166, 179, 193
national parties: Bill C-24 and relationship with local level, 139; independence of, 77; individual donations and, 77; and local candidates, 139; polling by, 77; public funding and EDAs, 12, 17; taxing of EDAs, 117-18, 128; transfer of individual donations to EDAs to, 77; transfers to EDAs, 113-14, 116-21
National Women's Liberal Commission, 166
Natural Law Party of Canada, 42
Netherlands, public funding in, 39
New Brunswick Commission on Legislative Democracy, 51, 53, 55
New Democratic Party (NDP): Bill C-24 and, 8, 70-72, 96-97; building ownership, 71-72; and candidates' reimbursements, 128n1; cartel party model and, 71; CLC and, 181, 192; coalition with Liberals, 1; contribution limits for leadership campaigns, 156; corporate donations and, 70, 96, 200; disclosure of contributions to leadership contests, 157; disclosure of leadership campaign expenses, 156; and election expenses reimbursement, 101; election spending by, 93f, 96-97; as electoral competitor, 97; fundraising, 100; individual fundraising and, 91f, 91t, 92t, 96; intra-party transfers of money within, 118t; Layton's leadership and, 198; leadership campaigns/contests, 151, 152t, 153t, 154, 155, 156, 157; and Liberal Party, 97; local executive control in, 107; as mass party, 106; as part of syndicate, 82-83; and quarterly allowance, 87-89t, 90f, 96; in Quebec, 143n4; sources of revenue, 87-89t; and spending limits, 168; state subsidies and, 96; state subsidies vs. non-public donations and, 46, 47t; and syndicate,

11, 96; unions and, 70-72, 75-76, 96, 200
New Democratic Party EDAs: activities of, 122t, 123, 123t; contributions to, 114, 115t, 116; expenditures of, 123, 123t; financial balance by vote percentage, 125f, 126; financial resources, 109t, 110, 111, 112t, 113t, 118; fundraising, 124; intra-party transfers to, 119, 120f, 121t; union contributions to, 116
new parties: 1996 reforms and, 43; accessibility for, 54; Bill C-24 and, 69, 70, 95; and cartels, 65; disadvantagement of, 24, 25; state funding and, 22, 32
New Zealand, registration of political parties in, 3
nomination contests: of leadership candidates, 168; political parties and, 14; regulation of, 5; spending limits on, 168
normative institutionalism, 28-29, 32-33

Obama, Barack, 177, 183, 185
one-candidate rule, 17n1, 48
Ontario, regulation of leadership contests in, 159
opposition parties: and cartel party model, 74-75, 82, 84; and coalition, 48; and elimination of annual subsidy, 2, 48, 49, 200; in majority governments, 202
organized labour. *See* unions
Ostrogorsky, Moisey, 20

Paltiel, Khayyam, 43, 56n6, 72
Parliament, proroguing of, 1, 48
Parti Québécois, 93
participation in public life: leadership contests and, 148; public funding and, 41
Pearson, Lester, 150
Peck, Kevin, 70

per-vote subsidy: in Bill C-24, 44-45, 85; and campaign spending, 70; Green Party and, 12, 139; maximization of votes, 132-33; public awareness of, 138; and voter turnout, 12, 132, 139-40, 141
Peters, B. Guy, 28-29
Phillips, Sir Hayden, 23, 29, 30
Pierre, Jon, 23, 31-32, 33
Pinto-Duschinsky, Michael, 55n2
policy: corporations and, 9; delegation of issues to non-political agencies, 64; grants for, 53; internal elite and, 55; leadership selection and, 147; party leaders and, 146-47; restriction of competition in, 64
policy development: EDAs and, 121; foundations, 52, 193; parties and, 204; public funding and, 39-40, 53, 54-55, 204
political action committees (PACs): BCRA and, 177; business, 176; connected, 175; as 527 organizations, 185; formation of, 175; fundraising by, 188; numbers of, 175-76; replacement of corporate soft money, 188; spending limits on contributions to candidates, 175; spending limits on individual contributions to, 175; and voluntary contributions, 175
political parties: as agents of civil society, 23, 66; as brokers among social groups, 62-63; cadre, 106; centralization of, 24, 26, 32, 105, 118; centralization of revenue, 204; challenges facing, 204-5; and civil society, 61, 75, 83, 84, 203; and class, 63; collusion and, 8, 25, 26-27, 31; constitutional theory of, 2; decline in affective attachment to, 63; and democracy, 2, 12, 21, 45, 49, 80n7, 168-69, 201; democratization of, 65; distribution of resources within, 138; and

electoral economy, 26; elites in, 32, 55, 147, 148, 149; extremist, 24-25; foundations, 51-53; impoverishment of, 202; independent, 146; leaders of (*see* leaders of parties); as link between citizen and state, 21; maximization of numbers of seats, 16-17; membership of (*see* members of political parties); new (*see* new parties); numbers of votes for, 17; as part of state, 23; petrification of, 24, 32; and policy (*see* policy); political education within, 39-40; politicization of finances, 199-200; pressures/threats from within, 65; as primary political organizations, 49, 52; as private entities/organizations, 2, 12, 13, 49, 94, 150, 202; as public utilities, 12-13, 21, 40, 49, 54, 168-69, 204; registration of, 3, 41-43, 48, 54; research, 39-40; rising expenditure of, 20-21; role of, 39, 45, 48; as semi-state agencies, 25; sources of revenue, 87-89t; as syndicate, 82-83; volunteer workers in (*see* volunteer party labour). *See also names of individual parties*

political parties (US), 13-14; BCRA and, 183; as 527 organizations, 185; fundraising by, 183, 184f; spending limits on individual contributions to, 175; spending limits on PAC contributions to, 175. *See also* Democratic Party; Republican Party

Prentice, Jim, 155

presidential elections: 527 organizations and, 186; fundraising in, 177, 183, 184f; public funding for, 40, 67, 177; restriction of access to public finance in, 67; spending limits and, 175, 177; voluntary public funding for, 175

prime ministers, party leaders as, 145, 147

private donations. *See* donations

Progressive Conservative (PC) Party: Bill C-24 and, 8, 199; and corporate donations, 99; and disclosure of spending, 151; election spending by, 93f; financing of leadership contests, 152t, 153t, 154; merger with Canadian Alliance, 3-4, 44; in 1993 election, 3, 43; public funding vs. non-public donations to, 46, 47t; revenue from individual fundraising, 91t, 92t; and spending limits, 151

proportional electoral systems, 23

public funding. *See* state funding

public opinion: of bans on corporate and union donations, 201; of political parties, 37; of state funding, 27-28

Public Policy Forum (PPF), 48

Quebec: 1963 reform in, 41; Bill C-24 and, 69; BQ in, 94; corporate/union contributions in, 7; Election Act, 51; *financement populaire* in, 7-8, 200; Liberal Party in, 10, 16, 73; NDP in, 143n4; semi-proportional mixed electoral system in, 51

Rae, Bob, 162, 163t

Reform Party: corporate donations and, 72; and 1993 election, 3, 43; rise of, 193

registration: of EDAs, 104; of leadership candidates, 160; of political parties, 3, 41-43, 48, 54; of smaller parties, 67

regulation: and disclosure, 157; of elections, 4; historical institutionalism and, 30; of leadership contests, 5, 145-46, 150-51, 160-61, 169; of leadership financing, 158-61; of nomination contests, 5; and parties as public utilities, 54, 204; of parties' internal affairs, 12-14; of party election finance, 6t; of party finances, 6t, 150; and party labels on ballots, 41; of party personnel selection contests, 150; of political parties, 3, 4; provincial, 159; of US campaign finance, 175-78. *See also* Accountability Act (Bill C-2); Bill C-24; Canada Elections Act; Federal Election Campaign Act (FECA); Revenue Act of 1971 (US)

reimbursement: Bill C-24 and, 85; of candidates, 42, 128n1; and CPC, 101; of election expenses, 67, 85, 101; and Green Party, 69; and Liberal Party, 128n1; and NDP, 101, 128n1; of parties, 42, 43f; votes and, 42, 131

Republican Party: business groups and, 176; and cartels, 62; and hard money, 189; National Committee, 185

research, public funding and, 39-40, 53, 55, 204

Revenue Act of 1971 (US), 175

revenue maximization, 26-27, 28, 33

riding associations. *See* electoral district associations (EDAs)

Rock, Allan, 155

Royal Commission on Electoral Reform and Party Financing (RCERPF), 5-6, 8, 13, 39, 49, 50-51, 52-53, 158-59

Sayers, Anthony, 84
Scarrow, Susan, 26-28, 31, 33, 34
Sears, Robin, 52
Segal, Hugh, 152t
Seidle, F. Leslie, 13, 204
self-interest: BCRA and, 179; and finance reforms, 7, 8, 9
self-regulation, of leadership contest spending, 14, 151-56, 159, 169

Service Employees International Union, 185

smaller parties: Bill C-24 and, 131, 142; cartel party model and, 75; registration of, 67; spending thresholds and, 49; state funding and, 32

soft money: amounts of, 176; BCRA and, 177; corporate donations and, 185, 186, 188; and corruption, 177; and Democratic Party, 182-83, 191; hard vs., 79n6; organized labour and, 185, 186; PACs and, 188; party fundraising and, 183, 184f, 189; push-pull distinction and, 177, 188; solicitation of, 176; uses of, 176

Soros, George, 185

spending limits: and accessibility to electoral competition, 54; Bill C-24 and, 85; BQ and, 93; on campaigns, 15, 150, 158; on candidates in US, 175; and corruption, 130; in Election Expenses Act, 150; election spending as percentage of, 92, 93f; and equity, 194; exemptions from, 154, 162; on individual contributions, 7, 161, 175, 201; and intra-party transfers of financial resources, 114; and leadership contests, 151-56, 167-68; for nomination contests, 168; of parties, 169n3; and polling by candidates, 77; presidential candidates and, 175, 177; provincial regulation of, 159; public funding and, 177; Quebec and, 56n9; self-regulation of, 151-56; and size of donations, 38, 130

Stanfield, Robert, 150

state: and civil society, 84, 85; normative conception of, 32-33

state funding: and Aboriginal people, 50; and accessibility to electoral competition, 54; and BQ, 92, 94; Canadian Alliance and, 8, 99; cap

Index

on, 202; and cartel model, 8, 75, 78, 84; to central parties vs. EDAs, 108; changes to, 202-3; and collusion of parties, 8; comparative studies on, 33, 34; and competition, 84; concentration at national level, 204; and corruption, 32, 34; CPC and, 82; criticism of, 40, 53; dependence upon, 32, 48, 53, 61, 86, 130; donations revenue compared to, 45-46, 47t; of election expenditure, 150; Election Expenses Act and, 41-42; and electoral competition, 201-2; and equity, 39, 194; and higher standards for parties, 204; in IDEA report, 38; impact of, 10-12; and independence of central parties, 77; as inducement to run candidates, 131; and influences of big money on decisions, 44; large private donations and, 38; and leadership contests, 146, 167, 203; and Liberal Party, 98-99; modification of, 49; and national vs. local associations, 12; NDP and, 96; necessity of, 201-3; negative effects of, 31-32; and new parties, 32; opinions regarding, 20-25, 27-28, 34, 38-40, 48; and parties as private organizations, 202; and party centralization, 32; and policy development, 39-40, 54-55, 204; and political education, 39-40; and political participation, 41; and presidential candidates, 175, 177; and public policy objectives, 53; quarterly allowance, 84, 86, 87-89t, 90f, 99, 100, 101, 199-200, 202; and research, 39-40; and responsiveness of politicians to electorate, 194; review of, 55; and role of parties within democratic systems, 39; roots of, 38; and smaller parties, 32; and societal inclusiveness/diversity, 204; and society/party links, 75; and spending limits, 177; and stability of parties' financial base, 38-39; tax credits as, 85; tying to individual donations, 202; and visible minorities, 50; and voter turnout, 12; and votes, 119

Stewart, Ian, 90
Strahl, Chuck, 155
Stronach, Belinda, 154-55
Studin, Irvin, 52
SUN-PAC decision, 175
Supreme Court (US), 177-78, 189, 190
Supreme Court of Canada: and fifty-candidate rule, 54, 67; *Figueroa* decision, 17n1, 43
Svåsand, Lars, 23, 31-32, 33
syndicates, 11-12; coalition government and, 102; defined, 84; electoral competition and, 84-85; Green Party and, 96; Liberal Party and, 97, 99; NDP and, 96; political parties as, 82-83

tax credits: Bill C-24 and, 85, 86; for directed contributions, 167; for donations, 4, 132; as indirect subsidies, 85; for individual donations, 67; and leadership campaigns, 169; and policy foundations, 51-52; for private donations, 54
trade unions. *See* unions
transfers of resources: intra-party, 113-14, 116-21, 126, 127; and margin of victory, 119, 120f; spending limits and, 114
Trudeau, Pierre, 150

union donations: ban on, 7, 16, 49, 159, 163, 190-91, 200-201; Bill C-24 and, 5, 130; BQ and, 200; Canadian Alliance and, 99; direct solicitation of, 191; to EDAs, 104,

107-8, 115t, 116; and fundraising, 202; and influence, 191; and NDP, 70-72, 96, 200; to parties, 45; public reaction to ban on, 201; push-pull of, 179

unions: business groups compared to, 188; in Canada vs. US, 192-93; co-signing of bank loans, 71; communication with members, 191; and Labour Party (UK), 22; and NDP, 70-72, 75-76; reaction to restrictions on donations, 200. *See also* union donations.

unions (US): BCRA and, 177; and Democratic Party, 181, 186; donations from, 175; and 527 groups, 185; and "ground war" tactics, 190; limiting role of, 179; and pushed vs. pulled money, 191

United Kingdom: campaigning in, 21; cartel parties in, 77; Electoral Commission, 53; electoral economy model in, 28; historical institutionalism in, 30; leadership selection in, 159-60; normative institutionalism in, 29; party centralization in, 26; Phillips inquiry in, 23, 29, 30; policy development grants in, 53; Political Parties, Elections and Referendums Act, 160; political parties in, 20, 22; public survey regarding state subvention in, 27; registration of political parties in, 3; spending ceilings in, 30; state funding in, 20, 29, 33-34; voluntary funding in, 26, 29

United States: ban on contributions in, 16, 200; business groups in, 187-89; campaign finances (*see* campaign finances [US]); candidates in (*see* candidates [US]); cartel model and, 62, 67; corporate donations (*see* corporate donations [US]); corporations (*see* corporations [US]); cultural differences between Canada and, 181-82; election campaign professionals in, 180; institutional differences between Canada and, 180-81; interest groups in, 174-75, 180-81, 182; labour unions (*see* unions [US]); organized labour in, 186-87; political culture compared to Canada's, 173; political parties (*see* political parties [US]); presidential elections in (*see* presidential elections); primaries, 13-14; regulation in, 175-78; resistance to public funding in, 40; Watergate scandal, 41. *See also* Bipartisan Campaign Reform Act (BCRA); US-Canada comparisons

United Steelworkers, 181

US-Canada comparisons: advocacy issues, 182; campaign finance regimes, 173-74; circumvention of laws, 173, 181; corporate and labour/union contributions, 181, 190-91; cultural differences, 179, 181-82; elections, 180; institutional differences, 179, 180-81; interest groups, 174-75, 179-80, 181-82, 191-92, 194-95; organized labour approaches, 192-93; parties in, 194; in reforms, 193-94; restrictions on campaign finance, 179-80

van Biezen, Ingrid, 13, 21, 32-33, 168
visible minorities, public funding and, 50
Volpe, Joe, 164
voluntary funding. *See* donations
volunteer party labour: paid professional labour vs., 24, 204-5; and party expenses, 21
voter turnout: Bill C-24 and, 131-39, 141-42; candidates and, 135; cartelization and, 78; closeness of election and, 131-32, 133-34, 141;

efforts of parties and, 134-35; electoral competition and, 132, 133-34; Green Party and, 139-41; individual-level, 135-38; individuals' preferences and, 132; per-vote subsidy and, 12, 132, 139-40, 141; reimbursement and vote totals, and, 131; state funding and, 12

voters: alienation of, 24; computer-generated lists of, 182; mobilization of, 119; third-party, 136-37

votes/voting: diminishing marginal returns of, 133; fundraising and share of, 90, 91, 94; individual donations and share of, 96; maximization of, 17, 119, 132-33; for party leadership, 149-50; public funding and, 119; reimbursement for, 42, 131; UK state subventions based on, 23. *See also* per-vote subsidy

wealth: and campaign fundraising, 165; of candidates, 14, 30, 165; and competition, 23; and electoral performance, 124; and leadership contests, 14; and political advantage, 30; and political influence, 22

Weekers, Karolien, 31

welfare states, distribution of resources within, 63-64

Westminster political tradition, 2, 3, 10; cartel party thesis and, 84; minority governments and, 101; and parties as private entities, 12; Phillips report and, 23

Widfeldt, Anders, 23, 31-32, 33

women: Commission on Legislative Democracy (NB) and, 51; in House of Commons, 13, 50-51

Working America, 187

Young, Lisa: on action groups, 182; on cartel party thesis, 84; on CLC and NDP, 192; on corporate Canada-Liberal Party relationship, 76; on differing impacts of reforms on parties, 15; on financial dependence on donor base, 67; on fundraising based on individual contributions, 75; on goals of campaign finance, 193; list of action groups active in 2000 election, 181; and policy foundations, 52; on regulatory tools, 30; on syndicate, 11-12

youth involvement, 39, 40, 52

Printed and bound in Canada by Friesens
Set in Futura Condensed and Warnock by Artegraphica Design Co. Ltd.
Copy editor: Judy Phillips
Proofreader: Stephanie VanderMeulen
Indexer: Noeline Bridge